Nephrology for nurses

A modern approach to the kidney

SECOND EDITION

Nephrology for nurses

A modern approach to the kidney

J STEWART CAMERON, MD, BSc, FRCP
  Professor of Renal Medicine

ALISON M E RUSSELL, SRN
  Formerly Ward Sister

DIANA N T SALE, SRN, RNCT
  Renal Clinical Tutor

GUY'S HOSPITAL, LONDON SE1

WILLIAM HEINEMANN MEDICAL BOOKS LTD
23 Bedford Square, London WC1B 3HT

First published 1970
Second edition 1976

© J S Cameron, A M E Russell and D N T Sale, 1970, 1976

ISBN   0 433 05111 6
(First edition 433 05110 8)

Typeset in IBM Press Roman
by Reproduction Drawings, Sutton

Printed and bound in Great Britain
by Redwood Burn, Trowbridge and Esher

Contents

Introduction

Since this book was written in 1970, the nursing care of patients with renal disease, especially those requiring dialysis and transplantation, has become a recognised specialty. We have revised all the material; in some areas progress has been such that it has been necessary to rewrite the chapter completely. In other areas it is sad to see that little or no progress has been made, and the description of the scene six years ago is substantially that today. The chapter on diet in renal diseases has been curtailed, and the recipes omitted, since information on the practical aspects of diets in patients with chronic renal failure are now readily available. An additional chapter on fluid balance, intravenous fluids and nutrition, and electrolyte disorders has been incorporated into the text, concentrating upon aspects of particular importance to the patients with renal disease. A few omissions have been made good: hepatitis now, alas, has a necessary place in any text on renal diseases, and analgesic nephropathy is now well recognised as a common and important disorder. Paediatric nephrology is also well developed and the care of children with renal disease is given even more prominence than in the previous text. Finally, we have included a number of suggestions for further reading from medical and nursing texts at the end of each chapter.

Guy's Hospital   D Sale
October 1976   J S Cameron

CHAPTER 1

The function of the kidneys

This chapter can be used as a reference chapter, turning to it for individual items of information when a particular disease situation raises questions about what normally happens. The section "Renal Functions in General" is, however, essential if the rest of the book is to be useful. One does not have to know all about physiology to be a good and useful nurse, but to understand what is going on in your patients, and to *anticipate* problems, some understanding of normal kidney function is necessary.

THE NEPHRON (Figures 1.1 and 1.2)

Each kidney is made up of about one million units called *nephrons*, each ·of which is similar and all of which seem to perform similar functions. For most purposes, each nephron can be considered as though it functioned alone, and renal failure can be regarded as the progressive reduction in the number of nephrons. For some functions, particularly the way the kidney excretes water in concentrated or dilute urine, the nephrons must be considered together as an organ.

The structure of the nephron is shown in Figure 1.1. It consists of a *glomerulus* and a *tubule*. Each *glomerulus* is a tuft of capillaries, just visible to the naked eye. Here the first stage of urine formation takes place. This is the pressure filtration of water from the plasma by the action of the heart; that is, cells and protein are held back and everything else is allowed to pass unrestrictedly. About 20% of the whole cardiac output goes through the kidneys (a little over 1 litre per minute). The renal arteries are short and wide, as are their branches, and the blood pressure is transmitted with the minimum drop to the glomerulus. This consists of a number of capillary loops, the lining cells of which are stretched thinly, and present no barrier even to large molecules. The end of the tubule, however, is spread thinly over the outside

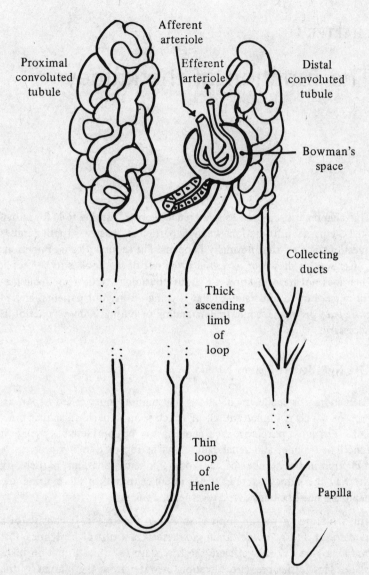

Fig. 1.1 A nephron. The glomerulus is formed from the conjunction of tuft of capillaries (here diagrammatically represented by only two) and Bowman's capsule. This is the upper end of the renal tubule, with the cells spread out very thinly and closely applied to the capillaries of the tuft. The space depicted for clarity between capillaries and Bowman's capsule does not, of course, exist.

The space formed by the invagination of the capillary tuft into the expanded and thinned end of the tubule is called Bowman's space, of the capillary tuft, and acts as a barrier to large molecules such as proteins. About 120 ml of glomerular filtrate are formed every minute — nearly 200 1/24 hours. Since there are only 40 litres of water in the whole body, and common observation tells us that only one or two litres of urine are passed each day, almost the whole of this filtrate must be reabsorbed back into the body. This appears clumsy and inefficient, and requires some explanation.

Two facts are worth remembering: (1) our kidney is the product of evolution. At some point our fish-like ancestors may have migrated from salt to fresh water. They then had a strong electrolyte solution in their blood and fresh water ouside. They would face the problem of excreting large volumes of water attracted into their bodies by the osmotic pressure of the substances dissolved in their blood. A kidney which pressure filters water is a simple and elegant answer. What if this "fish" moved to dry land? It must then conserve water and electrolytes, and could have done this by developing the second portion of the nephron to its present level — the tubule (see Figure 2.2). The tubule keeps all those waste products for which the body has no use in the tubular fluid which becomes urine. It also reabsorbs the bulk of the useful water and electrolytes, and is then in a position to manipulate according to the body's exact requirements, the much smaller volume

---

after the investigator who first described glomerular function and anatomy accurately. Blood flows through the glomerulus at high pressure from the renal artery, and filtration takes place through into Bowman's space from the tuft. The blood leaves the glomerulus by the efferent arteriole to join the renal vein.

The cells of the renal tubule, unlike those of Bowman's capsule, are large and metabolically very active. Some of them are shown in section near the glomerulus. The proximal part of the tubule is very convoluted, and forms the proximal convoluted tubule. By the time the filtrate has traversed this part of the nephron, its volume has been reduced to only one third of that filtered. This filtrate then passes down through the loop of Henle, which may pass deep into the medulla and papilla of the kidney. If the longest nephrons were to be drawn to the scale of the glomerulus and proximal convolution shown here, then a page about two feet long would be required. Not all nephrons have such long Henle's loops, however (see text). The ascending limb of the Henle's loop is thicker, with again metabolically active cells lining it. The tubule then passes by the vascular pole of the glomerulus, where the afferent and efferent arterioles run, to form part of the juxtaglomerular apparatus. The tubule then convolutes again before passing through the medulla to join the collecting ducts and pass to the tip of one of the renal papillae.

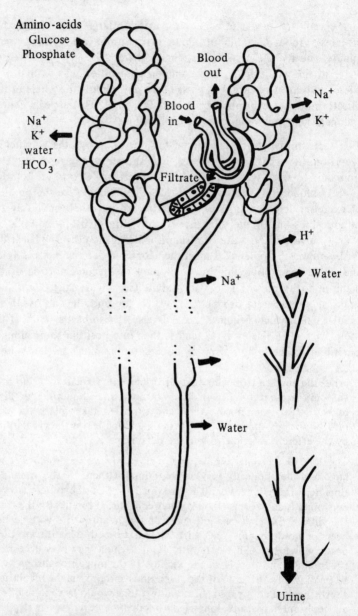

Fig. 1.2   Urine is elaborated by the tubules, acting upon the glomerular filtrate. Glomerular filtrate is an almost protein-free ultrafiltrate containing all electrolytes present in the plasma, in virtually the same concentration as in the plasma. This filtrate is modified into urine by a selective process of absorption of water and solutes, and by the secretion of some substances.

of fluid reaching the more distal parts of the nephron. (2) An advantage of the apparently wasteful business of passing all the body's water five times through the kidney each day is that very small adjustments on the tubular fluid can be multiplied up to large changes in final excretion by the end of the day.

Recently, we have realized that the cortex of the kidney contains *two* rather different organs. The outer cortical nephrons have only short loops of Henle, and perform most of the *filtration*; the inner cortical nephrons, in contrast, have long loops of Henle which pass deep into the medulla and form the countercurrent *concentration* mechanism (see page 8). This may be of importance when considering diseases affecting mainly the outer cortex (e.g. acute renal failure) or the loss of inner nephrons (e.g. papillary necrosis); since loss of the medulla will lead to a great fall in concentrating power but little fall in the filtration rate.

Considering a single nephron, we will now examine how it handles a number of substances of importance in the order they appear to be handled by the nephron (Figure 1.2).

1 Urea (and other nitrogenous waste products)

These are waste and ideally would simply be filtered and completely excreted. In practice the kidney cannot achieve this. Some is "trapped" in the papilla (q.v.) and contributes to the high concentration of solutes

---

In the proximal tubule, sodium chloride, bicarbonate and water are absorbed in very large amounts so as to reduce the volume of filtrate to one third. Even so, this still means some 60 l/24 h to be processed by the remaining nephron. In the proximal tubule also, all the glucose, almost all the amino-acids and most phosphate is reabsorbed, so that the urine is free of the first two. These are all valuable metabolites.

In the loop of Henle, osmolar equilibration with the high concentration of solute in the medulla occurs, and little transport is seen. In the thicker ascending limb of the loop, however, sodium is selectively transported to maintain this concentration gradient. This, and its role in concentrating the urine, are discussed in the text. By the time the tubular fluid reaches the distal tubule a further reduction in volume has occurred, and the fluid is dilute again. In the distal tubule and collecting duct potassium and hydrogen ions are secreted into the fluid, and as the urine passes down the collecting ducts water is absorbed to reach the final concentration of the urine. Some urea is absorbed in the distal part of the nephron, especially when the urine is being maximally concentrated and urine flows are low.

in this are of the kidney. Each healthy person produces and excretes 15 – 25 g of urea each day, derived from the breakdown of 45 – 75 g of protein.

2 Glucose and amino acids

These are filtered in the fairly high concentrations present in the plasma, and are almost totally reabsorbed in the proximal tubule (see Figure 1.2). If the blood level rises, or if tubular damage or inefficiency are present, the reabsorbing mechanism may be overwhelmed and the substance appear in the urine. This is particularly important with glucose. The level of blood glucose at which appreciable quantities appear in the urine is referred to as the "glucose threshold". Actually, it is the rate at which the glucose is delivered to the tubule which is most important, and this depends not only on the glucose concentration, but upon the filtration rate. These points will apply to any substance handled like glucose.

3 Phosphate

The phosphate excreted largely results from phosphate in dietary protein and fat. Phosphate, like glucose, is mainly reabsorbed in the proximal tubule but much less completely so that large amounts of phosphate normally appear in the urine. Phosphate excretion is influenced by a number of factors, particularly by *parathyroid hormone*, which decreases the phosphate reabsorption and therefore leads to loss of phosphate in the urine and a fall in the plasma phosphate.

4 Sodium (Na^+)

Most of the filtered sodium (probably 80%) is reabsorbed in the early part of the tubule along with an equal quantity of water, so that the salt concentration of the tubular fluid does not change. This smaller volume of fluid which remains is then manipulated according to the body's needs in the distal parts of the nephron. The amount of sodium reabsorbed is under hormonal control and may be greater or less than the equivalent water reabsorbed at the same time. The hormone principally involved is *aldosterone* from the adrenal cortex. This promotes reabsorption of Na^+ and excretion of K^+ (q.v.). It is probably this distal reabsorption of sodium that we alter by giving diuretic drugs. Aldosterone secretion itself is stimulated by

(1)   a fall in the volume within the circulation, either from loss of blood or of Na^+ and water.

(2)   renin/angiotensin, themselves produced when renal blood flow falls.
(3)   by the Na^+ concentration in the fluid within the distal tubule.

These hormonal mechanisms normally ensure that however much Na^+ is taken in the diet, or however little, the appropriate amount is conserved to keep both the volume and the Na^+ concentration of the extracellular fluid constant. The amount of sodium in the urine varies enormously with dietary intake from about 50 - 150 mmol/day.

5 Hydrogen ion (H^+)

H^+ is excreted in two forms by the distal tubule and collecting duct:

(i)   as H^+ in association with chloride, sulphate or phosphate
(ii)   as ammonium (NH_4^+) formed from H^+ and ammonia (NH_3) in the tubular cells. (Most of the "ammonia" one can smell in urine, especially when not fresh, comes from breakdown of urea by micro-organisms).

The H^+ is produced in vast quantities by cells all over the body. Most of this acid is excreted as carbon dioxide and water from the lungs. A tiny proportion, about 70 mmol/day on a normal diet, can only be lost through the kidneys and therefore assumes an extra importance. All H^+ must first be transported from its site of production (the cells) to the organs of excretion (lungs and kidneys) through the circulation. If this acid were simply added to the blood, the acidity would be so great that all cell activity would stop. It is therefore carried in the blood in a concealed, or "buffered" form, so that the actual concentration of free (unbuffered) hydrogen ions in the blood is very small (about 0·00000004 mmol/l at pH 7·4). The concentration of free hydrogen ions in the urine is about 100 times greater, the remainder again being buffered. Acid can be excreted very rapidly as free or buffered H^+, but if the body's production of acid remains high for long periods, ammonium comes to form a greater proportion of the acid secreted.

6 Potassium (K^+)

We are fairly certain that all the filtered K^+ is reabsorbed in the early part of the nephron, and that the K^+ we find in the urine is added in the distal tubule. As just mentioned, this process is influenced by aldosterone. The more H^+ is excreted the less K^+ and *vice versa* since they share a common secretion mechanism. We know very much less about how the body regulates its K^+ balance since 95% of the K^+ is within the cells.

THE ORGANIZATION OF THE KIDNEY

7 Water

So far, we have confined attention to the individual nephron. Now, in considering water excretion and reabsorption, we must look at the architecture of the kidney as a whole (Figure 1.3). The long loop of Henle was present in Figure 1.1 but has not yet been discussed. These loops are only present in mammals living in a dry environment, and are longest in desert animals; the longer the loop, the more concentrated urine the animal is capable of making. Inner cortical nephrons have much longer loops than outer cortical nephrons, whose loops in many instances do not reach the medulla at all. The proportion of these "short-loop" nephrons is about one in five in man, which is much higher than in most other animals. The concentrating ability of the kidney depends upon the "long loop" nephrons so that man is not capable of elaborating as concentrated urine as most rodents, for example.

An individual nephron is probably incapable of concentrating urine above plasma concentration, although it could dilute. The arrangement of large numbers of loops together, (with blood vessels running in parallel) does allow a concentrating mechanism to be built up. How this operates is not exactly known, but one well-known fact is that the concentration of substances (particularly urea and sodium) steadily increases as one proceeds from cortex to medulla to papilla (Figure 1.3). The loops of Henle, lying in parallel, build up this concentration by transporting Na^+. Each step in building up the concentration is small, but the arrangement of loops allows the steps to be built up into very high concentrations; in doing this, the loops act as a *countercurrent multiplier*; counter current, because the loops run into the medulla and out again; multiplier, because the small concentration steps applied one after the other to the same fluid multiplies the concentration gradient. This arrangement allows the "trapping" of solutes in high concentration in the medulla. At the tip of the papilla the concentration of solutes is equal to the most concentrated urine.

This means that the urine in the collecting ducts must travel (Figure 1.3) through a part of the kidney where the tissue fluid becomes more and more concentrated. If water were allowed to pass across the collecting duct wall, then it would do this in large quantities because of the concentrated fluid surrounding it in the medulla and papilla; eventually the urine concentration would equal the concentration of the papilla. If no exchange were permitted, the fluid from the distal tube (which is usually about as concentrated as plasma, or a little less) would remain dilute. It appears that antidiuretic hormone (ADH) "de-waterproofs"

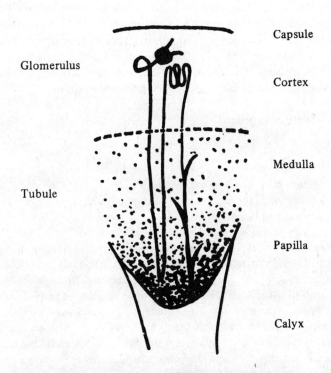

Capsule

Glomerulus

Cortex

Medulla

Tubule

Papilla

Calyx

Fig. 1.3 A nephron is shown in position in a small segment of kidney. The glomerulus lies within the cortex of the kidney, and the tubule loops deeply into the medulla, reaching to the tip of the papilla in this case. The concentration of solutes in the medulla steadily increases toward the papilla, reaching a maximum at the tip. The collecting duct of the nephron must traverse this region of high concentration before the urine formed within it can pass out into the calyx. If the urine equilibrates with the high concentration then a concentrated urine will be formed. If, however, the walls of the collecting duct do not allow water to pass into the concentrated papilla then dilute urine will result. Whether water is allowed to pass, and equilibration of the urine within the tubule with the papilla take place, is under the control of ADH (pitressin).

the collecting duct so that concentrated urine is made by equilibration with the concentrated papilla. Normally, the secretion of ADH from the posterior pituitary (where it is stored after manufacture in the hypothalamus) is stimulated by a rise in the osmolarity of the blood and corrects this by making the kidney retain water. By these mechanisms, the water excretion appropriate to intake and uncontrolled losses (such as from the skin is sweat) can be smoothly regulated. For a variety of reasons, diseased kidneys are incapable of regulating water excretion and they do not respond to injected ADH (pitressin).

Renal functions in general

The kidneys have four main roles in the body's economy:

(1)   excretion of waste products of metabolism
(2)   conservation of essential substances
(3)   regulation of the composition of the body fluids
(4)   secretion of hormones

(1) Excretion This is the function with which everyone is most familiar. Carbohydrate and fat can be burnt in the body to carbon dioxide and water, and the carbon dioxide excreted through the lungs. A number of other metabolic activities, however, lead to residues which can only be excreted through the kidneys. The breakdown products of protein, principally from nitrogen, but also from phosphorus and sulphur; breakdown products of nucleoprotein (DNA and RNA) metabolism, principally uric acid; and organic acids, such as oxalic acid must be excreted by the kidneys. A number of these processes generate acids, which may dissociate in solution to give hydrogen ions, H^+. In uraemia all these compounds may accumulate in the body, and in the absence of renal function the dialysis must remove them.

(2) Conservation The kidney discriminates between the waste compounds and those which the body can use. Some which are normally not allowed to escape in the urine, but which may appear in diseased states, are protein, glucose and the amino-acids from which proteins are constructed.

(3) Regulation This is the most subtle and difficult of the kidney's functions. Metabolism takes place within cells, in solutions of protein and across membranes of structures within the cell. The amount and type of electrolytes within the cells which maintain these processes have evolved over 500 million years. These electrolyte concentrations must be maintained for the cells to synthesize new compounds and produce energy. Human beings are, of course, organized aggregates of very large numbers of cells, bathed in extracellular fluid (ECF). The composition of the ECF may reflect in part the composition of the primitive sea where lived the single celled organisms from whom we are distantly descended. Again, the composition of this fluid must be maintained constant if the cell membranes are to function, transporting substrates into, and waste products out from the cell. The kidney is the final arbiter of how much water and electrolyte there is within the body as a whole.

The cells expel nearly all the salt that diffuses into them, while potassium can diffuse into, and remain in the cells. Sodium is therefore the kation (positively charged ion) found in the ECF and potassium that of the intracellular fluid. The cells allow water to move freely and this keeps the difference in total concentration of solutes within and without the cell at a minimum. *The amount of water in the body is therefore roughly determined by the total amount of sodium plus the total amount of potassium.* The kidney varies the output of sodium, potassium and water so that the concentrations of electrolytes inside or outside the cells change as little as possible. In addition the total amount of water remains constant. How well it performs this function is easily seen by how constant we keep our bodyweight, which is about 70% water and in the short term is an excellent guide to total body water.

In health, the kidney receives information on which proportion of sodium, potassium and water to excrete by hormones secreted in response to changes in these three quantities. In disease, the kidney may be incapable of responding to the instructions it receives and the regulation of the body's water and electrolytes may suffer.

(4) Secretion It is easy to forget that the kidney is an endocrine organ. Two hormones are known to be produced from the kidney:

(a) Renin This is an enzyme which acts upon one of the blood proteins splitting off a short protein chain (a polypeptide) *angiotensin.* This acts in at least three ways:

(i)   it influences directly the handling of salt and water by the kidney;
(ii)   it raises the blood pressure by making the arterioles constrict;
(iii) it stimulates the outer layer of the adrenal cortex to secrete the hormone *aldosterone,* which in its turn promotes sodium retention and potassium loss in the kidney.

Clearly renin is of importance in the regulation of salt, water and blood pressure.

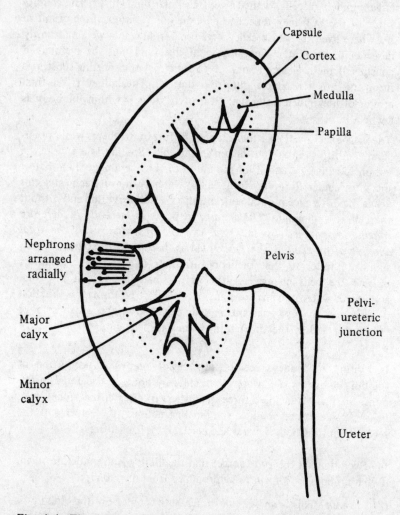

Fig. 1.4 The kidney. The outer areas of the organ, containing the glomeruli, are called the cortex. The inner area, containing the loops of the tubules, is referred to as the medulla. The nephrons are arranged radially around the collecting system, which starts at the collecting ducts of the nephron. These open into a minor calyx, which in turn leads into one of the three major calyces which fuse to form the pelvis of the kidney. The pelvis drains into the ureter.

(b)   Erythropoietin   Much less is known about this than renin, but it appears that this, too, may be an enzyme acting on blood proteins. The substance it generates stimulates the bone marrow to produce red cells, and obviously may be important in the maintenance of the red cell mass, in preventing anaemia, and in producing the polycythaemia sometimes seen in some renal diseases.

(c)   Vitamin D   Vitamin D as taken in the diet or manufactured by irradiation of precursors in the skin by sunlight is inactive; requiring transformation in the body before it can exert its influence on calcium in the gut and in the bones. This transformation takes place in two stages, the first of which is in the liver, leading to a weakly active compound (25 - hydroxy vitamin D). The second step, to the highly active compound 1,25 - dihydroxy vitamin D, only occurs in the kidney. The kidney thus elaborates a hormone from the precursor vitamin D, and in the absence of functioning renal tissue, or in chronic renal scarring, the production of vitamin D in its active form will be reduced. This is obviously of importance in the bone disease of uraemia. In passing, it is worth noting that some synthetic analogues of vitamin D do not require transformation (for example DHT (AT 10)) and that synthetic analogues of the active form of vitamin D (such as 1α OH vit. D) are now being manufactured.

(d)   Prostaglandins   The kidney is a rich source of these compounds especially the outer medulla. There are many prostaglandins which have a variety of actions of smooth muscle and cell metabolism, but the principal interest in renal prostaglandins centres on their possible role in regulating the distribution of blood flow within the kidney.

The maturation of renal function

In general, renal function increases along with renal size as the child grows. During the neonatal period, however, the kidney is relatively immature; the glomerular filtration rate is very low and remains relatively so for several months. The ability to excrete acid and to concentrate urine is also limited. This ability to concentrate urine depends also upon the type of food being given, that richer in protein enabling the infant to concentrate its urine to a greater extent. A greater proportion of the infant is water than in the adult, and upsets of fluid regulation and balance are correspondingly more frequent and more severe. For example, urinary tract infection in the first month of life may cause a raised blood urea and occasionally severe renal failure.

This tendency towards a high blood urea in young infants is made worse by the world wide tendency away from breast milk towards bottle feeds using cow's milk, which has a much higher concentration of protein, salt and phosphate than human milk. If this cow's milk feed is prepared from powder using a stronger mix than suggested on the packet, the baby may be fed so much solute and so little water that even making the most concentrated urine possible, the baby cannot excrete the urea and Na$^+$ in its feed. The inevitable consequence is dehydration, a high plasma Na$^+$ concentration and some degree of uraemia.

THE URINARY TRACT (Figure 1.5)

The gross anatomy and relations of the kidneys are considered in relation to renal biopsy (Chapter IV). From the end of the collecting duct in the papilla, the urine passes into a *calyx* of the collecting system (Figure 1.4). There are usually three major calyces – upper, middle and lower, with a number of branches on each; there is a great deal of variation in the number, size and disposition of the calyces. The calyces join to form the renal *pelvis*, which varies greatly in size and filling, and may lie almost wholly within or wholly without the kidney. The pelvis joins the ureter at a narrow point, the pelvi-ureteric junction. In all the structures mentioned – calyces, pelvis, ureter – there is circular and longitudinal smooth muscle and pain fibres. Stretching of smooth muscle in spasm is one cause of pain from the urinary tract. The renal substance has no pain fibres but the renal capsule is sensitive.

The *ureters* run downwards over the psoas muscle behind the peritoneum approximately over the tips of the transverse processes of the lumbar vertebrae as seen on X-ray. They cross the pelvic brim to enter the base of the bladder bilaterally. The ureter enters the bladder obliquely, so that on micturition the end of the ureter is compressed by the muscle of the bladder wall, and no reflux of urine occurs up to the kidney. Flow of urine down the ureter is intermittent, the ureteric muscle conducting slow peristalsis; this intermittency can be seen if ureteric catheters are left in place for drainage.

The *bladder* is a hollow sac, the greater part of the wall consisting of smooth muscle. It is lined, like the rest of the tract, by a fairly tough multilayered transitional epithelium. Up to 500 or 700 ml can be accommodated in the adult bladder without discomfort. Voiding urine can be automatic, but may also be begun voluntarily. The smooth performance of passing urine depends upon contraction of the bladder with simultaneous relaxation of the bladder neck.

This apparently simple act is still poorly understood. The innervation of both the bladder wall muscle (detrusor) and the bladder neck is through the nerves of the first and second sacral segments. Disease of these

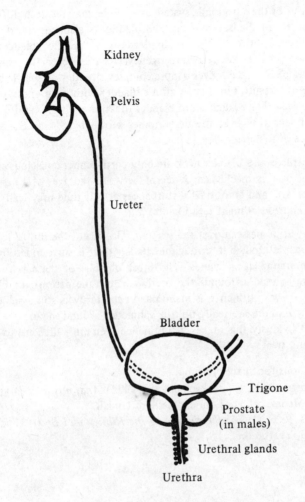

Kidney

Pelvis

Ureter

Bladder

Trigone

Prostate
(in males)

Urethral glands

Urethra

Fig. 1.5   The lower urinary tract. The ureters lead downwards over the
pelvic brim to enter the bladder obliquely. The ureter passes through
the bladder wall at an angle, which helps to prevent reflux of urine
up the ureters during micturition (see Figure 5.3). This "valve" is
much better developed in adults than in children. The ureter opens
at the outer angle of the trigone, the triangular area at the base of
the bladder. The junction of the bladder and urethra are surrounded
by extensions of the muscular wall of the bladder, and by specialized
muscle fibres. These muscles are concerned with continence, and act
like a sphincter although they do not, in the strict sense, form one.
The urethra is surrounded by a labyrinth of glands, the most promin-
ent of which (in the male) is the prostate.

nerves, or of the autonomic system as a whole, may result in difficulties in micturition. Sensation from the bladder is also important. Spinal cord disease above S1/S2 usually leads to a "spastic" bladder, with increased tone in the detrusor, urgency and small capacity. Disease at the level of S1 and S2 gives a more complex situation: a spastic bladder may be the result, but a large atonic bladder with poor emptying may also be seen. The evaluation of bladder function includes careful evaluation of sensation over the dermatomes served by S1 and S2, and the presence of the anal reflex.

The detrusor and bladder neck are only partly under conscious control. Control of this mechanism is learnt between the ages of $1\frac{1}{2}$ and four years of age, and emotional disturbances at this time may lead to persistent enuresis at night (see Chapter V).

Finally, urine passes down the *urethra*. This is not the simple tube it is so often pictured, but throughout its length it is surrounded by complex interconnecting glands. The most obvious of these is the male *prostate*, which surrounds the urethra below the base of the bladder. Exactly how continence is maintained voluntarily is still a subject for dispute, as there are really no true sphincters around the urethra at any point. Obviously this makes incontinence even more difficult to understand and treat.

Suggestions for further reading:
Armstrong, K. F., Jackson, S. M. (1972) *Anatomy and Physiology for Nurses*. 8th ed. London: Ballière Tindall.
Pitts, R. F. (1974) *Physiology of the Kidney and Body Fluids*. Chicago. Yearbook.

CHAPTER II

Acute uraemia and acute renal failure

A variety of conditions can lead to temporary loss of the kidney's ability to excrete waste products or to regulate the body's electrolytes. These are:

(1)   acute uraemia from poor renal perfusion (sometimes called pre-renal uraemia),

(2)   acute renal failure from "acute tubular necrosis".

(3)   acute on chronic renal failure,

(4)   acute obstruction of the urinary tract,

(5)   acute glomerulonephritis with oliguria.

A major problem for the doctor in uraemic emergencies is to determine as soon as possible into which of these groups the particular patient may fall, since the management and the outcome will depend on this. "Acute tubular necrosis" is the classical form of acute renal failure, and is discussed in detail below. Probably poor renal perfusion, acute tubular necrosis and the irreversible destruction of the outer cortex sometimes seen (acute cortical necrosis) are three, progressively more severe stages of an insult to the intrarenal circulation. This has causes besides purely cardiovascular events, however, and the doubt about its real nature leads to the term "acute tubular necrosis" being placed in inverted commas. The older "vasomotor nephropathy" has much to commend it. Because this is the commonest and most important state of acute renal failure, we will consider it first.

I ACUTE TUBULAR NECROSIS (VASOMOTOR NEPHROPATHY)

The striking contrast in this condition is the appearance of the kidneys which is normal or nearly so, and the almost complete loss of function they display. Probably the primary events are vascular and involve the

17

glomeruli as much if not more than the tubules. Several processes are involved. These include diversion of blood flow away from the outer cortex of the kidney, widespread clotting within the minute blood vessels of the kidney (intravascular coagulation) with removal of the clot by the clot-dissolving activity of the blood (fibrinolysis), and an increased activity of the renin-angiotensin system. Which of these is the primary event is unknown, but it is clear that despite the great variety of clinical circumstances listed below in which acute renal failure may be seen, all the varieties seem to operate through the *same final common pathway* of damage. From this arises the similarity of clinical course, whatever the cause of the acute renal failure.

The circumstances in which the nurse may encounter acute renal failure are only too familiar. They are:

(a)   In prolonged poor renal perfusion ("shock") This may occur with a low blood pressure, but sometimes the blood pressure is fairly well maintained at the price of diverting blood away from the kidney and other organs. In this type of "shock" the central venous pressure (CVP) is low and the hands and feet cold. Hypoxaemia as well as tissue hypoxia will contribute to kidney damage.

(b)   When there are pigments circulating, toxic to the kidney The commonest is free *haemoglobin* from broken down red cells. The causes of this are various, but include mismatched blood transfusion. *Jaundice* pigments (such as bilirubin) are highly toxic to the renal tubule, and make the kidney more vulnerable to poor blood flow.

(c)   When toxic drugs and chemicals have been taken Many drugs are at least potentially damaging to the kidney — for example, virtually all antibiotics in very high doses. There are also a number of chemicals which can damage the kidney, the most familiar being the cleaning fluid carbon tetrachloride.

(d)   In severe infections Infection, particularly where there is septicaemia, makes the kidney more vulnerable. It may do this by putting the patient into circulatory collapse, by haemolysis, or by direct effect of bacterial toxins. Some severely infected patients also become jaundiced.

(e)   After trauma This, whether accidental or surgical, may lead to all the factors a – d being present. Products from damaged tissues themselves (for example, myoglobin) may also be toxic to the kidney.

(f)   Obstetric accidents The uterus seems to be linked by nervous reflexes to the nerves of the renal circulation. In the placental separation of severe eclampsia (toxaemia of pregnancy) the renal circulation may constrict severely and renal failure result. Another common obstetric event leading to acute renal failure is abortion, particularly septic abortions.

(g)   Acute cortical necrosis In a small number of patients with acute renal failure, spontaneous recovery of renal function cannot be expected. In these patients very prolonged and very intense failure of renal perfusion leads to the *infarction* of all or nearly all of the renal cortex; this is called acute cortical necrosis. This is seen in severe eclampsia of pregnancy, after very severe trauma, and in the haemolytic-uraemic syndrome of childhood (see below).

(i) Symptoms and signs

The effects of acute renal failure are numerous. They will, of course, be seen against the background of the very different circumstances which precipitated the acute condition. For example, a fit young woman with an uncomplicated septic abortion and brief renal shutdown will present very different nursing problems from an old man with acute renal failure following a major surgical operation, or after a severe road traffic accident. These patients will have all the problems of surgical nursing, and may also be on a ventilator.

Acute renal failure may be divided into two stages:

(a) The oliguric phase This may last from a few days to several weeks. As the name indicates, during this period the urine output is very low. The principal dangers of this period are:

(1)   Failure to excrete salt and water taken by mouth or infused intravenously. This results in the low urine output, which in most patients with acute renal failure is between 200 and 500 ml/day. Complete anuria is uncommon, except in cortical necrosis and acute glomerulonephritis. The nurse is usually the first person to observe the fall in urine output, and prompt reporting of this finding may save the doctor and patient much trouble. If intake is not restricted while the urine output is low, then circulatory overload will occur with heart failure, breathlessness, raised jugular venous pressure, pulmonary congestion and oedema. If water without sodium is the principal intake then the plasma sodium may fall as well and the patient become weak and confused.

(2)   Rise in plasma potassium. This is aggravated by tissue destruction or breakdown, infection, haemolysis, hypoxia and poor tissue perfusion from poor cardiac output. The danger of a high plasma potassium is cardiac arrest, in asystole. There are usually no symptoms of the rising plasma potassium, but the ECG may show gross changes.

(3)   General consequences of uraemia (which are discussed in detail in Chapter VI) such as nausea, vomiting, itching, bleeding, lowered

resistance to infection, twitching, drowsiness, confusion, convulsions, coma, retention of administered drugs and pericarditis with or without tamponade. The endocrine, bone and connective tissue complications of chronic renal failure are not seen in the acute situation. Anaemia may be present, but usually takes a week or so to develop. The patient with acute renal failure is frequently desperately ill, and sometimes dying, before treatment and investigation of the condition can be begun.

(b) The diuretic phase This begins as the oliguria relents, after days or weeks. The transition is usually abrupt, taking one to three days before the large urine volumes found at this time are being excreted. The volume of urine is usually about 3 l/day but may be as large as 7 l/day. This diuresis usually lasts several weeks, and on occasion may persist for a month or two. The length and severity of the diuretic period depends upon the severity of the damage to the renal tubules, and upon how much excess urea, salt and water have to be excreted. The signs during this period are:

(4)   Excess loss of water and sodium leading to saline depletion, hypotension and possible circulatory collapse.
(5)   Excess loss of potassium, leading to a fall in plasma potassium and possible cardiac arrhythmias or fibrillation, especially if the patient is digitalized.
(6)   Continuing lowered resistance to infection, and retention of drugs, because although the urine volumes are impressive, renal function is still very impaired.

(ii)   Investigations (Chapter XI)

The *immediate* investigations are aimed at confirming the diagnosis of acute tubular necrosis. When a patient becomes oliguric or anuric, there are several possible diagnoses besides acute tubular necrosis:

(1)   Retention of urine
(2)   Blockage of the urinary tract (post-renal obstruction) e.g. by tumour involving the ureters, or by stones
(3)   Acute on chronic renal failure (see below)
(4)   Very poor renal perfusion ("pre-renal uraemia"). This is an important distinction because if it continues, acute renal failure will arise; and if the renal circulation can be restored, renal function will immediately return to normal.

The doctor will therefore order a number of *immediate* investigations to help the diagnosis and provide a baseline for future management. A urinary catheter will usually be passed (Chapter V) to confirm the presence of oliguria. The nurse must remember the special susceptibility of the patient to infection. The catheter is connected to a measuring cylinder, and the urine output measured hourly to begin with. In acute renal failure this will be less than 30 ml/h for an average adult. The catheter specimen may also be sent to the laboratory for culture, for estimation of urea and sodium concentration, and osmolarity. In acute, or acute on chronic renal failure, the urine will usually be dilute with respect to osmolarity and urea (Chapter XI) and will contain a fair amount of sodium (40 mmol/l or more). In very poor renal perfusion ("pre-renal uraemia") the urine will be very concentrated with respect to urea and osmolarity, and will have a very low sodium concentration (less than 10 mmol/l).

The doctor may also ask for a therapeutic investigation to be carried out: the injection of a powerful diuretic, usually frusemide, intravenously. Often very large doses are used (for example 250 – 1000 mg of frusemide) and it is important that these should be given slowly, over four hours or so, into an infusion rather than by bolus injection. In established acute tubular necrosis there is usually no change in urine volume, whereas in acute oliguria and uraemia from renal hypoperfusion there will be a brisk diuresis. Repeated doses of diuretic may then be given. Mannitol was formerly used in this fashion, but is difficult to prepare in very concentrated solution, may precipitate circulatory overload (especially if no diuresis is obtained) and make the blood very hyperosmolar to the cells, and in some patients does not work when frusemide or other diuretics will. It is now little used for this purpose.

The blood urea and electrolytes will be estimated and blood allowed to clot for serum, for grouping and cross matching. A straight X-ray of the abdomen will be taken, which is usually not very satisfactory done as a portable X-ray in the bed, and may mean the patient's transfer to the X-ray department if his condition permits. More use is now made of an IVU employing the injection of a high dose of contrast medium, (e.g. 2 ml/kg of meglimine iothalamate) plus tomography of the kidney area. The radiologist will usually want the patient back into the department for late films up to 24 hours later. The straight X-ray may show stones, or the high dose IVU scarred or small kidneys, suggesting that the acute episode is only one phase of chronic renal failure. X-rays of the bones may also show evidence of renal osteodystrophy, again evidence of chronicity, and a raised plasma alkaline phosphatase may also help here. At some point, consultation with the genito-urinary surgeon may be made, especially if the X-rays suggest obstruction. Finally, a radioisotope scan or gamma camera series may be done to determine the presence or adequacy of the renal blood flow, if this is not clear from the high dose IVU. Scanning techniques have the advantage that they do not overload the circulation with the high osmotic load of contrast. Often dialysis will be necessary before many of these investigations can be carried out, and the doctor will have to decide upon a plan of action for each patient at the outset. For example, the early management of a patient whose acute renal failure follows a severe burn, open heart surgery or a road traffic accident will be different from one who has taken some nephrotoxic substance. Usually, the management and investigation of the acute renal failure is only one of many problems the nurse will face in these interesting but exacting situations.

There will also be *continuing* investigations, performed as the doctor directs either 12 or 24-hourly. All urine is saved and sent for analysis or culture, as directed. A daily or twice daily blood sample will be taken for electrolytes and haemoglobin estimation and white cell count. Swabs will be taken for culture, depending on the state of the patient and the precipitating condition. If dialysis is being performed there may be other investigations concerned with this procedure. The patient may be connected to an ECG recorder, or ECGs performed as directed. Chest X-rays will also be done at frequent intervals.

If after two or three weeks the patient's kidney show no sign of returning function, the doctor may begin investigations to determine whether acute tubular necrosis alone is present, and spontaneous recovery can still be expected. These investigations may include renal arteriography (or possibly venography), renal scanning, or radioactive renogram to determine whether the renal vessels are patent; or a renal biopsy to see the renal histology. The genito-urinary surgeon may perform retrograde ureteric catherization at this time, if this has not already been done. These investigations will usually require the patient's transfer to the X-ray department or operating theatre.

(iii)   Observations and nursing

The patient in acute renal failure is best nursed in an intensive care area in a side ward to minimize cross infection, both to and from the patient, who is frequently already infected. Barrier precautions should be observed. In many instances the patient will be very ill from the condition, accident or postoperative circumstances leading to his acute renal failure. All the necessary observations relating to this will need to be carried out in addition to those relating to the acute renal failure, and to the dialysis if this is being performed; the patient will always need a special nurse, and some severely ill patients may need two from time to time. Wherever possible the patient should be nursed out of bed either in a chair, or ambulant, but this can rarely be achieved. If in bed, a large-cell Whittington type ripple mattress should be used, and the patient turned two-hourly; uraemia, infection and the tissue destruction often found in acute renal failure make skin breakdown particularly likely, and if this does occur widespread tissue necrosis may be seen with severe infection and an intractable ulcer.

The mouth and nose are also particularly vulnerable. The doctor may wish to keep the patient in slight negative fluid balance, which does not help salivary flow; the urea secreted in the saliva breaks down to ammonia and the patient's defences against infection are poor.

If a nasogastric tube is necessary, it should always be a soft one; attention should be paid to keeping it free of encrustations and the site should be changed frequently. If a urinary catheter has been inserted initially, the doctor will usually ask for it to be removed as soon as possible. The presence of a catheter in an anuric bladder inevitably leads to severe inflammation. When the catheter is removed, chlorhexidine, or Noxyflex, 150 ml of 2·5% solution, should be instilled. If the patient is very ill the doctor will often elect to pass a central venous catheter to measure the central venous pressure, to provide an easy means of obtaining blood samples, and to allow intravenous administration of fluid or drugs.

Temperature, pulse rate and respiratory rate will usually be observed and charted four-hourly, as will the blood pressure and the central venous pressure. An accurate fluid balance, recorded and cumulated 12 or 24-hourly as directed, is a vital part of the management. This should include the balance achieved by peritoneal dialysis if this is being performed. If the patient can be weighed this should be done once or twice daily. Unfortunately, this is often not possible in severely injured patients, or those on artificial ventilation. Use may then be made of a weighing bed. These, although simple in principle, require a great deal of attention since everything attached to or on the bed is weighed. In practice it is very difficult to maintain meaningful weights for periods of more than a few days, and often a new "baseline" weight will have to be taken.

Observations concerned with peritoneal dialysis are detailed in Chapter XIV, and those for arteriovenous shunts for haemodialysis in Chapter XV. The nutrition and care of intravenous infusions in the patients with acute renal failure is dealt with in Chapters XII and XIII.

(iv) Complications

Most of the "complications" seen in patients with acute renal failure
are either problems concerned with the precipitating condition, or consequences of the failure of renal function discussed above and in
Chapter VI. Two particular conditions require comment:

(a) Infection This has been laboured several times already, since it is
one of the main factors causing death. The nurse should be meticulous
in her handling of situations which might lead to entry of micro-
organisms, such as mouth care, nasogastric tube, wound, catheter,
peritoneal dialysis cannula, arteriovenous shunt, tracheostomy or cuffed endotracheal tube, and intravenous infusions. If chemotherapy is
given, the nurse will often notice that the dose has been modified to
suit the inability of the patient to excrete the drug, as discussed in
Chapter XVI.

(b) Hyperkalaemia The actual concentration of the plasma potassium
is often less important than the rate at which it is rising; but a concentration of more than 6 mmol/l will cause concern, above 7 mmol/l
alarm, and above 8 mmol/l is an indication for immediate action. The
patient will often already be connected to a cardiac monitor; if not, one
will be required. A defibrillation trolley and a cardiac emergency set
should always be immediately available. In addition to the sodium
bicarbonate provided, the nurse should see that the following are
always available should the doctor wish to use them to counteract a
very high potassium:

(1)   50% dextrose, 250 ml bottle; and 540 ml 33% dextrose
(2)   Insulin, 40 u/ml
(3)   Calcium gluconate, 10% or calcium chloride, 2·5%

Insulin and glucose, calcium or sodium bicarbonate may all be used to
minimize the effects of a high potassium on the heart, but the only
definitive solution is dialysis.

(v) Treatment

The treatment of acute renal failure consists of

(a)   The management of the primary conditions
(b)   The general management outlined in the previous section
(c)   Measures aimed at minimizing the uraemia. This may be done by
    (1)   conservative treatment
    (2)   dialysis

All three are continued until recovery of renal function takes place spontaneously. At present there is no way of shortening the period of renal failure once it is established.

(a) Conservative management This centres around the avoidance of overhydration, and minimizing the rise in plasma potassium and urea.

Overhydration is avoided by accurate fluid balance. Input is determined by the previous days' output, plus an allowance for insensible losses. This is about 500 ml in an average adult, but may be larger if fever is present. This usually means a daily intake of less than a litre. The aim is to produce a small weight loss each day.

Electrolyte intake should be negligible, since there is virtually no output.

Tissue breakdown, and hence the rise in plasma potassium and urea, are minimized by feeding an adequate energy intake. 1500 calories (6·2 MJ) should be aimed for, and the difficulty is giving this in the face of the fluid restriction. Details of dietary measures used are given in Chapter XII.

Intravenously, the energy may be given as 30% fructose, sorbitol or glucose. The first two solutions have the advantage that they cause little thrombophlebitis but depend on a well-functioning liver for their conversion to glucose in the body. The vein troubles with glucose may be minimized by using a central venous catheter in the right atrium, or a peripheral vein, and a polythene catheter and hydrocortisone hemisuccinate 5 mg and heparin 500 u in each bottle. Other measures which the doctor may order to help reduce the rise in plasma potassium are the injection of an anabolic steroid, such as norethandrolone, and oral calcium Resonium resin to bind potassium in the gastrointestinal juices. The nurse should not forget that hypoxia and infection are potent causes of a rise in the plasma potassium, and take the appropriate steps to avoid either.

(b) Dialysis The substitution of artificial means for the activity of the patient's own kidneys while they are not working has many advantages. The plasma biochemistry can be maintained more nearly normal than with conservative management, the fluid balance problem is solved and dangerous levels of plasma potassium are efficiently treated. Above all, the patient may then eat a relatively normal diet, and while not actually dialysing (if his illness permits) he may even be up and about the ward. His general nursing and medical management are greatly simplified, and some treatment for his primary condition — for example surgical operations — are made possible when otherwise they would be out of the question.

It is impossible to be dogmatic about when patients in acute renal failure should be dialysed. This will depend upon the patient, but also on the facilities that the ward and hospital where the patient is being nursed may have. The general tendency has been to dialyse patients early rather than late, to dialyse if there is any doubt that it is necessary, and to dialyse intensively (usually every day) so that the patients' fluid balance and biochemistry are as near normal as possible. This has resulted in the majority of severely ill patients with acute renal failure being dialysed at some time in their illness. The only group where dialysis is frequently unnecessary is that following uncomplicated abortions.

It is also impossible to be dogmatic about when to begin dialysing a patient. Some factors the doctor will take into consideration in making his decision are:

(1)   An acute rise in the plasma potassium may be an emergency. As conservative measures are taken (see above) dialysis may be arranged.

(2)   If the patient is very ill, especially if he is comatose or convulsing, then whatever his plasma biochemistry may show, dialysis will usually be begun.

(3)   If the patient's biochemistry is grossly disturbed, then even if he is well dialysis will be considered. As a very rough guide, a blood urea above 40 mmol/l or a plasma bicarbonate of less than 10 mmol/l.

(4)   If the patient is severely overloaded with salt and water, or very hypertensive.

(5)   More and more, dialysis is begun as soon as it becomes obvious that it will be necessary, at elective times to suit the other investigations and procedures the patients may undergo, and to ensure that wherever possible dialysis takes place in a predetermined fashion rather than as an emergency.

There are two types of dialysis available: *haemodialysis* and *peritoneal dialysis*. In both, the metabolites accumulating in the blood and tissues of the patient are removed by allowing them to diffuse across a membrane, into a fluid, which is then discarded. Haemodialysis requires the removal of blood from the body through an arteriovenous shunt. The blood is passed through a dialyser (the "artificial kidney") and returned to the body again. In peritoneal dialysis the blood vessels of the peritoneum are used, with the peritoneum acting as the dialysing membrane.

The principles of dialysis, details on the performance of peritoneal dialysis, a discussion of haemodialysis and notes on the care of arteriovenous shunts are to be found in Chapters XIV and XV.

The choice between peritoneal dialysis and haemodialysis will be made by the doctor for each individual patient, taking into account the local facilities and experience. Most patients will do well with either treatment, but a minority must have haemodialysis. These are usually patients in whom the peritoneum is unsuitable for dialysis, because of a burst abdomen, recent surgery with drains in place, or dense adhesions from old peritoneal inflammation. Recent abdominal surgery, provided that the abdomen is closed, is not a bar to successful peritoneal dialysis. Another group of patients who should have haemodialysis are those badly injured, heavily infected patients who produce very large quantities of urea and other products of tissue breakdown ("hypercatabolic acute renal failure"). The more powerful haemodialysis may be needed to keep the patient well with a relatively normal plasma biochemistry. The dialysis, of whatever type, will be continued through the oliguric phase, and into the polyuric phase until the patient's own renal function is sufficient. Dialysis can usually be stopped when the urine volume is over about 2 litres per day and contains more than 250 mmol of urea per day. If the patient is still catabolic, however it may be necessary to wait even longer before stopping dialysis.

(v) Prognosis

Provided that the nursing, medical and surgical care of the patient with acute renal failure are good, then with dialysis the outlook is almost entirely dictated by the circumstances which precipitated the acute renal failure in the first place. Return of renal function may take from one to six weeks, the longer periods of acute renal failure are found in the more severely affected patients. Over 80% of patients with acute renal failure from abortions or from toxic chemicals recover, but only about 10% or less of those with severe burns. Patients with postoperative acute renal failure have about a 50% chance of recovery. Acute renal failure is therefore still a very serious condition, with an overall mortality of some 40%. The biggest single factor contributing to this mortality, apart from the initial insult, is infection.

If acute cortical necrosis is present, the outlook is grave. If the necrosis is patchy, then recovery of renal function is possible, but it is more usually diffuse, and no recovery takes place.

(vi)   Acute renal failure in childhood

This is, fortunately, rather rare in children. Apart from primary renal disease, it may result from acute dehydration in gastrointestinal upsets, from hypovolaemia and circulatory collapse in the nephrotic syndrome, from trauma, particularly burns, from accidental poisoning with nephrotoxic chemicals or drugs, or very rarely after severe surgical operations. In general, children have a lower mortality for acute renal failure than adults, and rarely have such prolonged oliguria. In infants and young children also one of the causes of acute renal failure is a syndrome known as the haemolytic uraemic syndrome.

II   THE HAEMOLYTIC URAEMIC SYNDROME

This occurs usually in the first three or four years of life and is of unknown aetiology, although it may be viral in origin and seems to come in small "epidemics". The infant first has a gastrointestinal upset, but becomes steadily more ill with the appearance of uraemia, oliguria and severe anaemia. The small blood vessels are full of fragmenting clot, which both uses up the clotting factors of the blood and breaks up the red cells as they filter slowly through. If the coagulation is severe, then the kidneys are particularly affected and cortical necrosis appears. The outlook depends how complete the renal lesions may be; if the child is transfused, dialysed and generally supported, complete recovery can be seen, however, a number of children die in the acute attack, usually because diagnosis is late. As well as the management of a patient in acute renal failure, frequently on peritoneal dialysis, the nurse may also find that the patient is having a continuous heparin infusion which she must control. This is given in the early stages in the belief that it will limit further coagulation within the blood vessels. Usually the heparin is given as a continuous slow infusion of a very strong heparin solution (say 50,000 u in 500 ml), the rate being determined by an infusion pump, and adjusted according to clotting times, again usually performed by the nurse. This treatment is unproven, as is the infusion of clot-dissolving substances (fibrinolytic agents) directly into a catheter placed in the renal artery by the radiologist, under X-ray control. Again, a pump infusion is used. Clearly, extreme and untried treatments such as these will be used in only the most severe cases.

Occasionally so much of the patient's clotting factors are used up that the child begins to bleed. Even then, heparin may be given to try to reverse the primary event – the excess clotting.

The management of acute renal failure in a child is essentially that for an adult in acute renal failure. If dialysis is required this will more often

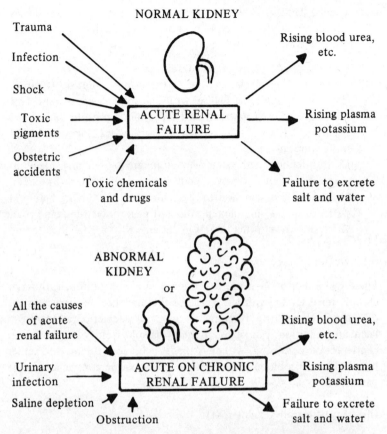

Fig.2.1 Acute and acute on chronic renal failure. A normal kidney is represented in the upper part of the diagram, and the two commonest forms of chronic renal disease in the lower half: a small, contracted kidney and a large, polycystic one.

be peritoneal dialysis than haemodialysis, especially in the very young child, provided that the amount of tissue breakdown is not excessive and the peritoneum allows free drainage.

III "ACUTE ON CHRONIC" RENAL FAILURE

This may be indistinguishable from acute renal failure occurring in a patient with normal kidneys (Figure 2.1).

(i) Causes

All the causes which may bring about acute renal failure in a subject with normal kidneys are even more likely to affect a patient with pre-existing renal damage. However, there are three particular circumstances which are important in this type of patient, and which may throw him out of his precarious balance:

(a)   Infection, particularly urinary tract infection

(b)   Salt and water depletion due to the osmotic diuresis (Chapter XVI) of chronic renal failure, with inadequate replacement. This may occur during gastroenteritis. The blood pressure falls, renal perfusion and renal function decline, with worsening uraemia and more vomiting.

Both infection and saline depletion are particularly likely to occur in patients with pyelonephritis or with polycystic kidneys. It is much less common to see acute on chronic renal failure in patients with glomerulonephritis, but acute infections can occur.

(c)   Acute blockage of the ureters in patients with partial obstruction.

(ii)   Symptoms and signs

These will either be identical to those of acute renal failure; or those of chronic renal failure with worsening of the uraemia, and perhaps signs of acute pyelonephritis (Chapter V), or of salt depletion and hypovolaemia in addition. The signs of hypovolaemia from saline depletion centre round confusion, withered tissues with low turgor, and either hypotension or a blood pressure which falls considerably on sitting the patient up.

(iii)   Investigations (Chapter XI)

Apart from the investigations as for acute renal failure, it is important for the doctor to establish whether two normal sized kidneys are present, or whether any of the stigmata of long standing renal failure — (such as bone disease) — are present. It is also important, even in a known chronic uraemic patient, to attempt the distinction between the final slow irrevocable decline in the patient's renal function from the sudden reversible fall-off in renal function we call *acute on chronic* renal failure. The reason is obvious: that in acute on chronic renal failure the patient will go home on his own renal function, whereas if he is in terminal renal failure wholly different circumstances may arise.

(iv)   Observations

These will be as for a patient in acute renal failure. The patient in acute on chronic renal failure will sometimes receive large quantities of fluids intravenously, and the observations of weight, fluid balance and sitting and lying blood pressure may be crucial. The urinary losses of sodium and potassium will be measured on 24-hour urine collections, and if urinary tract infection is suspected it will be managed as usual (Chapter V).

(v) Treatment

This centres round the treatment of the factors which caused the acute worsening of renal function, and dialysis if necessary, to tide the patient over until the fluid replacement or treatment of urinary tract infection can be effective. Often the doctor will have to begin dialysis without knowing whether the patient will in fact recover enough renal function to continue independently.

(vi) Prognosis

This is very variable. Patients with polycystic kidneys seem to be both particularly prone to develop acute on chronic renal failure, and particularly successful in surviving it with adequate treatment. The subsequent management is either that of chronic renal failure (Chapter VI) or of dialysis and transplantation (Chapters VIII and IX) that is if the patient survives, but this is very much dependent on the doctor's ability to offer substitution therapy if spontaneous recovery does not take place.

IV   ACUTE URAEMIA FROM RENAL HYPOPERFUSION

If the initial investigations establish that the patient is in uraemia because of a failure of perfusion of the kidneys, then the management will be quite different from the patient with acute renal failure. The main pointers the doctor will take into account are:

(1)   the composition of the urine (see p. 161)
(2)   the level of the right atrial pressure (see Chapter XIII)
(3)   the response to intravenous diuretic.

The patient with concentrated urine containing almost no sodium, who has a central venous pressure (CVP) of less than 5 cm of water and who has a brisk diuresis after frusemide may still require dialysis, but his central problem is lack of renal perfusion. Management therefore centres upon restoring this, and in the shocked patient with a low CVP who has received a diuretic much of the nurse's attention will be diverted towards rendering the CVP normal using the regime prescribed by the doctor. It will often be his or her responsibility to adjust the rates of infusion to maintain the CVP within prescribed limits (see Chapter

XIII). Further diuretic may be given judiciously to maintain urine output, but this can be a two-edged weapon since a large diuresis may further deplete the patient of vital circulating volume.

The second group of patients with acute uraemia from renal hypoperfusion have a raised CVP and their central problem lies in a poor cardiac output. This is most commonly seen in patients in severe congestive failure, immediately following cardiac surgery, or after a myocardial infarct. The management of these patients centres round restoration of cardiac output, and is outside the scope of this text.

V ACUTE URAEMIA FROM URINARY TRACT OBSTRUCTION

Again, this group of patients may well require all the management outlined above, including dialysis, while the diagnosis is established and the patient is rendered fit for treatment. The two large groups of patients seen here are those with obstruction due to stones — often in a single remaining kidney — and those with extrinsic blockage of the ureters. Sometimes this is benign, as in *retroperitoneal fibrosis*, but more often is *malignant*, with retroperitoneal lymphosarcoma and secondary spread from carcinomata elsewhere the most obvious. Carcinomas in the bladder and prostate may also involve the lower ends of the ureters.

After the patient has been made well enough, the aim is to relieve the obstruction and determine the precise nature of the obstruction. Sometimes it is necessary to drain the kidneys without knowledge of the underlying pathology. Close cooperation with the genito-urinary surgeon in the management of these patients is, of course, essential and the nurse will often find that the peritoneal dialysis catheter is replaced by tube or needle nephrostomies to look after. Sometimes the surgeon will elect to drain the kidneys from below by retrograde catheters left in place and strapped to the bladder catheter. Accurate observations of the volumes of urine passed via these different routes is crucial, especially any sudden falloff in output.

VI ACUTE URAEMIA FROM GLOMERULONEPHRITIS

This is managed as for acute renal failure from other causes, but the diagnosis and the prognosis will depend very much upon the appearances seen in the renal biopsy tissue, and this investigation is usually performed as soon as possible after suspicion of primary glomerular disease has crossed the doctors' minds. In some nephrotic patients, acute renal failure may follow a period of hypotension and renal hypoperfusion brought about by large protein losses in the urine, and particularly by superadded septicaemia (see p. 50). These patients can be very ill indeed, but although they may have a prolonged period of oliguria the outlook is usually good.

Suggestions for further reading:

Andrews, I. D.   Physiological response following trauma. *Nursing Times*. 14.3.74.

Cattell, W. R. (1975). Acute Renal Failure: *Advances in Renal Disease*. Ed. Jones, N. F. Edinburgh: Churchill-Livingstone.

Flynn, T. (1974). (Ed). Acute Renal Failure. London: M.T.P. Publications.

Friedman, E. I., Burton, B. T. (1974) Acute Renal Failure. Proceedings of a conference. Washington, D. C.: National Institutes of Health.

Kerr, D. N. S. (1973). Acute Renal Failure: *Renal Disease*, p. 417. Ed. Black, D. A. K. Oxford: Blackwell.

Lennon, P. (1974). A foreign patient suffering from acute renal failure: *Nursing Times* 31.10.74.

CHAPTER III

Acute nephritis

Diseases which predominantly affect the glomeruli of the nephron fall into two main groups:

(1)   Diseases affecting the kidney alone, called primary renal diseases. These are usually given the general name "glomerulonephritis". The name implies an inflammation ("-itis") but this is actually not visible in all types.

(2)   Diseases affecting small blood vessels throughout the body, in which the glomeruli (being mainly made of capillaries) may be involved along with all the other small blood vessels. There are many such secondary renal diseases, but the three most important are amyloidosis, diabetes and "connective tissue" disorders (Henoch – Schönlein purpura, lupus erythematosus, polyarteritis).

THE NATURE OF GLOMERULONEPHRITIS

The various forms of glomerulonephritis appear to be a group of disorders of *immunity*. Immune mechanisms are directed against the invasion of the body by foreign organisms or proteins. An elaborate system ensures that the blood, the body secretions and the tissues are capable of defence. This defence system includes:

(1)   Circulating substances, such as the various antibodies and the complement system. Together these breach the cell walls of invading organisms and initiate inflammation.

(2)   Lymphocytes and plasma cells which make the antibody.

(3)   Substances which increase capillary permeability, and attract leucocytes, so that exudate forms. Some of these are part of the complement system.

(4)   The leucocytes, which ingest organisms coated with antibody.

The effects of all this are seen as *inflammation*. Normally these mechanisms are triggered appropriately, for example during bacterial invasion, and act to the body's benefit. But if they are active inappropriately, or act against the body's own cells, then diseases will result.

In all forms of glomerulonephritis studied, some of these immune mechanisms appear to be involved, and may well be the starting point of the disease. Brief inflammation of the kidney (as in acute nephritis) may cause no permanent effects, but chronic inflammation heals with scar formation, and in the kidney a scar can do no work. Only a small distortion of the delicate glomerulus is needed to ensure that eventually the whole nephron to which it belongs will atrophy and cease to function. How exactly these immune mechanisms are triggered in glomerulonephritis is being investigated. At the moment it seems most likely that glomerulonephritis results from a distortion of normal immune responses, as discussed below. Patients who develop glomerulonephritis seem to be unable to rid themselves of foreign antigen as efficiently as normal individuals, so that antigen may persist for long periods in blood stream and tissue. The combination of antigen *and* antibody circulating sets the scene for the development of nephritis.

THE SYNDROMES OF GLOMERULAR DISEASES

Glomerulonephritis, and the other secondary glomerular diseases mentioned, can affect the kidney in such a way that the patient may suffer from one of several different clinical conditions. These are what brings his disease to the attention of the doctor, and causes his admission to hospital. The collections of symptoms and signs with which the patient presents are called "syndromes". There are only a few by which glomerular diseases may come to notice:

(1)   the acute nephritic syndrome
(2)   the nephrotic syndrome
(3)   symptomless proteinuria or haematuria
(4)   chronic renal failure.

Since there are a fairly large number of different underlying diseases, it follows that each of these clinical syndromes may be caused by a variety of diseases. Some of the diseases may pass through several of these syndromes during their course in a single patient; others are only found in one or other of the syndromes.

THE ACUTE NEPHRITIC SYNDROME

Characteristic: acute onset with haematuria.

There are several varieties of acute nephritic syndrome, the most important of which is acute nephritis itself.

A   Acute Nephritis (Figure 3.1)

(i)   Causes   The precipitating factor is a streptococcal infection, usually of the throat, occasionally of the skin. The organism is generally a *strep. pyogenes*, β-haemolytic on culture, and of a few specific strains. Rarely, other types of streptococcus, other bacteria or viruses may precipitate acute nephritis. Only some subjects will get acute nephritis when infected with these organisms, however, and most of them are children of school age. They appear to be individuals who are rather poor formers of antibody against the organisms. Antibody, complement, and streptococci form "complexes" which instead of being ingested by the white cells, circulate in the blood stream because the amount of antibody is too small. These "complexes" are caught up in the kidney and initiate an inflammatory process. As part of this inflammation, the cells of the glomerulus divide, or proliferate; the glomerulonephritis is therefore called *"proliferative" glomerulonephritis* and this is one of several forms of this particular type of glomerular disease.

(ii)   Signs and symptoms   Suddenly, one to three weeks after the streptococcal infection, the patient's urine volume drops markedly, and is seen to be rusty coloured from haematuria. It contains protein, is highly concentrated and has a very low sodium concentration. As a result of salt and water retention the face becomes puffy, the blood pressure may be elevated and the lung fields congested clinically and on X-ray. Mild uraemia is frequent. In the great majority of patients, all these signs and symptoms disappear within a week or two at most, but the haematuria and proteinuria may persist for up to six months before disappearing.

(iii)   Investigations   (Chapter XI)   All urine should be accurately measured, tested for blood and sent for microscopy. Initially 24 hour saves should be maintained for laboratory measurement of protein excretion, electrolytes, or creatinine clearance, as directed by the doctor. The throat should be swabbed on admission and the swab sent for culture to see if β-haemolytic *strep. pyogenes* is still present. Blood will be taken for the measurement of blood urea and plasma creatinine, electrolytes and for the performance of special tests such as the serum complement level, or the level of an anti-streptococcal antibody in the

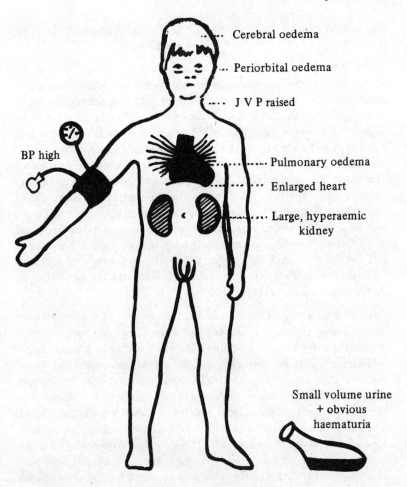

Fig. 3.1 Clinical features of acute nephritis. This is most common in children of school age, and is rather rare in infancy or adult life.

blood (anti-streptolysin) – the ASO titre or ASOT. The complement is initially low, and the ASOT high in acute nephritis. The doctor will order a chest X-ray to determine the heart size and to examine the lung fields.

(iv)   Observations and nursing Because of the salt and water retention, there is the risk of severe hypertension and heart failure. The patient should rest quietly in bed until the diuresis has occurred. Temperature, pulse, respirations and blood pressure are checked and charted four hourly, and the patient weighed daily. An accurate fluid intake

and output chart is kept, along with a chart of the urinary findings, which should be observed daily (blood and protein).

(v)   Treatment   The aim is to preserve a stable situation until the kidneys make their spontaneous recovery from the inflammatory process. While the patient is oliguric, fluids are kept to a minimum – for an adult 500 ml plus the urine output. For a child, the intake will be adjusted for bodyweight. Salt is restricted to 30 mmol/day, and it is usual, but not essential, to restrict the protein intake (see Chapter XII for details of diet). When the diuresis begins (as it usually does within a few days) and as the blood pressure becomes normal, the intake can become more liberal in all respects, and the patient is allowed out of bed. The condition is frequently mild, and prolonged bedrest has no advantage if the patient feels well, even if the urine still contains blood and protein on testing. There is no specific therapy for the renal lesion, but the doctor will usually order a 7 or 10 days' course of penicillin after the throat swab has been taken, to eliminate the possibility of continuing streptococcal infection.

(vi)   Complications   Occasionally the disease may take a more severe initial course, especially if the salt and water intake has been excessive during the early period of oliguria. Heart failure may be present, severe hypertension may be seen, and with the overhydration and high blood pressure convulsions may occur. In these circumstances the patient should be nursed sitting up and oxygen will be given. The doctor may elect to perform a venesection, which can produce immediate relief. The most useful apparatus to provide for this manoeuvre is a straightforward blood letting set as used for blood donation. This has the added advantage that the blood may be refrigerated and reinfused later after treatment. Alternatively, a large dose of a powerful diuretic such as frusemide or ethacrynic acid given intravenously may produce sufficient diuresis to avoid venesection. The doctor may elect to treat the blood pressure if the diastolic exceeds 110 or 115 mmHg, and several drugs may be used for this: hydralazine, reserpine, or alpha methyl DOPA intravenously. If fits occur the best drug is intravenous diazepam (Valium) which is not eliminated through the kidneys.

A very few patients may be so oliguric, and become so uraemic, that peritoneal dialysis may be necessary to control the uraemia and fluid balance (Chapter XIV). Even this, and the complications of heart failure, hypertension and convulsions, do not exclude complete recovery.

(vii) Prognosis   The glomerulonephritis heals completely in about 95% of children, but some slight scarring of the glomerulus may lead to persistent mild proteinuria, or less commonly haematuria. It may take

up to two years before these disappear, and on occasion they persist indefinitely. Some of these patients *may* develop hypertension and chronic renal failure in later life, decades after the initial attack, but this is far from proved. The other 5% of children, and a larger proportion of adult patients with acute nephritis, do not make a full recovery but seem to have more sinister forms of underlying glomerulonephritis. Two of these can now be distinguished.

One is called *rapidly progressive nephritis*. In these less fortunate patients, the glomerular inflammation is more severe and involves the cells of Bowman's capsule, which form masses of cells called "crescents" from their appearance in histological preparations. This form of glomerulonephritis is therefore often called glomerulonephritis with crescents. The patient may have acute nephritis, with severe oliguria, fails to recover and dies in the acute phase; or recovers a little renal function, retaining heavy proteinuria and haematuria, perhaps developing a nephrotic syndrome (see below) and declines into uraemia within a few months.

The other is usually called mesangiocapillary or membrano-proliferative glomerulonephritis, understandably abbreviated to MCGN or MPGN; The patient's kidneys fail to heal after the attack of acute nephritis, and there is often such heavy proteinuria that a nephrotic syndrome appears. Tests of the serum complement show that the condition is still active since the complement remains low. Proteinuria persists, with actual oedema on occasions, until after several years, or even longer, the patient develops severe hypertension and declines into chronic renal failure. The glomerular changes are again different, with a thickening of all the capillary walls of the glomerulus with complement and sometimes antibody deposits, as well as the usual inflammation of glomerulonephritis.

The management of these patients with progressive forms of nephritis will often be that of the nephrotic syndrome (see below) or of progressive nephritis with persistent symptomless proteinuria (see below). If chronic renal failure appears, it will be managed as for other patients with renal insufficiency, with allowance for the fact that heavy proteinuria is present.

B Recurrent Haematuria

(i)   Signs and symptoms   This is another variant of the acute nephritic syndrome. It is common in children and young adults, especially males. Attacks of gross macroscopic haematuria occur repeatedly, immediately after non-specific upper respiratory tract infections, or

after severe exercise. Frequently urine tests reveal a little protein between attacks. In contrast to acute nephritis, there is no hypertension or alteration in urine volume. The patient may feel a little "off colour" and have a slight fever during the attacks but is often quite well throughout.

(ii)   Investigation (Chapter XI)   Other causes of repeated haematuria, such as tumours of the urinary tract, may need to be excluded by urological examination. Sometimes tubular casts containing red cells can be seen in the urine, thus proving that the bleeding arises in the nephrons of the kidney, and this may avoid a needless cystoscopy. The doctor will usually wish to assess renal function and the urine should be carefully tested and recorded for both blood and protein. Fresh urine will be needed for microscopy, and an IVU will be done to show the kidneys and whether the urinary tract contains a tumour. Sometimes a renal biopsy will be necessary. Full investigation is frequently necessary because the repeated attacks of red urine may cause a great deal of anxiety to the patient or his parents, and reassurance is only possible after the fullest search.

(iii)   Treatment   There is no specific treatment. The patient may go to bed during each attack if he feels off colour, but prolonged bed rest simply because the urine contains red cells on microscopy has nothing to commend it and may be physically and psychologically harmful. Some doctors advise long term antibiotics to avoid upper respiratory infections but these are frequently due to viruses.

(iv)   Prognosis   Usually the kidney shows only a mild patchy ("focal") nephritis and sometimes appears completely normal. A common finding in this group of patients is the presence of immunoglobulin A(IgA) in the glomeruli. This is the variety of immunoglobulin characteristically found in secretions such as milk, tears and saliva, and its presence in the kidney is puzzling. In general the prognosis is good, with the haematuria ceasing in adult life. The problem is usually that of the disruption caused in the child's life by his tendency to have red urine from time to time. Haematuria frightens parents and they may reach the plausible conclusion that every time an attack of haematuria appears, the kidneys are being further damaged. Fortunately, this is usually not the case, although in a few patients, however, there is a more severe glomerulonephritis, hypertension develops and the patient becomes uraemic.

C Acute Nephritis in Generalized Diseases

Acute nephritic syndromes are occasionally seen as part of generalized diseases affecting small blood vessels. The commonest of these is *Henoch – Schönlein purpura* (anaphylactoid purpura) – a condition predominantly of childhood, in which haematuria is frequently seen. The other features of Henoch – Schönlein purpura which may be present are the purpuric rash, particularly seen on the legs and feet, joint pain and swelling, and abdominal pain, sometimes with diarrhoea. This condition is caused by a generalized vasculitis, but the precipitating agent is unknown. The rash, pain and joint swelling may come and go over several months, and in one attack there may be haematuria and proteinuria. The haematuria is usually of no significance and presumably is the purpura affecting the kidney. In a few patients, however a severe nephritis may be seen, sometimes with heavy proteinuria and the development of a nephrotic syndrome occasionally. The appearances in the kidney and the clinical course may resemble that of rapidly progressive nephritis. There is no specific treatment for the renal disease, although corticosteroids seem to quell the other features such as the joint pains. If, as rarely happens, the nephritis is a severe one, then cyclophosphamide or other immunosuppressive drugs may be considered by the doctor as treatment.

The serious nephritis with crescents around the glomeruli and a sinister course may also be seen in the rare vascular conditions, *polyarteritis nodosa, Wegener's granulomatosis* and *Goodpasture's syndrome.*

Suggestions for further reading:
Cameron, J. S., Jones, N. F. (1974). Glomerulonephritis and acute Nephritic syndromes. In: *Medicine*. pp. 1258 and 1282. Eds. Bayliss, R. I. S., Hall, R. London: Medical Education (International).

Cameron, J. S., Williams, D. G. (1976). The immunology of glomerulonephritis. In: *Medical Immunology*. Eds. Holborow, J., Reeves, D. G. New York: Academic Press.

Lancet Editorial (1975). Recurrent haematuria in children and young adults. *Lancet*, ii, 114.

Meadow, S. R. Glasgow, E. F., White, R. H. R., Moncrieff, M. W., Cameron, J. S., Ogg, C. S. (1972). Schönlein – Henoch nephritis. *Quarterly Journal of Medicine*, 41, 24.

CHAPTER IV

The nephrotic syndrome

I THE NEPHROTIC SYNDROME

Characteristic: insidious onset of oedema with albuminuria and hypo-proteinaemia.

(i) Causes

There are very many causes of the nephrotic syndrome, some of which are forms of primary renal disease (glomerulonephritis) and some of which are involvement of the kidney in generalized diseases:

(a) Glomerulonephritis (Figure 4.1)
    (1)   normal glomeruli ("minimal change", "lipoid nephrosis")
    (2)   proliferative glomerulonephritis
    (3)   membranous nephropathy
(b) Amyloidosis
(c) Diabetes
(d) Systemic lupus erythematosus (SLE)

and many rarer conditions which account for only 1% of all nephrotic patients.

(a) (1) Glomerulonephritis with normal glomeruli (Figure 4.1) This clumsy title conceals our ignorance of this condition's true nature. It is also called the "minimal change" lesion because there may be minor changes in the glomeruli, and the clinical terms "nephrosis", "lipoid nephrosis" and "pure nephrosis" are also used, especially by paediatricians. There appears to be a functional abnormality of the glomeruli which results in gross proteinuria, but which we cannot see even with the electron microscope. The slight changes we can sometimes see may be the result rather than the cause of the proteinuria. The condition appears to be an allergic state analogous to asthma. For example, it may be brought on by *drugs*, or by *pollen* and other sensitivities. In the majority of cases, however, the allergen is unknown. This condition is present in 80% of childhood nephrotics, but only in 30% of adults.

(a) (2) Proliferative glomerulonephritis (Figure 4.1) Several varieties of this may be seen in the kidneys of nephrotic patients, including all those described in the section on acute nephritis; some few seem to follow streptococcal infection. They range in severity from the most benign "focal" varieties to the severe rapidly progressive forms with crescents. Proliferative glomerulonephritis is the commonest finding in adult nephrotic patients, and accounts for almost all the children who do ,not have normal glomeruli. There are usually immune deposits within the glomeruli, but the antigens against which these are formed are unknown in the great majority of patients.

(a) (3) Membranous nephropathy (Figure 4.1) In this condition the capillary walls of the glomeruli are diffusely thickened by deposits containing antibody and complement, with scarring. These deposits lie on the ouside of the capillary wall, and we do not know what cause their deposition. From their nature, this is presumed to be a disorder of immunity involving the formation of circulating, soluble antibody-antigen complexes. As in proliferative glomerulonephritis, the antigens are usually untraceable but occasionally can be identified. For example, hepatitis B antigen (Australia antigen) has been identified as a cause of both proliferative and membranous nephropathy.

(b) Amyloidosis, (c) Diabetes, (d) Systemic Lupus Erythematosus (SLE) All these three conditions are characterized by involvement of small blood vessels. All may involve the kidney and produce heavy proteinuria. All may lead to renal failure, and commonly produce hypertension and haematuria. *Amyloidosis* appears as a complication of sepsis or rheumatoid arthritis (secondary amyloid) or sometimes on its own (primary amyloid). It is a fibrous protein, which infiltrates the blood vessels. We do not know how it appears. *Diabetes* similarly infiltrates the blood vessels (with glycoproteins) and eventually destroys the whole glomerulus. In *Systemic lupus erythematosus*, the kidney is damaged by the deposition of soluble antigen antibody complexes. In this instance the antigen is known, since it is the DNA of cell nuclei. From the deposition of DNA – anti-DNA antibody complexes, all forms of nephritis may result from the mildest to the most severe forms, leading to rapid renal failure. The pattern of glomerular reaction seen on renal biopsy influence the prognosis and treatment given.

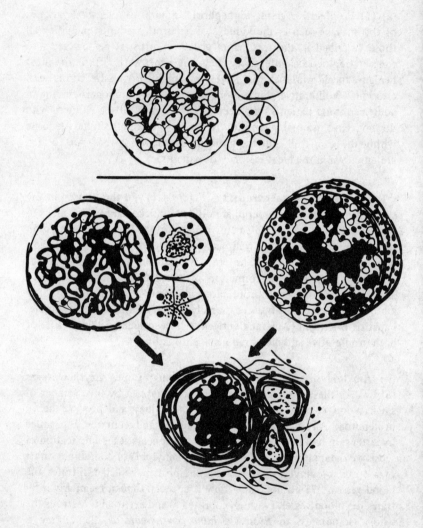

Fig. 4.1 The appearances of the glomeruli in glomerulonephritis, magnified about 400 times. The upper glomerulus has a normal appearance and is shown with two normal tubules. The glomerulus has a delicate lace-like structure of capillaries cut in section. There is little connective tissue, few cell nuclei, and thin capillary walls.

In the "minimal change" lesion, the glomerulus may look entirely normal, as here, or show very mild increase in the connective tissue (black). Functionally, however, it is grossly deranged and actually leaks large quantities of protein leading to a nephrotic syndrome. A glomerulus affected by *membranous nephropathy* is shown on the left. The capillary walls are diffusely thickened, and there is an increase of connective tissue in the glomerulus. Changes can also be seen in the tubules; in the upper tubule a cast is forming from protein-containing tubular fluid and damaged tubular cells, and in the lower tubule an excess of droplets from reabsorbed protein can be seen. These would be observed in any patient with proteinuria, whatever the glomerular disease. At this point the patient would probably have a nephrotic syndrome of proteinuria without symptoms; renal function would be rather less than normal, but still sufficient for normal life.

A glomerulus affected by a severe form of *proliferative glomerulonephritis* is shown on the right. There is an increase in the number of cell nuclei (represented by the black dots) and in connective tissue. As well as the glomerulus being affected, and the capillaries occluded by swollen proliferating cells, the cells of Bowman's capsule are also undergoing proliferation on the right side of the section. In section, the appearance is cresent-shaped and these are therefore called "crescents" and are usually of ominous significance, since the route for flow of urine to the tubule is blocked by cells. At the bottom a glomerulus in *chronic glomerulonephritis* is shown. It mostly consists of scar tissue, and scar tissue surrounds it and the two dying tubules shown adjacent. It may be impossible to tell from what variety of glomerulonephritis this appearance has arisen. As indicated by the arrows, both membranous nephropathy and severe proliferative glomerulonephritis may lead to chronic glomerulonephritis and renal failure. Milder forms of proliferative disease may not, and the "minimal change" lesion almost never scars enough to do this.

(ii)   Signs and symptoms of the nephrotic syndrome (Figure 4.3)

The essential feature of the nephrotic syndrome is that there should be prolonged profuse proteinuria, usually 3 – 5 g/day or more in an adult. The perceptive patient or nurse may notice that this proteinuria makes the urine more frothy than usual. Eventually, the heavy proteinuria will deplete the serum albumin to an extent where the plasma volume is no longer maintained. This sets in motion a chain of events leading to the oedema (Figure 4.2). Aldosterone and renin are secreted in excess, and salt and water retained. The salt and water reabsorbed by the kidney is promptly lost from the circulation because the plasma albumin is low. The end result is a grossly expanded volume of extracellular water, visible as oedema, and a plasma volume which may still be barely normal. In adults the oedema tends to appear first in the evening round the ankles, and to become gradually more obvious. In children, the oedema is often of more sudden onset, and with the better tissue turgor of children it is less affected by gravity and often first becomes visible round the eyes; it also tends to appear as ascites earlier than in adults, and round the ankles to a correspondingly smaller extent in the initial stages. The oedema may come and go in a patient with continued heavy proteinuria, both spontaneously and in response to treatment, so that this condition and heavy symptomless proteinuria merge into one another and have the same underlying glomerular diseases. On occasion the oedema may be massive, with gross swelling of the legs, genitalia and trunk, ascites and pleural effusions. The patient is distressed and unable to walk.

Microscopic haematuria, hypertension and reduced renal function may be present along with the nephrotic syndrome, depending upon the underlying disease and its severity. Usually those patients with the minimal change lesion in their glomeruli escape these consequences, but all the others are likely to develop them.

(iii)   Investigations (Chapter XI)

Investigations are of great importance in the nephrotic syndrome, both in establishing the diagnosis and in following treatment. The urine should of course be tested for protein and blood in all patients with ankle swelling. A clean mid-stream specimen of urine will also frequently be called for, since urinary tract infections are common in patients with the nephrotic syndrome, especially women. The presence of excess white cells in the urine does not always indicate infection; they may be the result of glomerular inflammation and may be seen in both acute nephritis and in some nephrotics. It is therefore wrong to refer to these

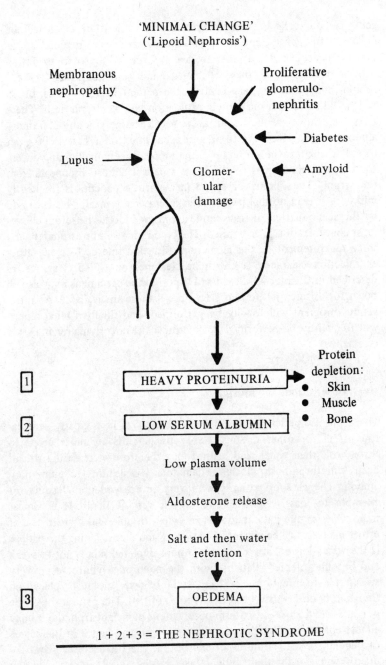

Fig. 4.2 Causes and consequences of the nephrotic syndrome.

cells as "pus cells". Twenty-four hour collections of urine will be collected frequently, and to begin with several consecutive collections may be needed and it is wise to save all urine. The protein excretion will be measured on these specimens and sometimes the 24-hour sodium and potassium, especially if the patient is on diuretics. Blood will be taken for plasma protein estimation and electrophoresis. These tests will show, in the nephrotic patient, a large amount of urinary albumin varying from 3 g to 50 g or even, in extreme cases, 100 g per day. The greater the proteinuria, the more the serum albumin concentration falls, sometimes to the point where it almost disappears from the serum. The plasma or serum in nephrotic patients is frequently milky, as it is in normal people after a large fatty meal. This is caused by the accumulation of triglyceride fat in the blood. The serum cholesterol concentration is also raised. The blood urea will be estimated, and some measurement of the glomerular filtration rate performed, either an injection clearance, a creatinine clearance or a urea clearance, as described in Chapter XI. Blood and "spot" urine specimens may also be taken for differential protein clearances if these are available. An intravenous urogram will usually be performed, and finally a renal biopsy will frequently be performed to determine the underlying renal disease (see below).

(iv)   Observations and nursing

The nephrotic patient need not be in bed, unless he is grossly oedematous or ill for other reasons. Nephrotic patients are more prone to thrombosis than usual, and bedrest may therefore increase the risk of deep vein thrombosis in the oedematous legs leading to pulmonary emboli. The care of patients with very severe oedema — leading for example to massive genital swelling — is very difficult. It is almost impossible for the patient to be really comfortable and a great deal of effort may have to be put into positioning and repositioning the patient if the water-logged, stretched and protein-depleted skin is not to break and become infected. Patients with the nephrotic syndrome are very susceptible to infection and at any spike of fever should be placed on four hourly observations and the doctor notified. The patient should be weighed daily, since short term observations of weight from day to day almost entirely reflect changes in body water, and hence in the degree of oedema. A daily fluid input and output chart is necessary, and the doctor will usually limit fluid intake as well as salt intake (Chapter XIII). The urine output may fall during the accumulation of oedema, and greatly increase during a diuresis. If the patient is hypertensive or

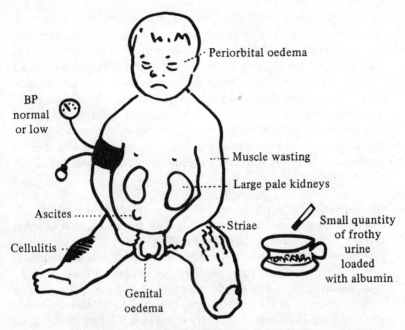

Figure 4.3 Clinical features of the nephrotic syndrome. Although it may occur at any age from birth to old age, it is most common at the ages of two or three years; hence the pictures shows a little boy with a severe nephrotic syndrome.

hypotensive a close watch is necessary on the blood pressure, and since both these states may arise it is wise to chart a daily blood pressure in all patients, taken lying and standing.

(v) Complications (Figure 4.3)

(a) Infection This has already been mentioned on several occasions and the nurse should remember this peculiar susceptibility of the nephrotic patient during any procedure which carries the risk of infection, such as injection, operation or catheterization. Prompt treatment with antibiotics has probably been the biggest single factor in improving the outlook for nephrotic patients. This susceptibility to infection is not surprising when one considers that the nephrotic patient is protein depleted, electrolytically imbalanced, water-logged and depleted of gammaglobulin (antibody) by his proteinuria. Urinary tract infection, cellulitis of oedematous tissues (frequently from E. Coli), infection of wounds or puncture sites, septicaemias and primary peritonitis with pneumococci are all seen. The doctor is presented with the dilemma of whether to give antibiotics prophylactically, and perhaps face infection with a resistant organism at a later date; or to treat infections only as they arise, recognizing that by the time he begins treatment the patient may already be severely ill. Some doctors will therefore place all nephrotic patients on antibiotics from diagnosis, others will withhold them. The nurse should not forget that other treatments the nephrotic patient may be having, such as corticosteroid therapy or immunosuppressive (cytotoxic) agents (see below) will not only reduce even further his resistance to infection but mask the early signs, both local and systemic, of the inflammation.

(b) Thombosis   The fibrinogen and fat concentration of the nephrotic patient's blood is increased, and along with them a number of other clotting factors, such as antihaemophilic globulin. The circulation is often poor, and the patient sometimes immobilized. It is not surprising that thromboses should occur, both venous and even arterial, in nephrotic patients. The nurse should be aware of this possibility because early observation of the complications may lead to treatment which is effective only if prompt. Pulmonary emboli are frequent in nephrotic patients. Any additional factor leading to thrombosis – such as a cut down on a vein, or an infected drip site – may easily lead to embolism. In addition, corticosteroid therapy increases the coagulability of the blood. It is now practice in some units to give nephrotic patients injections of heparin 5000 u bd subcutaneously, especially if they are bedridden, while they are oedematous.

(c) Hypovolaemia and hypotension   These may be so severe as to precipitate circulatory collapse. If this is prolonged, acute renal failure may appear, and in a nephrotic patient this is particularly severe because the tubules are full of protein-loaded fluid which sets into a jelly. The best way of detecting severe hypovolaemia of the circulation is to measure the blood pressure standing (or sitting up), and lying flat. A fall of more than 20 mmHg on sitting or standing up should be reported to the doctor. The same effect will of course be seen if the patient is on some hypotensive drugs.

(d) Protein depletion   This can be very severe, even when a high protein diet can be taken. Often the nurse may see, as the tide of oedema subsides, a grossly wasted patient appear. The skin becomes thin and atrophic, and may split, giving rise to wide purple stripes (striae) like those of pregnancy which fade but never disappear. These are worsened by corticosteroid therapy, which itself leads to protein breakdown. The protein of the bones is removed and osteoporosis may be seen in the nephrotic patient. Even after a successful remission of the disease, many months refeeding may be necessary to replenish the tissue protien stores.

(e) Hypertension and uraemia These may of course be present in the nephrotic patient but are features of the underlying disease and not complications as such of the nephrotic state (see Chapter VI).

(vi) Treatment of the nephrotic syndrome

Treatment of the nephrotic state is really palliation of the oedema. The real object of treatment is the removal of the proteinuria, but this is frequently not possible; this aspect is discussed below as treatment of the causes of the syndrome. All nephrotic patients, however, can benefit from the measures outlined here.

(a) Control of sodium balance This is one of the key manoeuvres to limit or reduce oedema. We may:

(1) limit the sodium in the diet (Chapter XII);
(2) prevent sodium absorption;
(3) increase sodium excretion.

Sodium absorption may be limited by the administration of resins which bind sodium in the food and that which is secreted in the intestinal juices, so that it passes out into the faeces. The resin (Katonium) is not very palatable, taken neat, but flavoured preparations are available. The resin may be rendered more acceptable by mixing well with a glass of milk, or by sprinkling it on the food. With the availability of newer powerful diuretics, resins are now much less used.

Diuretics (see Chapter XVI) are used to deplete the body of excess sodium, and with it the excess water visible as oedema. The doctor may order powerful diuretics, such as frusemide, ethacrynic acid or bumetanide, in the early stages. These can be dangerous if the plasma volume is very low and the peripheral circulation poor with a low blood pressure. The doctor may then elect to infuse a plasma expander while he gives a large dose of diuretic intravenously. Salt-free human albumin made up with 5% dextrose is best for this purpose but is very expensive. Plasma or high molecular weight dextran may also be used, but the plasma contains sodium. Often a very satisfactory loss of weight and oedema can be achieved by this combined therapy but it is only necessary in very oedematous patients. Another diuretic which may be used is the aldosterone inhibitor, spironolactone (Aldactone). This has the added advantage that it minimizes the potassium loss brought about by the other diuretics. When the patient is established on treatment, if it is possible, the doctor will often transfer the patient to a longer acting diuretic such as one of the thiazide diuretics (e.g. bendrofluazide or hydrochlorothiazide). These diuretics also cause some potassium loss so the doctor may well order potassium chloride supplements. These may be given as effervescent or resin-based tablets. An alternative is to use a potassium-sparing diuretic such as amiloride in combination with the thiazide.

(b) High protein diet   Details of this very important part of treatment are given in Chapter XII. Provided the liver is not diseased, the patient may be able to make sufficient albumin to raise his serum albumin and so minimize or lose oedema, even in the face of continuing proteinuria.

(c) Antibiotics   These will frequently be given, as discussed under "Infections" above.

(d) Acupuncture   Very occasionally a patient whose oedema fails to respond to all these measures is seen. Frequently this will be a patient who has, in addition, severe impairment of renal function, with uraemia of varying extent to add to his problems. It may then be necessary to perform acupuncture on the legs, after sitting the patient in a cardiac bed for a day or two to drain the oedema downwards. The doctor makes small cuts in the skin over the back of the foot and the shins, and the fluid is allowed to drain into a bowl under cover of sterile towels. Meticulous asepsis is necessary if cellulitis of the legs is not to appear. This rather brutal sounding manoeuvre is usually painless and is frequently followed by the maintenance of a relatively oedema-free state. It may convert a bedridden patient into one who can be mobilized. Sometimes patients perform "acupuncture" themselves by splitting the skin, and nurses frequently observe that injection sites in nephrotic patients will drain, sometimes for days. Again the risk of cellulitis is present.

While none of these measures tackle the real problem — the underlying renal disease and the heavy proteinuria it causes — they may render the life of the nephrotic patient normal, or nearly normal, in many instances where specific therapy is not possible. The nurse should not lose sight of the fact that often to the patient the disease *is* the oedema, and its relief brings more encouragement to the patient than to the nursing staff or doctors who may be conscious of their failure to eliminate the proteinuria.

(e) Corticosteroid and cytotoxic (immunosuppressive) drugs: the treatment of the underlying condition These drugs are of proven value only in patients whose nephrotic syndrome arises from the "minimal change" lesion ("lipoid nephrosis"). Some doctors use them for nephrotic syndromes caused by other types of glomerulonephritis, and this is discussed below.

(1) In patients with the "minimal change" lesion, it is possible to produce permanent remission with corticosteroid drugs such as *prednisolone or prednisone* – in practice there is no difference between these two drugs. It is well-recognized that patients with this condition may remit spontaneously but it is usual to treat them after waiting a week or two, since while still nephrotic the patient is at risk from the complications listed above. Often the doctor gives a large dose to begin with, then less for a period of four to eight weeks. The drug may be given on alternate days, or on three days a week, during this period to minimize the possibility of side effects; these are rarely seen in less than two months' treatment.

Almost all patients with the "minimal change" lesion will lose their proteinuria rapidly and have a prompt diuresis, shedding their oedema in a gratifying fashion. The doctor will then be able to taper off the steroids before the many side effects of these drugs appear. Meanwhile, the supportive measures outlined above may be employed.

About half of the patients will then remain well indefinitely. Unfortunately, the remainder relapse, sometimes as soon as the steroids are withdrawn. These patients need repeated, or even continuous steroid treatment and the problem turns into one of the side effects of the corticosteroid treatment, rather than of the disease itself.

The nurse should look for these effects in any patient on steroid therapy; they are only too familiar:

Growth failure in children, osteoporosis and fractures in adults
Hypertension and all its complications
A Cushingoid appearance
Cutaneous striae
Peptic ulceration
Protein wasting
Failure of puberty in children
Increased susceptibility to thrombosis
Increased susceptibility to infection
Masking of the signs of infection

When these problems appear, the doctor may consider the use of a cytotoxic drug, of which *cyclophosphamide* seems the most promising at the moment. How either cyclophosphamide, or prednisolone, act in this condition is quite unknown. Cyclophosphamide, of course, has side effects which may be immediately visible:

Marrow depression
Increased susceptibility to infections, especially viruses
Loss of hair
Nausea and vomiting

and it may well have long term effects of which we are ignorant. Doctors therefore employ this type of drug with extreme caution. However, the mortality in the group of patients who persist in relapsing is such that treatment is justified, especially since it need only continue for a few months at most. One important point for the nurse to remember, if cyclophosphamide is to be given orally, is that it should be given on a full stomach. It is preferable to give it last thing at night so that the doctor may give a sedative anti-emetic if he wishes. If this is not observed vomiting will be frequent. The white cell count in the blood will be watched closely and if a deliberate lowering of the white count is desired then it will be done on alternate days, or daily to begin with. The problem of hair loss should be discussed with patient or parent and many patients will wish a wig for the period of temporary baldness. The hair always regrows and the patient should be warned that it may be light coloured and curly to begin with. Hair loss is more frequent if larger doses (such as those to deliberately depress the white count) are used. Since results seem to be as good with lower doses as with higher doses which produce hair loss, this complication is much more rarely seen and most patients will only notice slight loss of hair if they are observant.

Cyclophosphamide does appear to control the disease in patients with "minimal change" lesions who no longer respond to corticosteroids, or who are suffering severe side effects from continuous dosage. After the cyclophosphamide is withdrawn there may be prolonged remission lasting many years, amounting to cure in some cases.

The nephrotic syndrome ("nephrosis") in childhood.   The nephrotic syndrome is twice as common in childhood as in adult life, and is particularly seen at the age of two or three years. About 80 or 90% of childhood nephrotics fall into the group of primary renal disease where no abnormality of the glomeruli is visible on light microscopy ("lipoid nephrosis", "minimal change lesion"); in most the aetiology is obscure.

The problem, as noted above, is the 50% of this group who have persistent or relapsing disease, and require maintenance corticosteroids to keep them free from oedema. The principal difference from the adult nephrotic is that these doses produce *growth failure*, leading to severe stunting as well as all the other side effects of corticosteroid drugs – a Cushingoid appearance and hypertension being most commonly seen. The repeated relapses or intermittent spells in hospital disrupt schooling and may lead to serious emotional disturbance in the younger child. It is in this group of children that cyclophosphamide has proved most useful, producing lasting remission in a high proportion of patients.

A few children with the nephrotic syndrome have other underlying renal conditions, such as proliferative glomerulonephritis, but secondary renal disease from diabetes or amyloid almost never occurs in childhood. A rare *congenital nephrotic syndrome* may be seen in the first three months of life. This appears to result from the action of a recessive gene. The babies fail to thrive or respond to treatment, and all eventually die by the age of eighteen months although a few have now received successful renal transplants.

(2) In patients with the *nephrotic syndrome from other conditions*, the use of both corticosteroid and cytotoxic drugs is much more controversial and different doctors hold contrasting views. *Corticosteroid drugs* do not appear to make much difference to the majority of adult patients with proliferative glomerulonephritis or membranous nephropathy, who of course form the majority of patients in this age group. Most doctors will therefore not use steroids on an adult patient unless they have performed a renal biopsy and seen that a "minimal change" lesion is present. In addition, the patient may have unsuspected amyloidosis (which steroids do not help) or even diabetes or systematic lupus erythematosus. This last disease is helped by steroid therapy but since it has to continue for long periods, often at quite high dosage, side effects are common and severe. The position with children is different; the great majority of children have the "minimal change" lesion, and unless some other feature is present (such as hypertension or haematuria) the doctor may well elect to try steroids without renal biopsy, reassessing the patient completely if he does not respond promptly.

Cytotoxic drugs such as azathiprine (Imuran), cyclophosphamide and chlorambucil have been tried in these other forms of glomerulonephritis and in the nephritis of SLE. Some results have been encouraging but only in SLE is there clear evidence of benefit. Even here, there is a price to pay and today one third of deaths in patients with SLE nephritis result from infections rather than from renal failure. There is no treatment for amyloid renal disease, except to treat the primary septic condition (e.g. osteomyelitis) if there is one. No drug seems to affect the renal disease of diabetes.

(vii) Prognosis

The outlook for the patient with the nephrotic syndrome depends much more upon the nature of the disease causing the syndrome than on the severity or duration of the oedema. This emphasizes the importance of the renal biopsy findings, as mentioned in the previous section. The only other test which will discriminate to some extent between patients with a relatively good prognosis and those who will do badly is the performance of differential protein clearances (Chapter XI). These are much simpler and of course, safer to do than a biopsy, but give less information.

Patients with the *"minimal change" lesion* generally retain good renal function, do not have hypertension and, in 50% of cases, never have another attack. Patients with other forms of glomerulonephritis (*proliferative glomerulonephritis* and *membranous nephropathy*) generally do not lose their proteinuria, generally develop hypertension and frequently suffer a decline of renal function to enter renal failure. A few patients (especially children) with proliferative glomerulonephritis provide an exception to this statement and do rather well. Since most children with the nephrotic syndrome have the "minimal change" lesion, and most adults do not, the prognosis for a child with the nephrotic syndrome is much better than that of an adult. However, if the child falls into the group with repeated relapses or continuous disease then it may suffer the complications of the nephrotic syndrome with those of steroid therapy in addition. The prognosis of *amyloid* renal disease depends upon whether the primary condition can be treated; occasionally there is no precipitating disease (primary amyloid) and the outlook is usually bad, as it is in the patient with the nephrotic syndrome from *diabetes*. The nephritis of *SLE* is, in general, progressive and is the commonest cause of death in patients with systemic lupus erythematosus.

From all this it can be seen that the outlook for the patient with the nephrotic syndrome, especially in adult life, is poor. The treatment is mostly symptomatic and all the problems of the patient with chronic disease arise. Should the patient enter chronic renal failure, then the oedema may remit, because so much kidney has been lost that the quantity of proteinuria diminishes. Some less fortunate patients have all the problems of a full nephrotic syndrome, with those of severe uraemia superimposed (Chapter VI).

II SYMPTOMLESS PROTEINURIA OR HAEMATURIA

Characteristic: fit patient, found by urine test.

(i) Causes

This state may arise from a partially healed acute nephritis, or a nephrotic syndrome, or be found in a patient with no history of previous renal disease at all. This can be deceptive, since many patients forget illnesses that they have had in childhood. Any of the diseases that may give rise to a nephrotic syndrome may give rise to symptomless proteinuria, that is, various forms of glomerulonephritis, amyloid, diabetes or systemic lupus, although the last two conditions are rarely without symptoms, even though they may not be renal. Symptomless proteinuria may also occur in patients with chronically obstructed kidneys or with pyelonephritis and tuberculosis. Symptomless haematuria may be found in a variety of urological disorders, particularly tumours of the urinary tract.

(ii) Signs and symptoms

None by definition, except for the proteinuria or haematuria. If the proteinuria is heavy, even if there is no ankle oedema, the serum albumin may be low.

(iii) Investigations (Chapter XI)

In general, this is the reason for admitting such a patient to hospital and all the investigations that may be applied to the patient with the nephrotic syndrome (see above), including renal biopsy, may be used in the patient with symptomless urinary abnormalities. It may be important to decide whether the patient has a possibly progressive condition, not only for his sake but because a job, emigration, service commission, insurance or other social circumstance rests immediately on the probable prognosis.

(iv) Treatment and prognosis

This will depend on the underlying condition, and whether renal failure is present or decline in renal function is observed.

III CHRONIC RENAL FAILURE FROM GLOMERULAR DISEASE

Most of the conditions discussed in this chapter can lead to chronic renal failure. They may first go through a nephrotic, or, less commonly, an acute nephritic state in the case of proliferative glomerulonephritis. They may be found in a patient with already advanced renal failure without any previous history. Patients developing chronic renal failure on the basis of glomerular disease almost invariably develop hypertension, usually severe and frequently accelerated in its final stages. This contrasts with pyelonephritis and polycystic kidneys where salt loss disproportionate to the renal impairment may be found, and hypertension may be mild or absent, even in the terminal stages. Chronic renal failure is discussed in detail in Chapter VI.

IV RENAL BIOPSY

If we can obtain a piece of renal tissue during life, it may enable us to say exactly what disorder is present. Clearly this may be important in deciding what treatment to give, or if no treatment is possible, and what the outlook may be. Since there are many *glomerular diseases* and their ways of presenting to attention are rather few, biopsy is sometimes indispensable if the patient is to be managed intelligently. Only a tiny piece of kidney is taken — with a needle biopsy this will usually contain 20 – 30 glomeruli and ten times as many tubules — so that only diseases which affect all the two million nephrons diffusely and equally can be studied in this way. In fact it is surprising how good the information gained from such a small piece of tissue can be.

Indications for renal biopsy

This is very much a matter for judgement and different doctors will manage their patients somewhat differently according to their experience. In general, however, the nurse will encounter renal biopsy in the following circumstances.

(1) The nephrotic syndrome Renal biopsy will not be necessary in young children with a nephrotic syndrome unaccompanied by hypertension, haematuria or renal failure, unless the patient does not do well. In all older children and adults, renal biopsy will be considered and usually performed.

(2) Acute nephritis or recurrent haematuria Only if the patient does not do well will a renal biopsy be considered — such as becoming anuric, nephrotic, or continuing with proteinuria and haematuria for a long period, or if there is great anxiety surrounding the child's future.

(3) **In persistent proteinuria** for the same reasons as the nephrotic patient. Particularly if there is a fall in renal function with time, hypertension or if a job or insurance policy depends upon a precise diagnosis.

(4) **In acute renal failure** when it is not clear whether a recoverable disease is present or if glomerular disease is suspected or known to be present.

(5) **After transplantation** to assess the viability of the graft if it is not functioning.

In general, renal biopsy is uninformative and may be dangerous by the time a patient has reached *chronic renal failure* if the kidneys are small and scarred. It is also not much use in patchy diseases, such as pyelonephritis, but in the patient with renal impairment, large kidneys on X-ray and no diagnosis a biopsy may well be considered.

Some other circumstances may make the doctor reluctant to perform a needle biopsy of the kidney:

A single kidney
Severe uncontrolled hypertension
A hypotensive, hypovolaemic patient.

In the case of a single kidney, open surgical biopsy may be done instead. Although a blind procedure, needle biopsy is quicker and simpler than open biopsy and has the added advantage that it can be repeated if required.

Procedure

Preparation An IVU, straight X-ray or tomogram of the renal areas is essential, unless the biopsy is being performed with intravenous injection of contrast under direct X-ray control. The blood group is determined and one pint of blood cross-matched and kept in reserve. Blood is taken for prothrombin and cephalin-Kaolin times, and platelet count. The procedure is explained to the patient by doctor and nurse, and the patient or his parent signs his consent to the local anaesthetic (or general, if it is to be employed). It is often useful to have the patient discuss the procedure with a patient who has previously had a biopsy. The patient is prepared in the usual way for theatres: gowned, identified and placed on a stretcher. The area will only occasionally have to be shaved. The doctor will usually order a premedication to be given one hour before the biopsy. The commonest drugs in use are pethidine, promazine, haloperidol and phenergan, alone or in combination. A light meal may be given a few hours before the procedure, unless a general anaesthetic is to be used, since post-operative vomiting is rarely a problem.

The biopsy The patient, with his notes and X-rays and accompanied by his nurse, is taken on a trolley to the treatment room, X-ray department or theatre. The treatment room of the ward is best since he remains in familiar circumstances. If direct X-ray control is to be used, this will mean going to the X-ray department and if a general anaesthetic is being given, then this will usually have to be given in theatres. A hard surface is needed for renal biopsy, an examination couch being ideal. A bed is usually too soft, even with fracture boards inserted, but may be used if nothing else is available. The nurse should remain at the head of the bed to reassure the sleepy but sometimes apprehensive patient. Details of the trolley to be prepared are given below.

The doctor checks the position of the kidney by palpating the patient and by measuring on the X-ray films. The patient is then turned face downwards and settled comfortably. The position of the kidneys is drawn on the skin (see Figure 4.4). The choice of kidney will be made by the doctor. The right kidney is a little lower than the left and therefore easier to biopsy. Unfortunately, the liver is very close by and can feel like a kidney when entered with the biopsy needle. Some doctors therefore prefer to biopsy the left kidney as a routine. If the patient has been biopsied before then the doctor will biopsy the other kidney on the second occasion. The point where the biopsy needle will enter is marked. It is over the lateral part of the lower pole of the kidney, and this usually is found deep to a point below the twelfth rib and just lateral to the sacrospinalis muscle. If direct X-ray control is being employed, the doctor will first inject the contrast intravenously and view the excreted dye on the image intensifier screen. This will enable him to identify his site of entry for the exploring needle exactly over the lower pole.

When the point for biopsy has been selected the doctor will first infiltrate the skin and then the deeper tissues with local anaesthetic. He then makes a small stab incision through the skin and passes the exploring needle vertically downwards towards the kidney (Figure 4.5). If the site has been selected correctly, the exploring needle enters the kidney and begins to swing with each respiration. This gives the depth of the kidney. The doctor may wish to place more local anaesthetic on to the

X-RAY   SURFACE MARKINGS

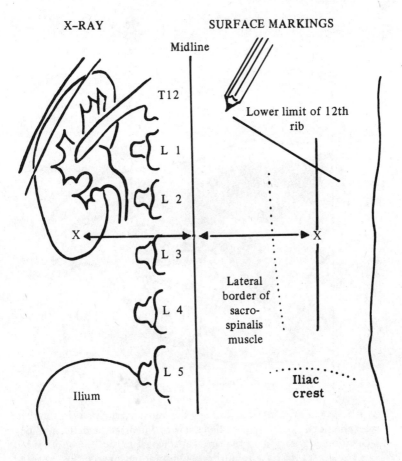

Fig. 4.4 Finding the site for renal biopsy. If direct X-ray control is used, then contrast injected intravenously will be seen being excreted by the kidney, whose substance will be faintly outlined (the nephrogram). If an IVU has previously been taken as a guide, then the X-ray will be examined first by the doctor, and the position of the kidney in relation to the surrounding palpable bony structures will be measured (spine, 12th rib, iliac crest). The measurements will then be drawn in on the back of the patient to be biopsied (right hand side of the diagram). The position is usually below the 12th rib and just lateral to the border of the sacrospinalis muscle.

capsule of the kidney, which unlike the other deep structures has pain-sensitive fibres in it. The exploring needle therefore must fit a syringe, and have a trocar, so that local anaesthetic can be injected through it; a lumbar puncture needle is excellent.

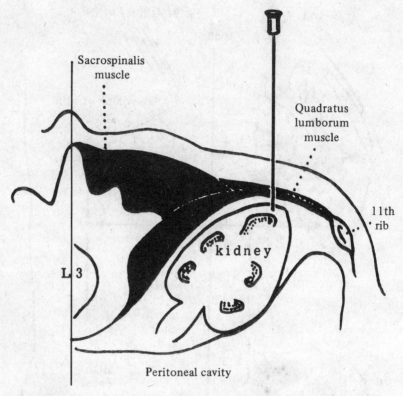

Fig. 4.5 A coronal section through the renal area. The third lumbar vertebra is shown on the left hand side of the diagram, in the midline. The kidney is very near the surface, separated from the exterior by peri-renal fat, fascia, the quadratus lumborum muscle, the subcutaneous fat and skin. When the exploring needle is passed vertically downwards at the correct point, the kidney is reached. The depth varies from 1 to 10 cm according to the size and fatness of the patient.

Having located the lower pole of the kidney and assessed its depth, the doctor then passes the biopsy needle down the same track into the kidney and takes two cores of renal cortex at successive attempts. The specimens are immediately placed in the fixative. A small adhesive dressing is applied to the biopsy site.

Post-operative care The kidney is a very vascular organ and some bleeding is frequent. The nurse must therefore direct her efforts to the early detection of excess bleeding. Immediately following the biopsy the nurse records the pulse and blood pressure while the patient is still in position. Remember that the premedication will make the blood pressure a little lower than the normal reading when up and about the ward; there should, however, be no tachycardia. If these observations are stable, the patient is lifted onto a trolley and returned to his bed. The blood pressure, pulse rate and biopsy site are checked at half-hourly intervals for four hours, and then less frequently as directed. The patient should remain quiet in bed for 24 hours after the biopsy and should be encouraged to drink one or two litres of fluid to keep up a good urine flow; if there is profuse bleeding down the ureters, then the likelihood of clot colic and clot retention are lessened. The first few specimens of urine passed are inspected and tested for blood; microscopic haematuria is almost invariable and minor macroscopic haematuria frequent. There should only be minor discomfort in the flank after the local anaesthetic has worn off. If the patient has pyelonephritis the doctor will wish the first post-biopsy urine sent fresh for culture. The presence of a rising pulse rate and a falling blood pressure, colic, profuse or persistent haematuria, or severe loin pain should of course be reported to the doctor.

Complications The commonest of these is immediate (surgical) haemorrhage; this occurs in about 1 : 100 biopsies. Very occasionally it may be a secondary (infective) haemorrhage at seven to ten days after the biopsy. Only about 1 : 1000 patients bleeds badly enough to require surgical intervention, and the risk of a fatal accident is probably less than 1 : 10,000. This of course will vary with the skill and experience of the operator and the type of patient biopsied.

The only late complication which has been reported is the formation of an arteriovenous fistula within the kidney from an artery and vein severed at biopsy by the needle.

Suggested trolley for renal biopsy

    1 small dressing pack containing   2 foil gallipots
                                          4 gauze squares
                                          8 wool balls
                                          2 pairs dressing forceps
7″ lifting forceps
chlorhexidine in spirit 1 : 200, or iodine
2 linen or paper dressing towels
5 ml syringe
nos. 1 and 25 needles
lignocaine 1% plain (or other local anaesthetic as ordered)

no. 11 or no. 15 Bard Parker blade
biopsy needle*
exploring needle (no. 9 Harris lumbar puncture needle)
6" bowl ⎫
sterile saline ⎭ for rinsing the needles
sterile gloves
masks
adhesive dressing
specimen jar containing fixative†
laboratory forms
(If X-ray control is to be used then a Thiopentone mixer, a 20 ml
syringe and contrast (eg 60 – 100 ml Conray 420) will also be needed)

*Most doctors use a Franklin modified Vim-Silverman needle, but
some prefer a Menghini needle. Disposable needles (Tru-Cut, Travenol
Laboratories) are also available.

†Various fixatives will be used, according to the doctor's preference
and what is to be done with the biopsy. For straightforward optical
microscopy. Dubosq-Brasil (Bouin) alcoholic picric acid-formalin is
probably the best, but straightforward buffered formalin will do. If
electron microscopy is to be done part or all of the biopsy will be cut
into 1 mm cubes and placed either in glutaraldehyde or osmic acid at
4° C. If immunofluorescent studies are to be done, then all or part of
the biopsy will be immediately frozen in liquid nitrogen. These last two
procedures will normally be carried out by the pathology technician.

Renal biopsy in children

This can be performed in children just as in adults. Usually a special
child's renal biopsy needle, which is a scaled down version of the adult
needle, is used[1]. Some doctors use a light general anaesthetic for
younger children, but it is usually possible to do the biopsy under local
anaesthetic. If this is the case, the nurse looking after the child should
always accompany the child into the treatment room or operating
theatre, to be at the head end of the table for comfort, reassurance, and
the presence of a trusted and familiar face. Often the presence and performance of the nurse will render the biopsy possible in a nervous child
when otherwise the procedure might have to be abandoned.

Renal biopsy in transplanted patients

Biopsy in this situation presents some special problems. Because the
kidney is single and the patient's life depends upon it, some doctors will

---

[1]   Such as the White modification of the Franklin Vim-Silverman (Down Bros.)

not perform needle biopsies on transplanted kidneys. Others, because the kidney is easy to localize, and usually fixed in its bed, do use needle biopsy where required. Surgical biopsy requires a small incision and the patient will go to theatres as for any other operation; usually the biopsy is performed because of a non-functioning kidney, and precautions must be taken to see that the biopsy is timed correctly in relation to the patient's dialysis, or that the heparinization is reversed. Similar precautions will of course be necessary for a needle biopsy.

The technique for needle biopsy differs from an ordinary biopsy because of the site of the transplanted kidney in the pelvis. After premedication, the patient lies on his back. The biopsy will usually be performed in the X-ray department, so that the clips inserted at operation, or the nephrogram of a high-dose IVU may be used to localize the kidney exactly. The skin is anaesthetized but deep infiltration is not necessary because the transplanted kidney capsule is anaesthetic. The biopsy is then taken as usual.

Suggestions for further reading:
Cameron, J. S. (1974). The nephrotic syndrome. *Medicine*, p. 1275. Eds. Bayliss, R. I. S., Hall, R. London: Medical Educational (International).

Robson, J. S. (1973). The nephrotic syndrome. *Renal Disease*, p. 331. Ed. Black, D. A. K. Oxford: Blackwell.

CHAPTER V

Urinary tract infections

Urine is an excellent medium for bacteria to grow in. The medulla of the kidney contains tubular fluid which approaches the composition of urine at the papillary tip, and in addition has rather a low oxygen tension, a high concentration of ammonia, and a high concentration of solutes. All these factors inhibit the normal defences of the body against infection, and it is not surprising that infections of the urine and the substance of the kidney are quite common, even in people with entirely normal urinary tracts. They are, however, strongly associated with abnormalities of the urinary tract, other renal diseases or urinary obstruction from any cause.

I ACUTE PYELONEPHRITIS ("Acute Pyelitis")

(i) Causes

In 85% of uncomplicated cases, the urine and kidney contain strains of *E. Coli*; other gram negative staining bacteria make up most of the remaining organisms, particularly Proteus. Mention must also be made of the gram positive coccus, *Streptococcus faecalis.* As its name suggests, this and the other organisms are those which can be found in the bowel of the patient with the infection. *Pseudomonas aeruginosa* (pyocyanea) also deserves mention because although uncommon, it can be particularly difficult to eradicate. In the patient with an abnormal urinary tract, particularly if he has been instrumented, or treated for long periods with chemotherapy, a variety of organisms may be found. Occasionally the sugar-laden urine of diabetics may contain yeasts such as candida albicans.

How do the organisms gain access to the urinary tract and to the kidney? In women and girls there is little doubt that they enter the bladder from below, since the female urethra is much shorter and more exposed than in the male, and from there either gain direct access up the urinary tract to the kidney or enter the blood stream and colonize the kidney in this fashion. In some instances, particularly in men, the blood stream is the most likely first route of access. Normally the defences of the bladder ensure that the bacteria do not gain a hold on the bladder or urethral wall, although the bladder in women and especially in girls is continually subject to bacterial contamination.

In any patient, but especially a child, more attention may be paid to infection in a male, since abnormalities of the bladder outlet are commoner in males, leading to obstruction and infection. These abnormalities include valves in the urethra, urethral stenosis, and various forms of obstruction at the bladder neck. Unless these obstructions are corrected, recurrent infection almost inevitably occurs. Frequently these obstructions (and also recurrent infections without apparent obstruction in females) are associated with *reflux of urine up one or both ureters during micturition* (vesicoureteric reflux). Reflux is never normal and is particularly common in children because their ureters enter the bladder wall more vertically than in the adult so that the valvular mechanism during micturition is not so efficient (Figure 5.1).

In addition, the actual thickness of the bladder wall is much less in a child. Reflux can appear during an acute infection and disappear again, but if it persists then a setting for persistent infection is present because the urine refluxed into the ureters will fall back into the bladder. There is always urine in the bladder, therefore, to form a nidus for infection.

(ii)   Symptoms and signs

In its typical form acute pyelonephritis is easy to recognize. There is frequency and scalding on passing urine, sometimes with severe suprapubic pain; the patient then feels as though the bladder has still not been emptied and passes a further small quantity of urine. These are all signs of bladder and urethral inflammation. In addition there is pain and tenderness in both loins, nausea, headache, high fever, with sweating and rigors on occasions. The urine may be foul and examination shows that it contains bacteria and an excess of aggregated leucocytes. Protein may be absent, or present in small quantities. In children, especially infants, this typical picture may not be seen and the doctor may make the diagnosis on suspicion only, awaiting urine examination to confirm the diagnosis. The frequency of infection in *neonates* is little appreciated because it is difficult to collect uncontaminated urine at this age (Chapter XI) and even when the child has a urinary tract infection, the symptoms and signs may be non-specific. Most paediatricians practice routine examination of the urine for organisms in any neonate

At rest: ADULT   CHILD

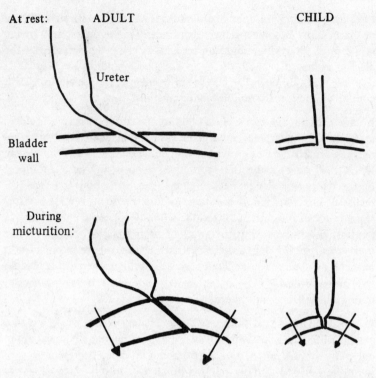

Ureter

Bladder
wall

During
micturition:

Fig. 5.1 The junction of bladder and ureter in adults and children. In
the adult, the ureter enters the bladder obliquely, so that during micturition the thick, muscular bladder wall contracts and seals the
junction so that no urine leaks back up the ureter. In the child, the
ureter enters the bladder more vertically, and the bladder wall is
much thinner. The valve action during micturition is therefore less
good, and reflux of urine more likely should some abnormal circumstance -- such as infection -- arise.

who is failing to thrive, has prolonged "physiological" jaundice, or is in
any way ill; and some screen all the babies passing through their
nurseries.

(iii)   Observations, investigations and nursing

The patient will be nursed in bed and four-hourly observations begun.
At the height of the fever there will be profuse sweating and the sticky,
uncomfortable patient will appreciate tepid sponging and changes of
fresh, cool linen. Fluid intake will be kept high (at least three litres a
day in an adult) both to replace that lost by sweating and to ensure a
good urine output. In children the dehydration may be severe and a

high fluid intake correspondingly more important. In very ill children or infants, this will need to be administered intravenously. In children also, the blood urea is more frequently and more severely raised during the acute attack.

Diet may be as desired but few patients will wish to eat a great deal in the acute phase. An MSU is taken for immediate microscopy and culture, and chemotherapy *then* ordered by the doctor. If the patient has an apparently uncomplicated first infection, then treatment will often be with sulphadimidine or other sulphonamide four or six-hourly. Usually the dose during the first day is greater than the maintenance dose to produce good tissue and urine concentrations as quickly as possible. When sulphonamides are used, the doctor may also order sodium bicarbonate to alkalinize the urine; potassium citrate is also used but is probably best avoided until it is determined whether the patient has normal renal function or not, since potassium is toxic in renal failure. The urine culture will be available in 24 hours to guide the doctor in altering the chemotherapy and after 48 hours the sensitivities of the organism to the various antibiotics will be available and an exact choice of antibiotic made. The commonest chemotherapy other than sulphonamides is with cotrimoxazole (Septrin or Bactrim) or ampicillin. For resistant organisms, such as *proteus* or *pseudomonas aeruginosa*, the doctor may have to use other antibiotics such as carbenicillin, colomycin or gentamycin. If no organisms are found the urinary sediment will be examined for tubercle bacilli.

Normally it is possible to render the patient symptom-free very quickly, when he can get out of bed. The urine may continue to show organisms for a few days. The next stage of management, which may be completed as an out-patient, is the investigation of the patient's urinary tract and renal function to exclude urinary tract abnormalities.

II RECURRENT AND CHRONIC INFECTIONS: SYMPTOMLESS BACTERIURIA

(i) Causes

Even what appears to be a first attack of urinary tract infection may be an episode in more chronic disease. Between attacks the patient may be well but be excreting bacteria in the urine. This state is called *symptomless bacteriuria*. Sometimes it precedes an acute attack and the patient may be entirely unaware of the infection. The majority of single attacks in women are without significance in the long term, but in men even a single attack is often an indication that something is amiss in the urinary tract.

In school children, urine infection may be associated with negligible symptoms or none at all. Over 1% of girls at school have significant bacteriuria (at this age infection is 25 times as common in girls as in boys). At present there is some dispute about whether all these children need treatment, and if so, whether school populations should be screened for infection.

Enuresis   Enuresis means wetting at an age when continence is expected. Most children are dry by day at $2\frac{1}{2}$ years, and dry by night at $3\frac{1}{2}$ years.

"Primary" enuresis refers to a child who has never been dry, possibly because of developmental delay or inadequate training. Less often organic disease is responsible, such as an ectopic ureter dribbling into the vagina, or a meningomyelocele impairing bladder nerve function.

"Secondary" enuresis is more common and applies to a child who starts to wet having previously been dry. *Daytime wetting* is less common than nocturnal. By day many children under the age of eight, especially girls, will wet their pants slightly if "too lazy" or "too late" in getting to the lavatory. It is also girls aged 10 - 15 who suffer from "Giggle Micturition" – involuntary voiding when laughing. However, persistent daytime wetting requires full investigation and many children will be found to have an organic cause – usually urinary tract infection. *Nocturnal enuresis* is more common, 10% of 5 year olds wet their beds more than once a week. In many it is because of an emotional upset, such as moving home or the arrival of a sibling during their sensitive learning period from $1\frac{1}{2}$ - $4\frac{1}{2}$ years, when bladder control is acquired. Organic causes for nocturnal enuresis are uncommon but important; a large number of children with urine infection wet their beds. Therefore investigation of a child with enuresis will include assessment of the emotional state of the child and the home, examination for signs of spina bifida occulta, neurological tests, and careful microscopy and culture of a fresh specimen of urine.

(ii)   Investigation

Because the symptoms may be slight or absent (and bear no relation to the seriousness of the underlying renal infection) investigation of any patient who has more than one attack of obvious urinary infection, fails to lose his or her bacteriuria, or is found to have symptomless bacteriuria, is usual. The doctor will also consider investigating every male with a urinary infection, even in the first attack. The investigation will usually include a blood urea and some tests of glomerular filtration rate and an IVU. In many cases a micturating cystogram and in some a cysto-scopy or panendoscopy will be performed. Many patients with recurrent or persistent infections have abnormal urinary tracts. The abnormalities are very varied but the common ones are:

(i)   in the older child or adult the scarring of chronic infection may already be present in the kidney (Figure 5.2)

(ii)   urine may reflux up the ureter during micturition. This is particu-larly common and important in children (Figure 5.3)

(iii)   there may be congenital abnormality of the kidney which inter-feres with urine drainage; such as a double kidney and ureter on one or both sides, or a horseshoe kidney

(iv)   there may be stones somewhere in the urinary tract

(v)   there may be obstruction to the outflow of urine from the blad-der; such as congenital abnormalities in children, urethral strictures in young men, and prostate obstruction in older men. The definitive treatment of these abnormalities is, of course, surgical, and some patients will be managed jointly with the genito-urinary surgeon.

(iii) Treatment and prognosis

If a surgically correctable abnormality is present (such as an enlarged prostate causing obstruction) then the urological surgeon may be able to perform a corrective operation. This is particularly urgent where there is a bladder neck or urethral obstruction in a child or young man. The situation when vesicoureteric reflux of urine alone is demonstrated is somewhat more complicated. First, the results of placing the patient on long term chemotherapy with antibiotics or sulphonamides will be tried. If this fails to eliminate infection, or the reflux persists or becomes worse, then reimplantation of the ureters into a new site in the bladder wall may be considered. Occasionally, if the bladder is for some reason so badly affected that it cannot be used, then implantation of the ureters into an ileal loop may have to be considered.

In any case the attempt will be made to render the urine sterile and keep it so, by long term chemotherapy. If reflux is present, then the patient should also be taught double or treble micturition. The child is shown that if he passes urine again two minutes after emptying his bladder, the urine which refluxed into the ureters during the first mic-turition and fell back into the bladder can now be passed. Sometimes, if the reflux is gross, a third attempt will be necessary before the bladder is completely empty. This is important, since residual urine is one of the most important factors in maintaining infection.

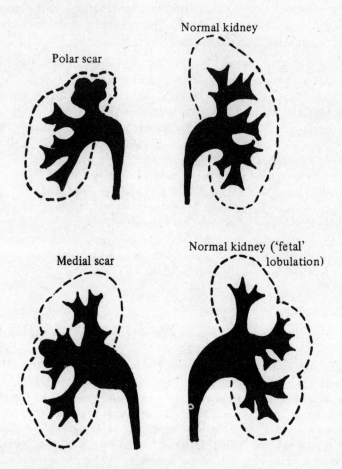

Fig. 5.2 IVU appearances in chronic pyelonephritis without reflux or obstruction. The upper pair of kidneys show a normal organ on the right, but a very severe atrophic scar affecting the whole upper pole on the left. Note that the thickness of the parenchyma is very much reduced, as well as the blunting and distortion of the calyceal pattern. This type of scarring may be seen as a result of pyelonephritis or as a result of vascular disease.

The lower pair of kidneys show a depressed pyelonephritic scar on the left. Note that it is opposite the middle calyx, which is blunted, whereas the indentation on the right kidney is between the calyces. This lobulated appearance is a normal variant.

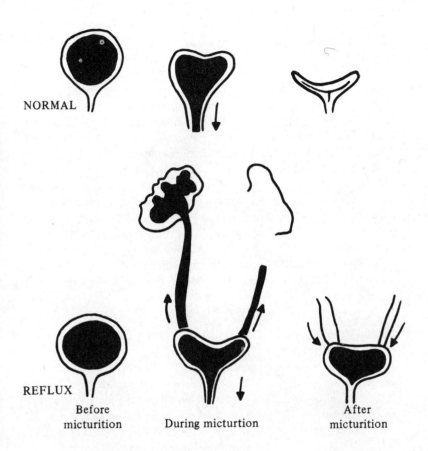

NORMAL

REFLUX

Before
micturition

During micturtion

After
micturition

Fig. 5.3 The micturating cystogram, demonstrating ureteric reflux of urine during micturition. In the normal state, urine is voided through the urethra, there is no reflux of urine up the ureters, and there is almost no residual urine in the bladder after micturition is completed. When reflux is present, there is reflux of urine up both ureters on micturition, worse on the left than on the right. On the left, a small, scarred kidney with distorted calyces is shown up by the contrast. After micturition, the urine descends from the dilated ureters so that urine remains in the bladder, and any bacteria present may continue to multiply.

Bacteriuria and pyelonephritis in pregnancy

Symptomless bacteriuria in pregnancy is often followed later in the pregnancy by a clinically evident attack of acute pyelonephritis. It has also been suggested that in pregnancies complicated by urinary tract infections with or without symptoms, the incidence of fetal loss is higher, although this is much less certain. It is worth while therefore, culturing the urine of all pregnant women at twelve weeks, or at their first ante-natal visit. Pyelonephritis is particularly common in pregnancy because during pregnancy the drainage of urine from the urinary tract may be slowed by the gravid uterus, and also because the ureter dilates and relaxes as part of the normal reaction of the pregnant state. In some patients, pregnancy may reveal underlying urinary tract abnormalities by precipitating frank infection, and after the pregnancy is over the doctor will wish to investigate the patient's urinary tract radiologically. This is not usually done during pregnancy because of the possibility of fetal damage by the X-rays. The effects of any drugs given to the mother for urinary tract infections upon the fetus must not be forgotten, especially during the first trimester. For example, most doctors will avoid co-trimoxazole during this period because it is a folate antagonist.

III   LOWER URINARY TRACT INFECTIONS ("Cystitis")

Many otherwise fit young women suffer from repeated attacks of pain on passing urine, frequency and other signs of urethral and bladder inflammation. At least 50% of women have this complaint at some time in their lives, and the percentage may even be higher. A few actually have pyelonephritis but have symptoms only referrable to the lower urinary tract. In the great majority, however, these attacks are a nuisance but not a threat to health. In many instances there is a mechanical irritation or bruising of the urethra and base of the bladder, particularly common after sexual intercourse ("honeymoon cystitis"). In others it is a flaring up of infection lying dormant in the glands around the urethra. This may be bacterial, but in about half the patients the urine is sterile by conventional tests. It may be that these attacks are due to rather unusual, fastidious bacteria which do not grow well on ordinary agar plates, or that the trouble is caused by viruses or organisms of the family Chlamydiae. Some women appear to be capable of dealing better with the frequent bacterial contamination of their bladders than others; there may be a minority whose defences are poorer and who are more liable to repeated infection. The doctor will wish to investigate such a patient to ensure that underlying renal disease is not being overlooked.

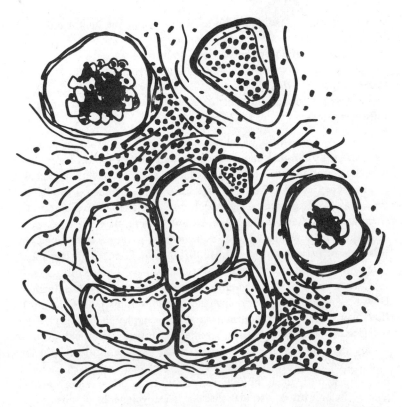

Fig. 5.4   The microscopy of the kidney in chronic pyelonephritis.
The renal tissue is grossly disorganized. There is a large increase in
connective tissue around and between tubules and glomeruli. In this
connective tissue can be seen aggregates of inflammatory cells,
mostly lymphocytes. The distortion and blockage of tubules leads to
large dilated tubules, such as those at the bottom of the diagram. In
the tubule at the top right can be seen a large aggregate of inflammatory cells. These might well be polymorphonuclear leucocytes. Two
glomeruli are shown. Both connect with tubules which are inflamed,
scarred and distorted and as a result the glomerular tuft has shrivel-
led and Bowman's space increased in size.

IV   "CHRONIC PYELONEPHRITIS"

This is a difficult subject at the moment. The term can be used for the
patient described above, with recurrent infections and perhaps an abnormal urinary tract, whose kidneys gradually scar with reduction in
renal function. Even here there is question whether bacterial infection

is the main agent leading to the renal failure but the doctor may well suggest long term chemotherapy. The role of vesicoureteric reflux appears greater at the moment. It is doubtful if kidneys ever develop coarse scars in the absence of reflux, and some prefer to call the coarsely scarred kidney *"reflux nephropathy"*. We know that reflux during childhood may later disappear, and this is probably the natural course of all refluxing ureters.

"Chronic pyelonephritis" is also used to describe a group of patients who arrive in chronic renal failure without any previous history, and who are found to have small, scarred kidneys without reflux. Especially if the kidneys show obvious, coarse scars – for example on the IVU – they may be diagnosed as having chronic pyelonephritis even though there are no bacteria in the urine, although there may be excess white cells and a little protein. This is done because we know that kidneys in this type of patient resemble, histologically, the kidneys of the patient with obvious infection (Figure 5.4), and we have assumed in the past that these kidneys were therefore the result of a burnt-out infection. Now we know that other circumstances besides primary bacterial infection may lead to these appearances. For example, the analgesic drug phenacetin has been shown with some certainty to be capable of producing the histological picture of "chronic pyelonephritis". To make things even more difficult, there is no doubt that *secondary* bacterial infection is more likely in kidneys, scarred from other causes, such as glomerulonephritis or vascular disease. The pyelonephritic changes in the kidney may be the most obvious, and the primary disease quite obscured by the time the kidneys are badly damaged and chronic renal failure present. So it seems likely that "chronic pyelonephritis" has been diagnosed too often and with too little evidence in the past; if the doctor is careful he will allocate a fair proportion of his patients with chronic renal failure as "chronic renal failure of undetermined origin" rather than calling them pyelonephritis. Their management is that of chronic renal failure (Chapter VI).

V CATHETERIZATION

The need for meticulous care in inserting and maintaining urinary catheters cannot be emphasized too strongly. Infection may all too easily be introduced, and once present, be impossible to eradicate in the presence of the foreign body in the bladder. One should approach catheterization with the intention of avoiding it where possible; the procedure is, however, essential in some cases, such as before a micturating cystogram, to deal with acute or postoperative retention, and often following urological or gynaecological operations. As a diagnostic tool, catheterization has its uses, such as after renal transplantation, or in acute renal failure, but as in every other case, the catheter must be removed as soon as possible. It should *never* be necessary to catheterize a patient to obtain an uncontaminated specimen of urine now that suprapubic aspiration of the full bladder (Chapter XI) is available, and the passing of a bladder catheter should be avoided *above all* in the anuric or oliguric patient.

Procedure

Catheterization should be carried out by a doctor or an experienced nurse, using gowns, masks and gloves under aseptic conditions; these can rarely be obtained in the bed and where available the treatment room should be used for the procedure. Two persons are nearly always required. The external urethral meatus is thoroughly cleaned with an antiseptic solution and the urethra in the male is filled with a sterile local anaesthetic gel (10 ml) which also contains antiseptic, such as chlorhexidine or Noxyflex. A sterile towel is placed over the patient's separated thighs and a receiver put in between. The sterile catheter is removed from its wrapping (held in the gloved hand), lubricated with the anaesthetic cream (1% lignocaine gel) and passed into the urethra. When the catheter reaches the bladder, urine flows into the receiver.

The choice of catheter is made by the doctor and it is outside the scope of this text to discuss in depth the wide variety of styles and sizes now available. However, the catheter used will depend upon the indications for its use, and the expected length of stay. All catheters are now made of non-irritant PVC, latex or silicone rubber. Catheters without self-retaining bulbs are less used nowadays, although the Gibbon catheter has something to recommend it. However it has disadvantages in that leakage of urine round the catheter is frequent, and it can easily be pulled out by a disturbed patient. The Foley catheter, self-retaining by virtue of its inflatable balloon, has the advantage of allowing no leakage of urine (provided that the right size is chosen) and requires no stabilization to keep it in place. Pressure of the catheter balloon on the bladder neck can cause inflammation and the 5 ml size is usually quite sufficient to keep the catheter in place; the 30 ml balloon need be used only rarely. Care must be taken to see no traction is exerted on the catheter from outside by strapping it to the patient's thigh, and by ensuring adequate support for the urine bag.

After care

The catheter should be connected with continuous drainage to a disposable, plastic bag with a non-return valve to prevent reflux of urine up into the bladder, and a separate emptying tube; those made by Portex and Aldon are satisfactory. If their use is long term, the bags should be changed weekly. A graduated, hard plastic cylinder (Uri-meter) is also available, but has the disadvantage in cases of severe haematuria of allowing clot formation at the outlet, which can cause complete obstruction necessitating frequent change of drainage apparatus. Continuous drainage means the prevention of urinary stagnation in the bladder, an important point in the prevention of infection. Catheters must never be clamped off.

Once *in situ* the catheter should be cleaned twice daily, the external meatus being swabbed gently with antiseptic to remove dried secretions, and the surrounding area washed with soap and water and thoroughly dried. Any signs of inflammation, swelling or complaints of pain should be reported. While the catheter is *in situ* urine is sent for culture as directed by the doctor, usually weekly. Catheters should be changed at least monthly.

The blocked catheter   This may be due to mucus and debris, blood or (in long standing catheters) phosphates. The bladder should be irrigated with sterile saline using a 50 ml syringe. If large clots are present in the bladder a bigger catheter may have to be inserted.

Removal   With Foley catheters, the catheter should not be cut to release the fluid in the bag; rather, it should be aspirated using a syringe. Before the catheter is removed, an antiseptic should be instilled into the bladder. This is particularly important when the patient has proved to be oliguric or anuric, as in acute renal failure. Chlorhexidine or Noxyflex are commonly used. Sometimes difficulty is experienced with the bag of Foley catheters, which will not deflate. If the catheter is made of latex, the bladder can be filled with 300 ml sterile water and 2 – 5 ml of ether injected down the catheter into the bulb. This will dissolve the latex. It is important to rinse the bladder well before removing the catheter, to make sure that any pieces of the bulb are removed. 5 ml of liquid paraffin will achieve the same result, but more slowly.

Catheterization in children

Because of the risk of introducing infection, catheterization is hardly ever used merely to collect urine for a routine test. However, it is necessary before micturating cystograms, and may also be needed in a severely ill child, to establish if any urine (and how much) is being produced.

Self-retaining Foley catheters are the most convenient and only the 3 ml balloon size should be used. This remains secure in all children; larger balloon sizes can damage a small child's bladder. The smallest No. 8 Foley can be used on most infants, but in very small babies or children with a narrow meatus, a narrower gastric feeding tube may have to be used (French gauge 6 or 4·5). It is best to try the larger size first because although the small one slips in easily, leakage around it is common.

The procedure will require at least two nurses, and unless the nurse is extremely skilled she will do it faster and more cleanly if the catheter is held in gloved hands rather than in forceps. Previous sedation is essential for a young child.

Suggestions for further reading:

Bailey, R. R. (1973). Reflux Nephropathy. *Clin. Nephrology*, 1, 132.

British Medical Journal Editorial (1971). "What is chronic pyelonephritis?" *British Medical Journal*, 2, 61.

Brumfitt, W., Asscher, W. A. (1973). *Urinary Tract Infection*. London: Oxford University Press.

Kaye, D. (1972) (Ed). *Urinary Tract Infection and its Management*. London: Kimpton.

Kunin, C. N. (1975). *Urinary Tract Infection*. Philadelphia: Lea & Febiger.

Rolleston, G. L., Maling, T. M. J., Hodson, C. J. (1974). Intra-renal reflux and the scarred kidney. *Archives of Disease in Childhood*, 49, 531.

CHAPTER VI

Chronic renal failure

Chronic renal failure is the condition which appears when the kidneys are progressively and irreversibly destroyed by disease. Usually this occurs over a period of years or decades. The kidney, unlike some organs such as the liver, cannot grow new tissue after maturity. This is not surprising in view of the complex organization of the nephron (Chapter I). The most we may see is an *increase in the size* of remaining nephrons when others are removed or lost. This may be seen in disease affecting both kidneys, but is particularly obvious when one kidney is removed, since the other kidney can be seen to grow in size over the following months (if it was normal originally).

Chronic renal failure is unfortunately one of the commonest renal conditions, and is a major cause of death. It has many causes, but the patients suffer the same problems, even though they are suffering from a variety of diseases. Clinically the major distinguishing feature between patients is often not their underlying disease, but whether hypertension is present or not, and how severe it may be.

I CAUSES OF CHRONIC RENAL FAILURE (Figure 6.1)

Many conditions can lead to chronic renal failure, but only a few are common:

(1)   glomerulonephritis: usually proliferative, sometimes membranous (see Chapter IV)
(2)   chronic pyelonephritis (see Chapter V)
(3)   polycystic kidneys
(4)   essential hypertension

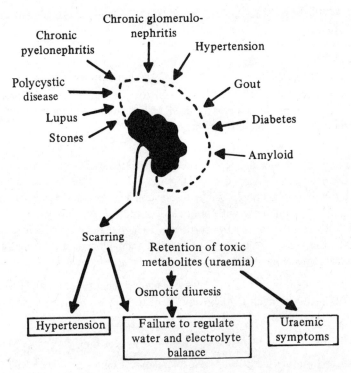

Fig. 6.1 Causes and consequences of chronic renal failure.

Other conditions which are less common but may lead to chronic renal failure include:

(5) analgesics
(6) gout
(7) amyloidosis
(8) "connective tissue" diseases (SLE, polyarteritis)
(9) stones and other obstructions (eg retroperitoneal fibrosis, malignancy)
(10) diabetes
(11) renal tuberculosis

All these causes of renal failure may lead, through the renal damage, to hypertension. Hypertension itself further damages the kidney. The combination of two assaults upon the kidney sets up a vicious circle and may lead to a rapid decline in renal function and great rise in blood pressure, accelerated or malignant hypertension, often after many years of relatively slow deterioration (see Chapter VII).

H   THE DISORDERS OF FUNCTION AND SIGNS AND SYMPTOMS
(Figure 6.1)

All the functions of every organ in the body are affected in severe renal failure. The uraemic patient, poisoning himself with the products of his own metabolism, and unable to control his water and electrolyte balance, presents an apparently bewildering variety of problems; many of these directly affect his nursing care.

Chronic renal failure can be looked upon as a progressive reduction in the number of working nephrons. It is worth remembering that one can enjoy a normal life in all respects with only one half of one kidney functioning. It is even possible to stay alive in reasonable health but with restricted activity with only two per cent of the kidneys functioning. This fact, in some ways fortunate, means that many patients may suffer the steady destruction of most of their kidneys until hypertension or some symptom draws attention to what is happening.

At the beginning of Chapter I we considered renal function under four broad headings. Each of these four is disturbed, as might be expected.

Retention of toxic metabolites ("Uraemia")

The condition usually but rather carelessly called uraemia should be thought of as "urine in the blood" rather than simply referring to the blood urea. Urea, it is true, is present in the blood and tissues in greater quantity than any other substance, in chronic renal failure. Urea is distributed throughout all the body water, within and without the cells. It is not in itself particularly toxic but it is secreted into the mouth, stomach and intestines in the various gastrointestinal juices and in some parts of the gut it is broken down into ammonia by bacteria. *Creatinine*, and a number of other toxic products of protein metabolism also accumulate in the blood, as does *uric acid*. *Phosphate* excretion is also impaired, with a rise in the plasma phosphate concentration. As a result of this the plasma calcium falls. Acidosis appears because the kidney cannot excrete the *acid* generated by the sulphur and phosphorus in the diet. The bicarbonate concentration of the blood is also low.

Loss of substances in the urine

Depending upon the underlying disease, red blood cells, white cells and protein may be found alone or in combination in the urine, but it is rare to find glucose except of course in diabetes. Salt, water and potassium are occasionally lost in excess.

Failure to regulate electrolyte and water balance

A striking feature of chronic renal failure is the production of large volumes of dilute urine. The composition of this urine is unvarying, whatever the circumstances. This is in striking contrast to the normal kidney, which can vary the urine composition according to the body's needs. As renal failure advances the ability to vary the composition of the urine is lost.

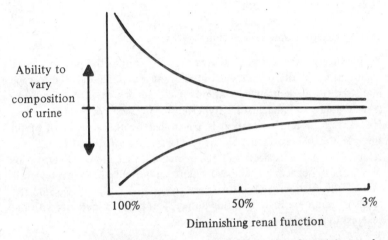

Fig. 6.2   As renal function declines and the number of surviving nephrons decreases, the ability to vary the urine composition gradually decreases. This applies to all renal functions, for example, both concentrating or diluting the urine, or producing a urine of high or low sodium content in response to varying intake. Eventually the urine is of fixed composition whatever the circumstances.

The constant flow of urine, unvarying in composition, leads to one of the striking symptoms of chronic renal failure – the need to pass urine during the night as well as during the day. The danger of salt and water depletion, or salt and water overload, is always present. Unlike acute renal failure, a high plasma potassium is uncommon except just before death, or when the patient is being maintained on regular dialysis.

Why does the failing kidney produce large, constant volumes of rather dilute urine? One clue is given by the fact that the concentration of the urine in this situation approaches that of the plasma – about 300 mOs/l, sp. gr. about 1010. A smaller and smaller number of nephrons must attempt to excrete the usual amount of waste products of metabolism of which the bulk is urea. After about two-thirds of the kidney is destroyed this is no longer possible, the blood urea starts to rise and each nephron has a greater and greater load of solute (urea) to excrete. The situation is that of an *osmotic diuresis* (Chapter XVI) in which a fixed urine concentration and sodium loss may be found. Urea can actually be used as an osmotic diuretic in neurosurgery but has obvious disadvantages. In chronic renal failure, as in an osmotic diuresis induced by mannitol injection, sodium, water and potassium are lost into the urine in uncontrolled amounts. Occasionally sodium or potassium losses are extreme: this state is sometimes called "salt losing nephritis" or "potassium losing nephritis".

Disturbance of hormone secretion

Paradoxically, the secretion of *renin* (and therefore the production of angiotensin) is often *increased* in chronic renal failure, and always increased in patients with the most severe degree of hypertension (accelerated or "malignant" hypertension). This arises because the mechanism of renin secretion is controlled by the amount of blood flow to the kidney tissue. In many diseases causing renal failure, the renal substance is scarred and the remaining tissue may be starved of blood. This ischaemic tissue will then secrete renin in excess which is one of the factors leading to severe hypertension. Hence we find the levels of renin are highest in the kidneys and blood of patients with the severest hypertension.

Erythropoietin secretion is, in contrast, low. It is lowest in diseases which scar the whole kidney very badly and cause it to contract, such as pyelonephritis. Erythropoietin secretion is least affected in polycystic kidney where the kidney is relatively well preserved, although it is grossly disorganized.

Vitamin D metabolism is altered in renal failure because of the reduced mass of functioning renal tissue, conversion of 25 – OH vitamin D to 1,25 di – OH vitamin D is very reduced, and this cannot be overcome by feeding extra vitamin D in the diet. The resulting fall in calcium absorption and failure to calcify bones properly are therefore resistant to vitamin D administration, unlike ordinary nutritional rickets or osteomalacia.

Symptoms and signs of chronic renal failure (Figure 6.3)

These disorganizations of function lead to a large number of events which the nurse may encounter in patients with chronic renal failure. The patient's initial complaint and state varies a good deal:

(1)   he may be well, but have had his urine tested routinely;

(2) he may be suffering from hypertension and its consequences, such as breathlessness or angina;
(3) he may have an unexplained anaemia;
(4) he may present critically ill in "acute on chronic" renal failure (Chapter II),
(5) he may just be feeling generally unwell, tired and "run down".

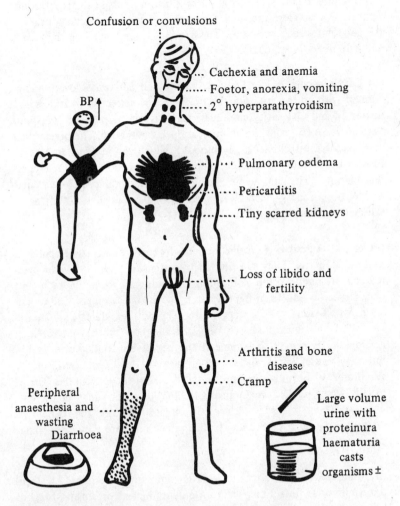

Fig. 6.3 Clinical features of chronic renal failure. Not all of the very many primary and secondary effects of chronic renal failure are shown.

This gives some idea of the range and variety of the symptoms and signs of chronic renal failure. It is convenient (although arbitrary) to consider these according to the body system they effect or from which they arise.

(a) Gastrointestinal Anorexia, vomiting and unpleasant taste in the mouth are common symptoms. The mouth is often foul, the breath foetid, the gums in poor condition, infected and bleeding (see below). There may be diarrhoea, which can be blood-stained. Hiccough can be prolonged and exhausting. A good proportion of these gastrointestinal symptoms arise from the breakdown of retained urea which appears in the gastrointestinal secretions. The product is ammonia, which is toxic and irritant to the mucosae.

(b) Cardiovascular Heart failure, due to salt and water overloading, with or without hypertension, is common. The patient is breathless and distressed and may be cyanosed. Pericarditis can be present, and spontaneous recovery from this complication is rarely seen. The pericarditis may cause an effusion (usually bloody), which can be large enough to cause cardiac tamponade, and causes typical precordial pain. Hypertension and all its consequences may be seen, including cerebrovascular accidents, coronary occlusion, angina, and as already noted, heart failure and pulmonary oedema.

(c) Neuro-muscular Convulsions are frequent, and some patients present with fits. They are due to hypertension, salt and water overloading or, rarely, cerebral bleeding or occlusion. Retinal detachment may be seen, again from hypertension and saline overload. Vision may be impaired from hypertensive retinopathy with exudates, and papilloedema of the optic disc may be seen on retinoscopy. A peripheral neuropathy is always detectable if the nerves are studied electrically, but may cause actual sensory symptoms or, less commonly, motor symptoms, of burning numbness or weakness of the extremities. This is usually worse in the legs. Coarse twitching of muscles may be present, with severe cramp and occasionally tetany. Finally the patient is anxious, may be confused and hallucinated; and before dying becomes comatose.

(d) Pulmonary Pulmonary oedema is common, and primary or secondary pulmonary infections occur, often with bizarre organisms, fungi or yeasts. As always, pulmonary emboli may occur in bedridden patients. The deep slow respiration of severe acidosis is often present. The term "uraemic lung" is sometimes given to the appearances seen on chest X-ray in patients with chronic renal failure. These look very like those of pulmonary congestion, and appear to be organized, and often infected, chronic pulmonary exudate.

(e) **Haematological** Pallor and anaemia is always present, and parallels the severity of the uraemia. The anaemia is due to both defective production of red cells by the marrow and increased haemolysis. The marrow is poisoned by the uraemia and erythropoietin secretion is diminished (see above). The red cells also break down more quickly in a uraemic environment than normally. The anaemia is usually normochromic, but many bizarre red cells can be seen in a blood smear. Bleeding, from mouth, nose, gastrointestinal tract, or into the pericardium, lungs, brain or skin may occur. All the clotting factors seem to operate poorly in uraemia, particularly the platelets. Although these are usually present in normal numbers they do not work efficiently.

(f) **Bones, joints and connective tissues** Bone disease is very frequently found in long-standing uraemia. It may relate to the raised phosphate and lowered calcium concentrations in the blood, to the acidosis, and to the defective activation of vitamin D already mentioned, which is a consequence of diminished functioning renal tissue. A variety of changes may be present in the bones, including *osteoporosis, osteomalacia* and secondary *hyperparathyroidism*. Usually these are only visible on X-rays but may give rise to symptoms. The hyperparathyroidism is brought about by the persistently low serum calcium levels, and raises the plasma calcium to "normal" levels which are in fact high for the uraemic patient. The combination of "normal" calcium and high phosphate leads to calcium being deposited in the soft tissues and joints. In the joints it leads to a painful condition just like gout (*"pseudogout"*) and *calcification of soft tissues* and blood vessels may be seen on X-rays. Calcium phosphate may be deposited in the eyes, leading to soreness and inflammation (*"Uraemic red eyes"*). In children *ricket*-like changes are seen instead of osteomalacia, and bone age is less than the chronological age. Bony deformity and *dwarfing* occur (see endocrine).

(g) **Endocrine** In female patients the monthly periods usually cease and even mild uraemia leads to lowered fertility and increased rate of spontaneous abortion. The risk of toxaemia is greatly increased if hypertension is present. Males are subfertile and libido is reduced in both sexes. Hyperparathyroidism may be seen.

(h) **General** Patients with chronic renal failure feel generally unwell and tired. This has a number of components, including the anaemia, muscular weakness, anorexia and nausea. The urine volume is large and the patient usually rises once or more during the night to pass urine (*nocturia*). If vomiting or diarrhoea should occur for reasons unrelated to the uraemia, such as infective gastro-enteritis, then rapid worsening of his condition may occur, or even *acute on chronic renal failure* (Chapter II) with rapid deepening of the uraemia. Some patients present in this fashion, without any previous history. If *urinary tract infection* is present, any of the symptoms of this condition may be complained of (Chapter V) but infection is often silent. Patients with polycystic kidneys may complain of sudden pain in one or other kidney, or have sudden attacks of *macroscopic haematuria*.

Resistance to infection is diminished in uraemia because all aspects of the body's defences are reduced. This includes the ability of the body to mobilize white blood cells, which do not in any case ingest bacteria as well as white cells from normal individuals. Antibody production is inhibited, along with all protein synthesis. Gram negative organisms particularly relish the uraemic environment (just as they grow well in urine) and may occur in unexpected places such as in the lung. Septicaemias are frequent, and the usual local and general signs of infection, such as inflammation and fever, may be completely absent. *Drugs* are retained in the body and dosage may need modification; toxic effects are correspondingly more frequent (see Chapter XV). The *skin* shows many abnormalities in uraemia. Anaemia gives rise to pallor, and a brownish yellow pigmentation is frequent. This deepens on exposure to sunlight, and has several causes. Some of it arises from the retention of pigmented compounds normally excreted in the urine, some of which darken in sunlight. However the concentration of the melanin-stimulating hormone (MSH) released by the pituitary gland is higher in the blood of uraemic patients, so that increased pigmentation with the true pigment of the skin, melanin, is also present. Salt and water loss makes the skin dry, and itching may be intolerable. The reasons for this itching are not understood, but it may relate to urea, uric acid and calcium salts deposited in the skin. Occasionally, if the blood urea rises very high (over 100 - 120 mmol/l) then urea may be visible as a crystalline deposit in the skin, particularly around the beard area and the face; this is picturesquely called "urea frost".

III INVESTIGATIONS (Chapter XI)

At some time or another, almost all the investigations discussed in Chapter XI may be used in a patient suffering from chronic renal failure. The urine volume will be measured and will usually be increased; the urine will be found to contain protein, white cells, and frequently red cells. Organisms may be present. The urine is dilute, with a specific gravity around 1010, and an osmolarity around 300 mOs/l. It contains little urea but a normal or even increased amount of salt. The amount of urea, sodium and potassium in the urine are used to help with the construction of the appropriate diet (see below). The blood electrolytes will often be normal, but urea, creatinine, phosphate are present in the blood in excess. There is usually an anaemia. The determination of the glomerular filtration rate is, of course, of crucial importance and many doctors measure this by several different methods in each patient to ensure an accurate result. The commonest method is the creatinine clearance, but this overestimates the filtration rate when this is very low (say below 10 ml/min). This and other methods are discussed in Chapter XI. The kidneys will usually be X-rayed by IVU, and sometimes a micturating cystogram is performed if pyelonephritis with urinary reflux up the ureters is suspected. The warning not to dehydrate, purge or thirst patients with severely impaired renal function given in Chapter XI should be remembered.

IV OBSERVATIONS AND NURSING

The patient will be up and about unless he is critically ill, in which case his management will be that of "acute on chronic" renal failure (Chapter II); or unless he has active urinary tract infection (Chapter V) or heart failure. His temperature, pulse and respiration will be taken and recorded, more frequently if fever or heart disease is present. The blood pressure should be recorded four times a day, standing and lying, for the first few days to provide a baseline. If the patient is either hypotensive, hypertensive or on hypotensive drugs this may of course need to be continued. To begin with all urine should be saved as 24-hour collections, apart from fresh specimens for microscopy or culture, so that creatinine clearance and urinary electrolyte excretions may be measured. A fluid balance chart is kept, since the patient may be incapable of regulating his own fluid balance. The weight is of great importance, since short term weight changes reflect water balance, and long term changes nutrition. This will be recorded daily in most instances. Patients in chronic renal failure are often constipated because of dehydration, inactivity and failure of appetite and this may need attention.

V TREATMENT

This may be considered as attacking three problems:

(a)   treat the condition causing renal failure

(b)   minimize the uraemia
(c)   treat the secondary effects

(a) Treating the condition causing the renal failure Unfortunately, there is often little we can do to prevent further renal destruction. Some patients with *glomerulonephritis* may have corticosteroid drugs or cytotoxic agents such as azathioprine or cyclophosphamide, but the worth of these drugs in progressive forms of glomerulonephritis is doubtful, to say the least (Chapter IV). If there is *chronic urinary tract infection*, especially if there is a urinary tract abnormality, then treatment may be possible if the kidneys are not too badly scarred already. The doctor may well order long term chemotherapy to keep the urine sterile, and the patient may be investigated by the urologist to see whether the urinary tract abnormality is treatable, or the obstruction can be relieved. This type of patient may show very gratifying response, for example when the ureter is obstructed by some non-malignant disease, such as *stones* or *retroperitoneal fibrosis*. There is no treatment for *polycystic kidneys* apart from avoiding infection; the operation of puncturing the cysts is now little performed. *Gout* may be treated by reducing the amount of uric acid produced in the body. The doctor may order the drug allopurinol which blocks the formation of uric acid. There is no treatment which will affect *diabetic nephropathy* or *amyloidosis*, but the progression of the amyloid may be stopped by treating the primary infection, if one is present. Obviously, if the patient is taking a toxic drug such as *phenacetin* then it must be stopped; often this will help a great deal and the decline in renal function cease. The treatment of *renal tuberculosis* is usually carried out by the urologist, and involves both surgery and antituberculous drugs. The treatment of hypertension is considered below and in Chapter VII.

(b) Minimizing the uraemia This is achieved by ensuring a good salt and water balance and by adjusting the protein intake; both are considered in detail in Chapter XII. In brief, the *sodium and water* intake are adjusted to the levels where blood pressure, cardiac output are good, but oedema is absent, weight is constant and blood pressure is normal. The *protein* intake is made largely of animal protein, reduced to the minimum the patient can tolerate and remain in nitrogen balance without wasting. This usually involves avoiding ordinary flour and flour products such as bread, since they contain quantities of vegetable protein which does little for the patient in chronic renal failure except raise the blood urea. This protein restriction must be accompanied by a high energy intake to prevent breakdown of the patient's own muscle, and reinforces the need for special carbohydrate or fat energy supplements.

The success of this diet requires careful instruction and encouragement of the patient by dietician and nurse. The main benefit to the patient is improvement in gastrointestinal symptoms such as nausea, foul taste and increased appetite.

(c) Treatment of secondary effects The most important of these is *hypertension*. The doctor will always treat this vigorously. The blood pressure will be raised by salt and water overload, so attention to salt and water balance is the first step. It will often be necessary for the doctor to order hypotensive drugs, and the nurse may see that patients who cannot excrete these drugs through their kidneys are very sensitive to relatively small doses. The commonest drugs for maintenance treatment at the moment are α-methyl DOPA, propranolol or other blocking agents for sympathetic β-receptors, hydrallazine, bethanidine or guanethidine, and debrisoquine. A textbook of pharmacology should be consulted for information on their actions and use.

Cramp may be severe especially at night; quinine sulphate is sometimes used for this. There seems to be no way of relieving the *itching* of chronic renal failure. Phenothiazines such as chlorpromazine are sometimes used but these sedate the patient and are of little value. Hot baths with sodium bicarbonate with baby oil rubbed in afterwards seems to be the most useful manoeuvre. If the itching is related to *hyperparathyroidism*, the doctor will of course be considering parathyroidectomy if the patient is to be placed on maintenance dialysis, or is likely to survive for a good period of time. He may also consider using Vitamin D in very large doses if there is rickets or osteomalacia causing the patient pain, but this needs to be done cautiously since the calcification elsewhere may be made worse.

There is no treatment that will benefit the *anaemia* except to reduce the blood urea. Blood transfusions are only of temporary benefit. *Infections* may be troublesome in patients with chronic renal failure. The dosage of many antibiotics will have to be adjusted to the patient's renal function.

The management of the very ill patient with severe hypertension, heart failure, fluid overload, convulsions or pericarditis will often involve peritoneal dialysis (Chapter XIV) and will be that of acute or acute on chronic renal failure (Chapter II).

VI COMPLICATIONS

Most of the "complications" of chronic renal failure, such as bone disease and hypertension, are secondary effects of the uraemia or the renal scarring and have already been discussed. On occasion, the patient known to have chronic renal failure may suddenly deteriorate, or may come to attention for the first time in what appears to be acute uraemia; this "acute on chronic" renal failure is dealt with in Chapter II.

VII   CHRONIC RENAL FAILURE IN CHILDHOOD

Chronic renal failure is fortunately rare in childhood, if we ignore those babies who die in the neonatal period from gross malformations of the kidneys and urinary tract, including total absence of the kidneys. Under the age of five years, by far the commonest cause of chronic renal failure is small, scarred kidneys with associated reflux of urine up the ureters during micturition (Chapter V). A high proportion of these children with early renal failure have some underlying abnormality of the upper or lower urinary tract, such as an obstruction in the posterior urethra. We may, however sum up this situation under the heading of *congenital abnormalities plus pyelonephritis*, since infection is an almost inevitable secondary event. In children between five and fifteen years of age, this type of patient accounts for only half the children in renal failure, the remainder suffering from *glomerulonephritis* (Chapter IV). Usually this is of the proliferative or sclerosing types. A minority of children who have an attack of the *haemolytic uraemic syndrome* (Chapter II) do not recover renal function, or go into chronic renal failure a year or two later.

Children in chronic renal failure may present all the features seen in adults, and discussed above. In addition, however, they suffer two additional problems. First, the emotional and family consequences of chronic illness at a time when their siblings and friends are developing rapidly both at home and at school, intellectually, socially and physically. Second, their growth is stunted.

Growth failure in uraemia may be total, with no increase whatever in height; more usually some growth is seen, but at a lower rate than expected for a child of equivalent age. Progressively, the untreated uraemic child becomes dwarfed. In addition, bone disease is often present when uraemia appears in growing children, and this further stunts growth and may introduce the problem of bony deformity. In part, the growth failure may be seen as an adaptive response to the low energy intake usual in uraemia, itself the consequence of the poor appetite felt by most uraemic patients. To grow, a child requires proportionately about two to three times as much energy as an adult, and is therefore much more sensitive to the effects of energy deprivation. Growth failure certainly does not result from a lack of growth hormone itself, but some of the accessory factors needed for it to exert its action may be defective in uraemia.

The management of the child in chronic renal failure presents many problems. The impact of the renal failure on the child and its family may totally disrupt normal living, and one of the tasks the nurse and all those looking after the child is to show the parents how to cope with the situation, without turning the child into an "invalid" or neglecting other members of the family and then suffering guilt because of this. The nurse can play a vital role in this, most especially by the attitudes he or she transmits to child and parents, not always verbally. One of the most precious aids at this time is simply *information*, and the nurse should see that any advice she gives to the parents is accurate, and in agreement with the policy adopted for the child. It is better to say "I don't know, but I will find out", than guess. The drug and dietary régime for the child may seem overwhelmingly complex to the parents at first, and step by step rehearsal of the treatment and its rationale will help to place the parents in control of the situation. Diet is further discussed in Chapter XII, but it is worth noting here that this requires considerable modification for children. Because they tend to have lower blood urea and plasma creatinine concentrations for equivalent renal functional impairment, protein restriction below 1 g/kg/day is not used – indeed must not be used if normal or "catchup" growth is to be attained. As in adults, the key to successful diet is to *increase the intake of energy* to levels where normal growth can be resumed. Salt restriction in the hypotensive child, on the other hand, can be more irksome than in the adult because of the small bodyweight and body sodium.

When a child enters terminal renal failure, the problem arises whether it is best to offer or withhold dialysis or transplantation. It is not always the best course to continue treatment of a child beyond this point, bearing in mind the welfare of the whole family. Obviously, this is never an easy decision to reach. It is usual to discuss transplantation or dialysis earlier in the course of renal failure than in an adult whether considered in terms of blood urea or plasma creatinine, or of glomerular filtration rate. This is to avoid a prolonged period of severe uraemia with possible permanent loss in stature, and because for the smaller muscle mass of the child the same plasma creatinine represents more severe uraemia in a child than in an adult.

VIII PROGNOSIS

This is very variable. It mainly depends upon the rate of progression of the underlying condition. On occasion, as with some forms of glomerulonephritis, the deterioration in renal function is so rapid that the patient is dying within a year or two, but some patients with polycystic kidneys survive into old age. Hypertension, if it appears, greatly accelerates the rate of decline and determines the prognosis to a greater extent than any other secondary factor. The presence of secondary urine tract infection will again shorten the probable life span. The degree of renal damage when the patient presents to medical attention is obviously important; a patient with only mild renal impairment can obviously be helped more, and in any case will probably survive longer, than a patient appearing with kidneys almost destroyed and a glomerular filtration rate of less than 10 ml/min.

Eventually there comes a point when, in spite of careful control of salt balance and protein intake, the patient is no longer capable of continuing his existence. This point is reached when the glomerular filtration rate is about 2 - 3 ml/min. If there is also severe hypertension, then intractable heart failure is likely to be the terminal event earlier than this. Similarly, the patient cannot keep in nitrogen balance if he cannot excrete the urea produced by 18 - 21 g protein a day, that is 6 - 7 g urea/day. The daily urea excretion is obtained by multiplying the daily urine volume by the urea concentration. For example, 2000 ml of urine containing 800 mg/100 ml urea will give a daily excretion of 16 g urea.

When the minimum excretion point is reached, or if the patient suffers an acute deterioration of function from which he does not recover, then a decision must be made whether to begin peritoneal dialysis with a view to subsequent maintenance haemodialysis or transplantation, or to let the patient die. This may be a painful decision if the patient is already on peritoneal dialysis and is relatively well. The problems of this decision are discussed in Chapter XVII.

Suggestions for further reading:
British Medical Bulletin (1971). Renal Failure. vol. 27. No. 2.

Curtis, J. R., Williams, G. B. (1975). *Clinical Management of Chronic Renal Failure*. Oxford: Blackwell.

Moorhead, J. F. (1975). Anaemia in renal failure. *Advances in Renal Disease*. (Ed.) Jones, N. F. Edinburgh: Churchill-Livingstone.

Ross, E. J. (1973). Chronic renal failure. In: *Renal Disease*. 3rd Ed. p. 463. (Ed.) Black, D. A. K. Oxford: Blackwell.

CHAPTER VII

Hypertension and the kidney

The kidney is intimately related to hypertension, both through its control of sodium excretion and through the hormones it produces. At the moment we do not know exactly how renal disease may bring about hypertension in some patients and not others, but the damaging effect of high blood pressure itself on the renal blood vessels is only too obvious.

I CAUSES

(a) Essential hypertension

Most adult patients with hypertension (at least 95%) do not have any discernible disease which might lead to high blood pressure. They experience a steady rise of blood pressure with age, as does the whole population, but gradually their readings become more and more at the upper limit of normal until they exceed this level. There is no sharp cut-off between these patients with essential hypertension and the normal population in terms of blood pressure, and doctors argue about what figure should be used to define it in day to day practice. These patients are many times as liable to the vascular consequences that are associated with high blood pressure, such as cerebrovascular accidents. The condition is usually called "essential hypertension" because we are ignorant of the many factors which act together here to raise the blood pressure.

(b) Secondary hypertension

The 5% of hypertensive patients who do not have essential hypertension have some apparent precipitating cause; most of these causes are quite rare, but coarctation of the aorta, tumours of the adrenal cortex (aldosteronoma) or medulla (phaeochromocytoma) deserve mention.

However, the bulk of this 5% have a renal condition which appears to be bringing about the rise in their blood pressure.

Hypertension and renal disease may occur together several ways:

(1) a patient with known chronic renal disease develops hypertension, or

a patient with hypertension turns out, on investigation, to have advanced chronic renal disease, affecting both kidneys;

(2) a patient with a family history of hypertension develops essential hypertension in turn; after some years, the kidneys are damaged by the high blood pressure;

(3) a patient with hypertension has disease of one kidney which may be curable if the kidney can be operated upon.

(1) has been considered in Chapter VI, chronic glomerulonephritis in Chapter IV, and chronic pyelonephritis in Chapter V. The third commonest cause of chronic renal failure and hypertension is polycystic kidneys (Chapter X).

(c) Unilateral renal disease as a cause of hypertension

The majority of the small proportion of hypertensive patients with renal disease have diffuse disease of both kidneys. Patients with unilateral renal disease thus form a very tiny proportion indeed of all those with hypertension. The interest in this type of patient is mainly because, unlike other forms of hypertension, treatment of the affected kidney may lead to cure and the end of continuing drug treatment.

The most important form of unilateral renal disease causing hypertension is *renal artery stenosis* (Figure 7.1). This is a narrowing of the renal artery, usually by a congenital hypertrophy of the middle (muscular) coat of the artery. In old age, atheromatous narrowing of the outlet of the renal artery from the aorta is relatively common, but is rarely a cause of hypertension – although it may be found in hypertensive patients. The stenosis, if severe enough, reduces the renal blood flow so that the kidney is poorly perfused or "ischaemic". This leads to the secretion of renin, which then produces angiotensin (Chapter I); the alteration in sodium excretion, and the vasoconstriction that the angiotensin brings about leads to hypertension, which is usually severe and rapidly becomes worse. Renal artery stenosis from fibromuscular hyperplasia is most commonly seen in female patients aged fifteen to thirty, which is less than the age at which essential hypertension usually becomes apparent.

Other anomalies of the renal artery may occur, such as congenital *aneurysms* which compress the artery from which they arise. Sometimes they occur in one of several renal arteries, the presence of more than the usual single renal artery on each side is a common variant.

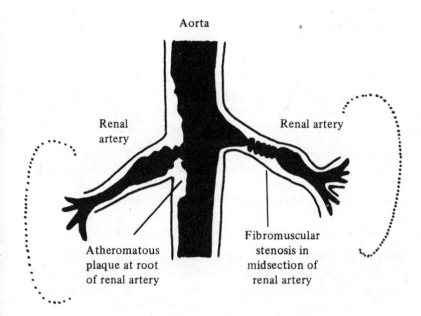

Fig. 7.1 Renal artery stenosis. The two commonest varieties are shown for convenience in a single patient, although this is most unlikely in practice.

On the left of the picture is shown the form found in older patients with renal artery stenosis; atheroma of the aorta has involved and obstructed the root of the renal artery. This may, of course, proceed to complete obstruction and loss of the kidney. This sort of partial obstruction is common in old age and may or may not be associated with hypertension.

On the right the congenital, fibromuscular stenosis is shown. This tends to be further along the renal artery, and may affect one of its intrarenal branches. The long, banded or "beaded" appearance seen on arteriograms in this condition is shown. This condition may be bilateral.

Note that immediately after each stenosis the diameter of the renal artery is a little larger than usual – "Post stenotic dilatation" due to the turbulent blood flow at this point.

Occasionally, *"pyelonephritis"* (reflux nephropathy) is predominantly unilateral. It is probable that this is in fact secondary pyelonephritis in refluxing kidneys or dysplasia but by the time adult life is reached it is impossible to tell.

Finally solitary *cysts* of the kidney may occur; they are rarely, if at all a cause of hypertension and if found in a hypertensive patient are usually a coincidental finding.

(d) Hypertension in children

Hypertension in children, unlike adults, is rather uncommon. When it does appear in a child there is almost always an underlying condition to which the hypertension is secondary. "Essential" hypertension, for which no cause can be found, is very uncommon in the child.

Any child who is found to have hypertension will usually be admitted so that investigations can be carried out. As in adults, renal disease affecting one or both kidneys is the commonest finding but adrenal tumours and renal artery stenosis of the fibromuscular type are also seen.

(e) Accelerated (malignant) hypertension (Figure 7.2)

As well as looking at hypertension by apparent cause, it may be considered by *degree*. When the diastolic blood pressure reaches and remains at an extreme level (usually above 140 mmHg) the damage to the small blood vessels (arterioles) changes in type from slow scarring and hypertrophy to an acute, destructive, inflammatory lesion (fibrinoid necrosis). This in turn results in a worsening of the blood pressure (at least in part from the damage to the small vessels in the kidney), and as renal function rapidly decreases, the blood pressure equally rapidly rises. Untreated the patient dies within weeks or months at the most and terminally the *diastolic* blood pressure may reach, or even exceed 200 mmHg. The damage to the arterioles is visible in the fundus of the eye, through an ophthalmoscope, and papilloedema and cerebral oedema are usually present. The urine contains protein, sometimes in large quantities, and blood.

II SYMPTOMS AND SIGNS

These do not differ from those of essential hypertension: headaches, breathlessness, angina, and if severe, left or right heart failure, convulsions or vascular catastrophes. Patients with renal hypertension are on the whole younger than patients with essential hypertension. The symptoms and signs of uraemia may be present (Chapter VI) but these may of course be due to secondary renal damage arising from prolonged severe essential hypertension.

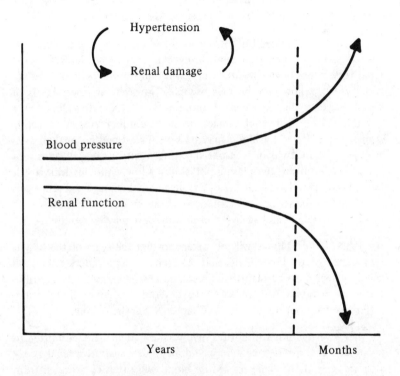

Fig. 7.2 The course of renal function and blood pressure in a patient with slowly progressive renal disease. While decline in renal function is slow, blood pressure rises slowly as a consequence of the renal damage. At a certain point (which may occur at any time in the course of the disease, but is more usual when the kidney is severely damaged) the blood pressure rises more rapidly with more rapid renal damage. The vicious circle of hypertension and renal damage accelerates, so that renal function declines over relatively short periods with a rise in the blood pressure to diastolic levels of 140 mmHg or more. If the blood pressure is not controlled, death usually occurs within months; survival for more than a year was rare before the introduction of effective hypotensive therapy, even when the underlying condition was hypertension itself, and the renal damage and decline in renal function entirely secondary.

III   INVESTIGATION OF THE PATIENT WITH HYPERTENSION
(Chapter XI)

Obviously it is important to decide whether the patient with high blood pressure has either a renal condition causing his hypertension, or renal damage resulting from it. Most doctors will therefore wish to investigate their patients with hypertension to decide this.

The urine will be tested for both protein and blood. Severe (accelerated or malignant) hypertension may bring about so much damage to the renal vessels that in all cases the nurse will find some protein and blood, which on occasion may be macroscopic. However, at lower levels of blood pressure the presence of proteinuria or haematuria may be a valuable indicator of renal damage, so that careful and repeated testing is necessary. Urine and blood may be sent for estimation of their electrolyte content, which is especially important in the diagnosis of hyperaldosteronism; the plasma potassium is low while the urine loss is large. Obviously diuretic drugs or advanced renal damage will make this observation useless. Some estimation of the glomerular filtration rate will be undertaken, and again 24-hour urine save may be required.

An IVU of the kidneys will be taken, so that the scars of the hypertension, or of pyelonephritis, may be seen, or polycystic kidneys too small to feel may be identified. A radioactive scan, dynamic scintillogram or renogram will be taken to determine whether there is any difference between the two sides (Chapter XI) in the tracing.

Further investigation will always involve the patient being admitted to hospital. Renal arteriograms may be done to demonstrate a renal artery stenosis, and at the same procedure blood will often be sampled from the renal veins to estimate the renin concentration. Peripheral blood may also be sent for renin, angiotensin and aldosterone concentrations. The nurse may notice that not only diuretics but also hypotensive drugs may be stopped for these investigations, if the patient's condition permits. It is particularly important to stop any β-blocking agents such as proporanolol, since some of these are renin antagonists. Now, much less use is made of *divided renal function studies* than formerly. In these, ureteric catheters are passed up so that urine can be collected from each kidney separately. The ischaemic kidney which may be causing hypertension passes urine of a characteristic composition: low sodium, but high urea and other solutes. The contribution of each kidney to the total renal function can also be estimated. Since so much information can be gathered from dynamic scintillography using the gamma camera, together with scanning techniques and renin estimations the need for this complicated and difficult investigation is now small.

Meanwhile, the investigation of the cardiovascular system (ECG chest X-ray) will proceed, so that the doctor may assess how the heart has stood up to the hypertension.

IV OBSERVATION AND NURSING

The most important observation on a hypertensive patient is, of course, the blood pressure.

Taking the blood pressure In renal disease, the determination of the diastolic blood pressure is usually of greater importance than the systolic. The mean blood pressure against which the heart has to work is much more dependent on the diastolic than the systolic. The diastolic blood pressure has now been internationally agreed as the point at which the sounds heard over an artery compressed by a cuff diminish suddenly; on occasion, sounds may be heard at pressures less than this, even to zero on occasion. The influence on the cuff size in relation to the arm circumference on the recorded blood pressure must not be forgotten. This is of special importance in two conditions; childhood and obesity. If the cuff is too large – for example if an adult size 15 cm cuff is used on a child – then the recorded blood pressure may be as much as 30 mmHg overestimated. Conversely, on an obese arm a standard cuff may underestimate the blood pressure.

It is frequently necessary to take the blood pressure both standing (or sitting) and lying. A large drop (of more than 10 mmHg in the diastolic reading) may indicate paralysis of the vascular vasoconstricting nerve endings by drugs, or more rarely disease; or poor filling of the vascular bed from bleeding, dehydration or saline depletion.

As with so many measurements in medicine, it is *changes* in the blood pressure with time rather than an individual observation that are of greatest value, especially when correlated with other measurements – for example with the pulse rate.

Other observations may be those as for chronic renal failure, or as directed by the doctor.

The nursing of the hypertensive patient will depend upon his general state; most commonly he will be admitted for investigation and be up and around the ward. If severely uraemic, or in heart failure, he will need the nursing care appropriate to these states (Chapter VI).

V COMPLICATIONS

Apart from the possibility of cerebral haemorrhage or myocardial infarction the principal complication of hypertension is, of course, renal damage, either in addition to the pre-existing renal disease, or as a result of the essential hypertension. This renal damage arises from damage to the small blood vessels of the kidney. It may be of the usual type found in chronic hypertension (arteriosclerosis) or may be the acute destructive changes of accelerated (malignant) hypertension (Figure 7.2).

VI TREATMENT

Treatment of chronic glomerulonephritis and chronic pyelonephritis, what little there is, has been discussed in Chapters V and VI. There is no treatment for polycystic kidneys; the operation of puncturing the cysts (Rovsing's operation) has little to commend it and is now rarely performed unless a cyst is causing obstruction, for example to the ureter. Infection in a polycystic kidney may be difficult to treat because of the lack of drainage from the cysts.

Salt restriction is a vital part of the management of hypertensive patients with renal impairment. Diuretics are, of course, less effective in this type of patient (although they can be employed in larger doses than usual to produce an effect). Salt restriction is therefore of greater importance than where renal function is normal. Details are given in Chapter XII.

Drug treatment of hypertension has become highly successful in the last fifteen years. Many powerful drugs are available which can render the blood pressure normal or nearly so. This is often only attainable at the price of severe side effects. Some of these affect other systems but most difficult are those which result from severe postural hypertension. The search is now for hypotensive drugs with few side effects, since potent drugs are already available. The use of these drugs in renal hypertension does not differ from that in essential hypertension, with allowance for reduced renal function if present. The drugs in common use include α-methyl DOPA, guanethidine, bethanidine, debrisoquine, propranolol and other β-blockers, hydrallazine and prazosin.

Treatment of unilateral renal disease varies with the type. Nephrectomy may be performed if it is thought by the doctor that the blood pressure will improve or be cured as a result. This he will decide on the results of the tests, and in particular what contribution the kidney to be removed is making to the patient's overall renal function. If this is much reduced and the affected kidney contributes a good deal, then nephrectomy will in general be avoided. In renal artery stenosis and aneurysm, an operation on the artery may succeed in relieving the obstruction as well as preserving the kidney, which may be of normal size. Unfortunately, the artery may thrombose after a successful operation upon it and the kidney be lost in any case. The number of patients who can benefit from surgery is small and selection will be very careful.

VII PROGNOSIS

The prognosis of patients with diffuse bilateral renal disease depends upon the rate of progression of the underlying condition; this is slower in patients with polycystic kidneys than those with pyelonephritis or glomerulonephritis. It also depends upon the success with which the blood pressure can be controlled. This is probably the most effective treatment we can offer – good control of blood pressure which requires the continued cooperation of the whole medical staff and the patient.

The prognosis of patients with unilateral renal disease and hypertension is generally good, provided that the opposite kidney and the rest of the vascular system have not been severely damaged by the time diagnosis is made. The blood pressure can usually be controlled by drugs, and for the patients who have operations on the kidney or renal artery there is the prospect of cure.

Suggestions for further reading:

Peart, W. S. (1973). Hypertension and the kidney. *Renal Disease*. 3rd Ed. p. 705. (Ed.) Black, D. A. K. Oxford: Blackwell.

CHAPTER VIII

The patient on regular haemodialysis

Patients reaching terminal renal failure can now be maintained on regular dialysis treatment. This is sometimes called, less accurately "intermittent dialysis" although "maintenance dialysis" has something to commend it. "Chronic dialysis" is inaccurate and should not be used, and "renal dialysis" is a misuse of language; it is not the kidney, but the patient, or his blood, that is dialysed.

Patients on regular dialysis lead relatively normal lives and may present in any department of the hospital for routine treatment of any condition, from toothache to pregnancy or surgical operations. In addition, before starting dialysis, and immediately thereafter in the terminal phases of their renal failure they will be nursed on general medical or surgical wards in many hospitals, so that large numbers of nurses encounter patients on dialysis in the course of their work, even if they do no special renal nursing themselves. The medical hazards of the life on regular dialysis (such as the dangers of salt and water overload, and the altered metabolism of many drugs) must therefore be appreciated by all nurses.

This chapter deals with the patient; arteriovenous fistulae and shunts, their use and care, and an outline of haemodialysis itself may be found in Chapter XV.

I THE PATIENT BEYOND TERMINAL RENAL FAILURE

When patients reach a stage when their own kidneys can no longer support life, then the doctor will consider substitution therapy to replace the failing kidney function. The events leading up to this point are described in Chapter VI. Severe hypertension, or the presence of a nephrotic syndrome as well as uraemia or a patient under fifteen, may well make the doctor decide earlier that the patient cannot continue; usually a glomerular filtration rate of less than 3 ml/min or a daily urea excretion of less than 120 mmol are taken as guides. The problems of selecting patients for limited facilities are discussed in Chapter XVII.

Once selected for substitution treatment for his or her renal failure, it is important to decide as early as possible whether the patient is to be offered regular dialysis at home as the main first line of treatment, or an early renal transplant. This decision will influence when and how the patient is dialysed, and whether a temporary external arteriovenous shunt will be used or arteriovenous fistulae needed (Chapter XV). In practice, many of the facts and opinions are not available, and often treatment must be begun without a firm commitment to one or other course. For example, the patient may be too ill to begin with to give his own ideas on the subject, or to allow the staff an assessment of his or her capabilities.

Many patients will spend time on peritoneal dialysis first (see Chapter XIV) and access of some description provided within a week or two at most, either for more permanent peritoneal dialysis (Chapter XIV) or vascular access for dialysis (Chapter XV). At first these initial dialyses may be performed with the patient in hospital, but then the patient will usually go home, and return to the hospital only to dialyse. If the decision is taken to train him for home dialysis, training will be begun as soon as possible, and later the patient's spouse (or if a child, the parents) will also attend for training. Most dialysis training is undertaken in daytime, so that the patient is unable to work or care for the family during this time, and this must be considered in timing the training programme. All throughout the early phases of the programme, independence is stressed. Unless the patient can feel independent of the hospital (as far as the situation permits him to) and in charge of his or her own future, he cannot be fully rehabilitated. Meanwhile, the nutritional, psychological and metabolic abnormalities of terminal renal failure reverse and relative well-being returns. The administrator and social worker will interview the patient and his family, and begin the modifications to the home necessary to accommodate the dialysis machinery.

If suitable for early renal transplantation (Chapter IX) the patient will be maintained on hospital peritoneal dialysis or haemodialysis. It may be necessary to remove the patient's own kidneys in a preparative operation. In either case, if the nurse is not directly involved with dialysis she should visit the unit with the patient and watch the dialysis procedure, since only then will she understand the stresses the patient is subject to.

II CARE OF PATIENTS ON REGULAR DIALYSIS TREATMENT

(a) General

The first principle of regular dialysis is that the patient must be made independent and taught to carry out procedures for himself. This is often difficult for nurses to appreciate, since it runs contrary to much of their routine ward nursing practice. It should, of course, be standard procedure within dialysis units. The patient should be got out of bed as soon as his illness permits, encouraged to wear his own clothes and to leave the ward as soon as possible for walks. A weekend at home as soon as the doctor thinks reasonable is a great step forward since many patients find it difficult to believe, initially, that they have a future. As soon as he is well enough to cooperate (if he is ill) or from the beginning if he is well, he should be introduced to his shunt (Chapter XV) if he has one and given instruction in its care and observation. He will need to spend time with the dietician, and so will his wife or whoever is to prepare his meals at home. Protein intake must not be restricted below 1 g/kg/day (about 70 g day) since many patients have months or years of protein malnutrition to overcome, and amino-acids are lost during each dialysis. Salt restriction is imposed by some doctors on all patients on regular dialysis, but some prefer to use this only in hypertensive patients. High potassium foods may need to be avoided.

Usually fluids will be limited to 300 or 500 ml per day plus his urine output, if any. Details of diet are given in Chapter XII but in general, apart from fluid and salt restriction, it is the *normality* of the diet that needs emphasis. Most patients find it an immense relief to be able to eat relatively normally again after the rigours of a low protein regime.

(b) Drugs

In general, the patient on regular dialysis will receive no drugs apart from vitamin supplements. These are generally thought necessary because water soluble B vitamins and folic acid are removed during dialysis, although on a really good diet they are not essential. Occasionally antibiotics will be necessary, especially for infections concerned with the arteriovenous shunt or fistula, and some patients will require hypotensive therapy if their sodium and water restriction is not good. Aluminium hydroxide gel or capsules may be given to lower the high plasma phosphate by binding phosphate in the gut. This is most frequently used in patients with a high plasma phosphate concentration, itching, bone disease, metastatic calcification or arthritis.

With every drug given the nurse must consider what influence the absence of renal function may have had on the dosage asked for by the doctor.

(c) Shunt

If the patient has a shunt this will require observation in the early stages (Chapter XV) but the patient will often be able to take over his shunt care. In the case of smaller children who will have a shunt on a long term basis for home dialysis, the child and parents will need careful instruction (Chapter XV). Arteriovenous fistulae usually do not require observation between dialyses, although oozing may be troublesome in the early stages from the needle sites when the fistula is still thin and mobile.

(d) Weight: hypertension

The patient's weight will be watched closely, being recorded daily whilst in the ward, and before and after each dialysis. Most patients beginning regular dialysis are overloaded with salt and water (frequently to the extent of being in heart failure), hypertensive and undernourished. One of the early aims of dialysis will be to establish the "dry" weight for that patient. Short term (day to day) changes in weight reflect almost entirely changes in body water.

Ultrafiltration during dialysis, using a high negative pressure (Chapter XV) to obtain large losses of weight (3 - 4 kg) may well cause cramp during this time. The aim is to remove sacral and ankle oedema, and to reduce gently the blood pressure to satisfactory levels over the first few dialyses. Weight reduction is continued until the patient is oedema free and begins to show a fall of blood pressure in the erect position, the lying down figure being satisfactory – say a diastolic pressure of 100 mmHg or less. The weight is then stabilized at this level, when a slow increase due to better nutrition may be seen over the next few weeks. Weight gain between dialyses should ideally be 1·6 kg or less, and certainly no more than 2 kg. A very small minority of patients, nearly always with glomerulonephritis, have blood pressure which cannot be controlled by ultrafiltration – indeed it may become worse. They secrete enormous quantities of renin and may need nephrectomy to control their blood pressure.

III COMPLICATIONS

Most of the secondary events in chronic renal failure discussed in Chapter VI can be reversed by adequate regular dialysis, and their appearance indicates that insufficient or inefficient dialysis is being given. However, a number of consequences of the mildly uraemic state in which the patient remains will be seen.

(a) Anaemia

Most patients on successful regular dialysis maintain a packed cell volume of 25 - 35% and a haemoglobin concentration from 7 to 11·5 g/100 ml. This degree of anaemia is remarkably well tolerated, patients undertaking even strenuous exertion and sport on occasion. A few patients, however, run much lower haematocrits in the range of 12 - 25%, and feel much less well. The reasons for this are sometimes obvious: for example, excessive menstrual loss in women, worsened by the heparinization during dialysis; blood loss during dialysis, either acute and external, or within the dialyser and more insidious; or the removal of large quantities of blood for investigation, which is one of the largest blood losses the patient may be subjected to. Most dialysis units give their patients a regular supplement of iron in addition to the folate already noted; some give this orally, others as an intermittent injection of parenteral iron every two or four weeks. Children on regular dialysis maintain much lower haemoglobin concentrations than normal in adults, rarely attaining haematocrits above 25% and often in the range 15 - 20%. The reasons for this are not clear, although dialyser blood losses are proportionately higher than in adults. Patients who have had a nephrectomy run lower haematocrits than those with their kidneys *in situ*, probably because even though almost useless from the point of view of excretion, the kidneys still have some residual function in secreting erythropoietin.

(b) Bone disease

Occasionally the secondary hyperparathyroidism continues and it may be necessary to remove the parathyroid glands. The patient may then require supplements of calcium and small doses of vitamin D or dihydrotachysterol. In some units rather than others, and for no reason at present discernible, patients commonly suffer severe osteoporosis and multiple fractures. This appears to be disease distinct from metabolic bone disease of uraemia.

(c) Itching

Usually this disappears in the first few weeks of adequate dialysis but a few patients experience intractable itching which persists in spite of otherwise good health. Hot sodium bicarbonate baths and glycerine or other oils rubbed on the skin may help. Some patients have itching which is relieved when their parathyroids are removed.

IV PSYCHOLOGICAL PROBLEMS

The psychological problems faced by patients on regular dialysis and their families should not be underestimated. Most are aware that they have undergone an experience akin to death, and all are aware that their life is considerably more precarious than usual. To this may be added the strain of awaiting a donor kidney at any time, the restrictions imposed by the need to dialyse regularly, by technical troubles during dialysis, together with the consequent anxiety. The judgement of when to support the patient and his spouse, and when to insist upon independent action can only be learnt for each patient. Always, the patient should be encouraged to ask questions, to discuss problems, and be reassured that straight answers will always be given to any question, however unpalatable. The patient must also often be made aware that we do not have the answers to every question, if his hopes are not to be aroused falsely. The patient's reaction to stress may not always be obvious. For example, when a hitherto well controlled patient is not restricting his fluid or potassium intake, this may well be a sign that he is asking for help. Frequently the strain is greater upon the husband or wife than on the patient dialysing and situations of reinforcing anxiety are often seen where the patient worries about his spouse worrying about his condition. Technical failures and difficulties with machinery destroy hard-won confidence, especially if frequently repeated. Anxieties of a general nature may emerge under the guise of specific anxieties. These may be related to the needling procedure if an internal arteriovenous fistula is present. The nurse may be able to explore, discuss and release the fears of death which may underlie these apparently specific anxieties. Aggressive behaviour is commonly seen, and must be understood and tolerated and even welcomed if it indicates the beginning of the patient's independence. Denial of the dialysis situation is frequent and must be overcome. Other fears may relate to the future of job and family.

The major problem for the dialysis patient is to get the dialysis procedure into perspective, in spite of the fact that its technical detail and complexity, and new terminology and way of life may overwhelm him at first. The patient must learn to dialyse to live, not live for dialysis, and with his every thought revolving round the procedure itself.

The role of the medical social worker in these psychological problems is discussed below (vi).

V   SOCIAL PROBLEMS

Many patients will lose income or employment during their terminal illness and be unable to restore their earning capacity after return to health. Jobs may be lost by repeated absences from work, and many patients find the morning after dialysis is a difficult one, if they are suffering from some degree of post-dialysis headache and some hypotension. Some patients find it more difficult than others to sleep during dialysis and again this reflects upon their performance the next day. Some patients may need to be rehoused to the detriment of their family, and of course are unacceptable at present for life insurance so that both borrowing money and protection for their families becomes more difficult. The stresses of dialysis, particularly in the home, may well expose underlying marital discord and precipitate a breach. The medical social worker (see (vi) below) should see each patient when they begin dialysis, since there are few who will not require some assistance.

VI   THE ROLE OF THE MEDICAL SOCIAL WORKER by Mrs J Harrison

The medical social worker is trained in order to help people to deal with their practical and emotional problems arising through illness or increased by it. She is able to employ the social services to suit the patients' needs, and has a wide knowledge of these services. She has knowledge of the theory of human growth and development and is a skilled interviewer, who consciously uses the relationship with the patient as a therapeutic one, geared to help the patient resolve his difficulties. The emotional problems she can help resolve are those which we all face, which are not so unusual as to require psychiatric treatment. These problems may include the emotional problems arising out of prolonged enforced dependence on dialysis and the inevitable ambivalence that this involves. The prolonged stress and uncertainty, greatest in patients awaiting transplants and their relatives, can be severe and can lead to increased marital and family difficulties. The emphasis is on helping the patient to help himself, and never to take the responsibility of decision making out of his hands. Social work help is not something from which every patient can benefit and the medical social worker must be aware of when it is appropriate to give help and when to withhold it. Many families cope extremely well with minimal support but in a situation as stressful as dialysis it is likely that at some time patients and their relatives will need some help, however minimal. It is important for the medical social worker to work as a member of the team treating the patients and that she should discuss patients with medical and nursing staff. Members of the team, because they have been trained differently, see people in different ways and it is essential that knowledge be shared.

Practical problems

(a) Financial   (1) The financial burden of visiting patients in hospital can also be great, especially as the catchment areas of dialysis centres are large. In many hospitals there is a Samaritan Fund which can be used for this purpose at the discretion of the medical social worker, although of course the fund is not unlimited.

(2) The cost of fares to attend hospital for dialysis may be large – up to £10 per week or more. The Department of Health uses officers of the Department of Social Security to assess need, and when this has been agreed patients may get their fares refunded through the hospital. In many hospitals this is done through a general administrative office and not the social work department. Application is made through the medical social worker to their local Ministry of Health and Social Security which sends an officer to visit them when they are discharged. Male patients usually get their fares paid whether or not they are in full-time work, but the wives of husbands in full-time work do not at present receive help in spite of pressure on the Department of Health and the regional committees. For families in real hardship some funds may be available to help. It is worthwhile referring patients with other financial difficulties to the medical social worker as she may be able to help or advise where help might be available.

(3)   Mothers on dialysis who have young children at home may need help with them whilst they are in hospital for dialysis, either overnight or during the day. Health visitors can arrange for day nursery care or a child minder, and child care officers can arrange short-term fostering if absolutely necessary. Payment has to be made for the last two services. The medical social worker can act as a liaison in making the initial contact between the family and the social service required. Home helps may also need to be arranged.

(4)   Most units insist that all patients on home dialysis and awaiting transplant have a telephone. The Department of Health will pay for the installation and rental of home dialysis patients' telephones, but not, at present, for transplant recipients. In cases of need the Department of Social Security may be reluctant to pay for this as they see it as a Health responsibility. It is sometimes necessary to raise money from other sources to contribute towards this cost.

(b) Employment As with any ill patient there is the problem of the interruption of work and consequent reduction in income. Help sometimes needs to be given with patients' sickness benefit and contacting their employer. Employment is generally used as a criterion of successful rehabilitation. There are two major attitude problems here; that of the prospective employer who may doubt that the patient is capable of doing a good day's work, and the patient's attitude towards his condition. Some patients see themselves as basically fit active members of society, and others as permanently too ill to do any sort of work, irrespective of their actual health. Those patients with a strong desire to work do not find great problems in finding suitable work, even if this means a change of job. Those with the opposite attitude are extremely difficult to help find employment. Obviously, in order to convince an employer that he will be a reliable worker the patient must be convinced of it himself. Basically what is required is a change of attitude. This may take a long time and is often associated with a rebellion against those who expect the patient to work, i.e. members of the treatment team. Unhelpful attitudes may also be encouraged in relatives. There are also practical problems in approaching employers because of the time off which may be required on the afternoon of a night dialysis. Another problem is that a man who has previously been an unskilled labourer with perhaps high earnings after overtime may need a lighter job.

His earnings may now be lower than he would receive through Social Security benefit. The Medical Social Worker's role in helping patients with employment problems is mainly to support the patients self-confidence so that they can come to believe they are capable of productive work. Help may also be needed in modifying relatives' attitudes to patients' work, in liaison between the hospital and the Ministry of Employment and Productivity.

If patients need re-training the Ministry of Employment and Productivity runs courses for this purpose but usually with waiting lists at present about eighteen months which is obviously unsatisfactory. There are, however, rehabilitation courses lasting about six weeks which assess the patient's aptitude and recommends the best type of training and are a useful halfway house, even though the patients may not receive training.

(c) Housing As in any group of hospital patients there are renal patients living in overcrowded, poor conditions. The Medical Social Worker can advise on housing problems and can sometimes help by contacting housing authorities. The housing problems arising from home dialysis are usually dealt with by the home dialysis administrator.

Problems may arise if a patient's self-esteem is very much tied up with his particular home. The compulsory move to accommodation which in his (and perhaps his family's) opinion is inferior to his previous accommodation, although suitable for dialysis, may precipitate a family crisis, and may also cause a financial burden if the rent is higher than before.

The Medical Social Worker can help in finding suitable accommodation for short periods for patients living far away during home training near the dialysis centre. The Department of Health is authorized to pay for bed and breakfast for the patient. It may be necessary to find similar accommodation for parents of children being dialysed, or husbands and wives. The expense of this can sometimes be met out of other funds.

(d) Problems relating to bereavement and death Initially the most important problem for the patient (and more especially for the relatives) is the fact that the patient has been extremely ill; and both he and his relatives will probably have been told that there was nothing that could be done until dialysis was mentioned. Thus the relatives may have been preparing for the patient's death and may have already partly mourned for him. Then, suddenly, the patient is very much alive again and a totally new situation arises. All patients and relatives have been anxious at some time to go over in great detail what they have experienced. The relatives are anxious to talk about this usually during the first few interviews, but the patient usually brings this up after health has been regained, after several dialyses. However, a few patients, even after two months on dialysis, are still convinced that they are going to die soon. Indeed, in a very real sense they have had a bereavement and their attitudes at this time are similar to other patients who have lost a leg or some other of their body function. Patients and relatives must be given an opportunity to express their negative feelings about their loss of freedom and the restrictions that the treatment imposes on them, and the Medical Social Worker can help them with these feelings in a positive way. The point in treatment when a bilateral nephrectomy is carried out is often a difficult one. It is much less easy for patients to persuade themselves that their kidneys will never start working again, and they may become very depressed at this time and need considerable support.

(e) Problems relating to dependence This is one of the most common emotional difficulties of chronically ill people. It is heightened and prolonged in the dialysis situation as the relationships between patients and staff are usually closer and there are fewer staff changes. The patient sees, and comes to know well, the doctors and nurses on whom he is to some extent dependent for life itself, even though he is always encouraged to be as independent as possible. How the patient adjusts to this situation depends largely upon his previous experience of dependency, e.g. his relationships with his parents or wife. He will inevitably regard the nurses and doctors in some way as "parents" and this situation inevitably produces ambivalent feelings which arouses such strong emotion that it may interfere with treatment. All members of staff are, at some time the target of aggressive feelings and must be able to accept and understand this. It is often easier for patients and relatives to express these negative feelings to someone like the Medical Social Worker on whom they are not dependent for treatment. Some patients need to be positively encouraged to do this, in order to conserve their energy for concentrating on more positive aspects of home dialysis training. Some patients on dialysis become passive and regress completely expecting to be treated like children or babies. Some may say they feel they have been reborn and most feel this to some extent. Those who have previously lacked affection and who do not receive much emotional support from their families may need considerable assistance in order to "grow up" again. Patients who have been very deprived (one in particular who was brought up in an orphanage) find the dependence of dialysis easy to cope with and this somehow fulfils their need. However, the problems may arise when they leave the hospital to begin home dialysis.

The fantasies that patients have about staff in charge of them should not be underestimated. One often hears remarks like "I feel I can't really say what I think because they can always stop treating me". Patients who are able to express their feelings are usually much less depressed than those who cannot.

(f) Marital and family difficulties The stress that chronic illness puts on a family may uncover problems which have been partially solved previously. An equilibrium has been maintained which is now upset. Relatives may feel left out of things unless they are involved in training for home dialysis or can be a kidney donor. Although they receive a great deal of support from nursing and medical staff in the ward and on the unit, when the patient is discharged this problem occurs especially when the family live some distance from the unit. Many feel slightly paranoid about the hospital's attitude towards them, especially those with marital difficulties. It can help if they know they can express their difficulties to someone (for example the Medical Social Worker) who they do not identify directly with the Renal Unit. There are practical problems in offering this sort of help on a long term basis, especially to male relatives at work all day and who may live a long way from the hospital. One can give limited help by telephone and some relatives find it enough to write down what they are feeling, whether they post the letter or not. Continuing stress and insecurity can cause total marital breakdown but many patients remark that the experience has increased the strength of their marriage and that they have learnt a lot from it. Another area of difficulty may be the sexual side of marriage. Illness can be used as an excuse through which partners can opt out. This general problem is especially relevant in transplant patients, nearly all of whom have made some comment about the sex of the donor, reflecting their anxiety about their own maleness or sexual identity since receiving the kidney. Whether this in fact causes any long term problems is unknown but is very likely. The role of the Medical Social Worker in helping patients resolve their marital difficulties is to provide some channel of communication to enable both partners to see the situation as realistically as possible.

Problems relating to the children of dialysis patients are common, especially if the patient is a mother with young children. Young children sometimes start bed-wetting, have other behavioural difficulties and are generally difficult. In one family a mother with young children was persistently called "auntie" by them because of her frequent admissions to hospital and prolonged absence from them. This is obviously upsetting for the mother who often needs to discuss ways of coping with this.

Social work help is not something from which every patient can benefit. Not all people find it easy to express difficulties and feelings and in some cases it would not be helpful for them to do so. Many people are ambivalent about accepting help initially and some are throughout the contact. It is important to get to know the families so they know what help can be offered when and if they need it, even if at the beginning they seem quite able to cope. Many families are more appropriately helped by nurses and doctors. Nurses spend a great deal of time with patients and are often the members of staff in whom patients confide. It is therefore essential that frequent discussions are held so that knowledge is shared between all members of the team which will lead to a greater understanding of patients' and relatives' problems.

VII PROGNOSIS

Dialysis is a very successful treatment for the invariably fatal situation of terminal renal failure. In well-managed units, the number of patients dying is usually very small indeed – perhaps only 5 or 10% over five years. The problems lie in two directions. The first is that dialysis badly performed and badly supervized keeps the patient just alive, in a miserable state and with a very high mortality, principally from heart failure. Like so many medical treatments of chronic disease it is only of use if done well. The second problem is that the expense of the procedure in time, money and trained personnel is very high. Even when home dialysis can be supervized after the initial training period by somewhat inexperienced staff, it still may not be possible to offer treatment at a cost acceptable to public and Government to all the patients with renal failure. As a prelude and back up to successful transplantation, regular dialysis has a permanent place. It seems that it will always also be necessary for the patient who is or who becomes untransplantable for immunologic reasons. It is probably possible to offer a decade or more of useful life at present, and this may improve in future.

VIII   HOME DIALYSIS

Home dialysis is undoubtedly the most successful way of performing regular dialysis. Although there is the extra initial cost of providing each patient with his own equipment, the removal of dialysis into the home from the hospital means that far more patients can be offered the treatment. In addition, the patient is to some extent liberated, and is free of the risk of cross infection.

Certain conditions must be met, however. The patient's home must contain a room in which the dialyser, the proportionating system, the water softener in hard water areas, a space for the preparation and a sink for the washing and rinsing of the kidney, and a bed can all be accommodated. It is preferable that this should not be a shared bedroom, so that the patient and his family are not continually reminded that dialysis is a part of their lives. Many patients will need to be rehoused, or extensions to their existing houses built, before the machinery can be accommodated. A room of ten or eleven square metres (about 100 sq. feet) is ideal but smaller rooms can be used. Extra plumbing and electricity will usually be necessary.

Next, the patient and his or her spouse must be capable of carrying out the dialysis safely and regularly. This does not require high intelligence but rather a certain practical ability and flair for organization. It also requires a toughness of temperament to survive the inevitable minor problems without crisis. The patient will be trained by the dialysis unit nursing staff, usually in a special "school" for dialysis run during the day. The period of training lasts six to nine weeks, depending upon ability and previous experience of dialysis. During the period of training social and psychological problems must be overcome. During the last two or three weeks of training the spouse will also be trained in a support capacity.

At the time of writing most home dialysis is being carried out using flatbed dialysers and fully monitored systems which also manufacture dialysate (see Chapter XV).

IX REGULAR DIALYSIS IN CHILDREN

Dialysis in children is surprisingly simple, and the children stand up to the stresses of dialysis perhaps better than adults. Certainly their survival is even higher: it is very rare indeed to lose a child maintained on dialysis especially in the home. Many units prefer to use dialysis only as a prelude to early transplantation, but a large number of children are now on regular dialysis and a growing number in the home. Provided they are well-dialysed and a sufficient energy intake can be attained, normal growth can be attained and in some children even "catchup" growth is possible.

Several aspects of dialysis create more difficulties in children than in adults. *Arteriovenous fistulae* can be used in children of 10 years or older, but below this age needling by parent or child presents difficulties which few can surmount. It may be that single needle techniques (see Chapter XV) may improve this situation, but for the moment *arteriovenous shunts* are still used for long-term access in children below the age of 10 or so. *Anaemia* is more profound than in adults, as already noted, and we do not know why this should be the case. *Bone disease* is more commonly present on beginning dialysis, and is often more severe during dialysis than in adults. *Growth* must be maintained or achieved, and this may be difficult if bone disease is present; both problems may be worsened by removing the kidneys and, thereby removing the only source of active vitamin D. Attaining the energy intakes required for growth means attention to *diet* at a level not necessary in the well-dialysed adult (Chapter XII). Finally (and perhaps most important of all) the impact of hospital or home dialysis on the *family* is even greater than that of the chronic illness which may precede it (Chapter VI).

X HEPATITIS AND HEPATITIS-ASSOCIATED ANTIGEN (AUSTRALIA ANTIGEN)

There are many forms of virus hepatitis, including that occurring in glandular fever due to the EB virus, or from cytomegalovirus infection (CMV). The commoner form of hepatitis in the general population is the epidemic hepatitis A, or infectious jaundice, but the jaundice most commonly associated with dialysis is that from the *hepatitis B virus*. This is also called serum hepatitis, because it was first recognized in association with injections of infected serum or contaminated needles. The particular association with renal disease and hepatitis B is that both uraemic and immunosuppressed patients tend, once they have acquired the virus, to keep it indefinitely circulating in their blood and growing in their tissues. This means that they act as a reservoir of the infection, and not only is their blood highly infectious, but virus may also be seen in their urine, faeces, saliva and seminal fluid. Those coming into contact with a uraemic patient on dialysis, which inevitably means handling some blood, are therefore put at risk of acquiring the disease. Unlike the uraemic patients, who experience in the acute phase only a mild transient illness, normal individuals have a severe disease which in some instances is fatal.

Because of this risk, and following several epidemics in dialysis and transplant units in the UK and elsewhere a code of practice in handling patients was drawn up (the Rosenheim report). Apart from elementary hygiene and normal cross-infection procedures on which this report is based, use has been made of a test for what is believed to be the coat of the virus concerned. This is called hepatitis-associated antigen (HAA) Australia Antigen (Au-antigen) or hepatitis B surface antigen (HB$_s$). This has enabled well, potentially infectious carriers to be identified and isolated, and normal individuals to be identified as incubating the hepatitis B virus, or actually suffering from it rather than one of the many other viruses capable of causing jaundice. Screening of blood donors and individual donations is now routine. Individuals who have recovered from the virus may have *Au-antibody* in their blood, but this requires no special action. It is usual to screen all patients who may come on to dialysis programmes from the presence of Au antigen, and all staff who may work in contact with these patients are screened at regular intervals.

A sense of perspective must be maintained in connection with hepatitis B carriers. Hepatitis B is transmitted by many insects, and in the tropics up to 10% of the population may be symptomless carriers of the virus. In the United Kingdom, however, the carriage rate in those born in the country is only 0·01%, so that those working with patients in dialysis units undoubtedly carry a higher risk than those workers in general medical or surgical areas. Should they themselves develop hepatitis and are unfortunate to become carriers, it is advisable that they do not work in contact with other dialysis patients in future.

Suggestions for further reading:
Dialysis and Transplantation (Journal) published from 15300 Ventura Boulevard, Los Angeles, California.
Harrington, J. de L., Brener, E. R. (1973) *Patient Care in Renal Failure*. Philadelphia: W. B. Saunders.
Oag, D. (1974). A realistic approach to the Rosenheim Report. *Nursing Times*, 7.2.74.
Proceedings of the European Dialysis and Transplant Association. Published by Pitman Medical, Bath (annual 1964 -).
Proceedings of the European Dialysis and Transplant Nurses Association (EDTNA) (annual 1973 -).
The Rosenheim Report. (1972). *Hepatitis and the Treatment of Renal Failure*. A report of the advisory group. Department of Health and Social Security.
Transactions of the American Society for Artificial Internal Organs. Published by the University of Georgetown Press (annual 1962 -).
Waterson, A. P. (1974). Serum hepatitis in hospital practice. *Nursing Times*, 7.2.74.
(see also the reading list for Chapter XIV).

CHAPTER IX

Renal transplantation

PRINCIPLES OF ORGAN TRANSPLANTATION

The surgical problems of transferring a kidney from one person to another are solved. The unsolved problems relate to establishing and maintaining the function of the transplanted kidney.

TISSUE COMPATIBILITY

Through immunization produced during pregnancy, following blood transfusion and skin grafting in volunteers we have learned that all the cells in the body carry as an integral part of their cell membranes sites which allow recognition of the tissue — "tissue antigens". Some of these probably relate to the species we belong to, but others appear to relate to us as individuals and to be inherited in a regular fashion from parent to child just as blood groups are. We recognize one large system called the *HL-A system* which contains more than forty antigens grouped into two sets called *loci*. Each individual has four HL-A antigens, two from each of two loci; one on each locus comes from one parent, the other two from the other parent. There may even be a third locus. When presented with cells from an individual with a different HL-A type, we are capable of "recognizing" these cells as different, probably through cells of the lymphocyte series. More recently, we have recognized another set of related tissue antigens which, unlike the HL-A antigens, are not detected by antibody tests but by *cells*. This cell-mediated locus is recognized by the *mixed lymphocyte test (MLC)* in which cells from the individual to be typed are mixed with lymphocytes from other individuals and potential donors. The rate at which they divide and react to this stimulus is the basis of the test. This is also called the lymphocyte-determined or LD locus.

120

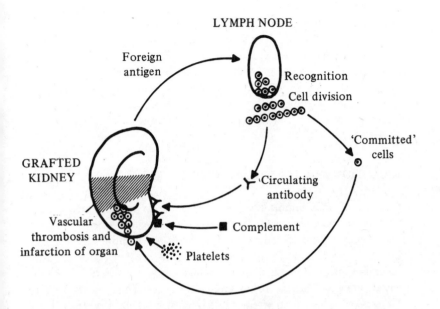

Fig. 9.1 Some mechanisms involved in the rejection of kidneys grafted
between non-identical individuals. Tissue components are released
into the venous blood draining from the kidney. These have not
been characterized, but can be "recognized" as foreign antigens,
probably by lymphocytic cells in the lymph nodes. Cell division takes
place, and a group of cells which are "committed" against the grafted kidney appears in the circulation. These infiltrate the grafted
organ. Other cells produce antibody directed against the tissue components of the grafted kidney. These are particularly important in
very acute rejections. The cells and antibody, together with complement, damage the lining (endothelium) of the small blood vessels in
the grafted kidney. Platelet thrombosis of the small blood vessels
takes place. At this acute inflammatory stage the process is reversible
by anti-inflammatory drugs such as prednisolone. After a day or two,
the thrombosis organizes, collagenous scar tissue is deposited and the
changes are irreversible. Prolonged occlusion of the blood vessels
leads to infarction of the kidney.

We can now "tissue type" individuals, much as we can determine the blood group. To do this, living white cells are separated from the blood and reacted with sera against the various HL-A antigens. If the antigen is present on the cells they will be killed, and can be stained to make this visible. This is a quick test available in a few hours at most, but the MLC test takes several days at the moment and can only be used prospectively in living donor transplantation, although the result can be analysed after a cadaver transplant has been done. Cells from the recipient are mixed with the prospective donor and a "panel" of lymphocytes of known reactivity, and the culture incubated for several days. A radioactive tracer is added and the result available after 5 - 7 days.

REJECTION AND ITS AVOIDANCE

This has obvious importance when we come to consider how we can circumvent the body's well-developed defences against foreign antigens. Once recognized as foreign, the body mounts a comprehensive attack on the organ (Figure 9.1). This involves cells, antibody and a host of secondary mechanisms including complement and platelets. The blood vessels are blocked, the organ infarcts and dies. This process is called *"rejection"*. There is an afferent side (recognition) and the efferent side (mobilization and attack). Obviously it would be better to prevent the mechanism ever reacting, by *blocking recognition*, but at the moment we are most concerned with *blunting the reaction*, which is, of course, only second best.

It is worth looking at the different ways we might be able to modify the situation, since it is likely that in the future we will be able to use some methods that at the moment are only experimental or theoretical.

(1)   we could transplant between identical individuals only
(2)   we could prevent the foreign antigens being recognized as such
(3)   we could try to desensitize the recipient to antigens he does not have before being transplanted.

(1) is of course possible between identical twins, but this is a rare curiosity. More important is the tissue typing of individuals, and the organization to match donor to recipient. On the basis of HL-A typing, this has now been done through the National Organ Matching Service (NOMS) in the United Kingdom and Ireland, and similar bodies elsewhere in Europe, such as Scandia transplant and Eurotransplant. There is no doubt that when this technique is applied to matching recipients

and donors who are close relatives (mother, father, brother, sister) it improves results considerably. When applied to cadaver transplantation, however, the results have been much less spectacular and at the moment there is much argument whether the effort of typing and organ transport actually improves results at all! The reason for this is clear; using the HL-A typing only we are neglecting other, more important systems of tissue matching. One of these is the MLC locus mentioned above, but until we can match prospectively and quickly for this we cannot use it as a means of improving results. In short, we do not yet have complete or accurate tissue typing.

(2) and (3) are in some ways same thing, since repeated exposure to a foreign antigen *can* lead to a state of desensitization; for example, when allergic individuals are desensitized to some pollen or dust to which they may be allergic. At the moment this technique is in its infancy so far as organ grafting is concerned. It is possible that some patients react to blood transfusion (which contains white cells and platelets, both carrying tissue compatibility antigens) with the production of antibody which *blocks recognition of the antigen*, rather than antibody which leads to an exaggerated response and accelerated destruction when the individual next encounters it. The results of transplantation in relation to previous blood transfusion are being eagerly studied at the moment to see if they contain a clue to this paradox.

CLOSING THE GAP AND BLUNTING THE REACTION IN PRACTICE

At the moment we have achieved some success by combining techniques to minimize the antigen gap between donor and recipient, together with techniques to blunt the recipient's reaction on recognizing the gap. First, the donor and recipient must be blood group ABO compatible; other blood groups such as rhesus (Rh) do not seem to matter:

Recipient with group:	Can have donor kidney from:
O	O
A	A, O
B	B, O
AB	AB, A, B, O.

The situation is the reverse of blood transfusion. The great majority (over 80%) of the British population are groups O or A.

Next the HL-A tissue type will be considered, and (if the donor is a close relative, and therefore living) the results of the MLC test. The tissue types of all patients awaiting cadaver transplantation are indexed in the computer of the NOMS in Bristol, and should a kidney become available which is a good or identical HL-A match for this particular recipient, the doctors looking after the recipient can be quickly made aware of his existence and the kidney sent. Many factors must be taken into consideration – the urgency of the recipient's need for a graft, whether or not the patient is fit at the time, how good the match is in relation to other possible recipients. Different units have different policies with regard to matching.

Various agents have been used to minimize the reaction of the recipient to his foreign kidney. These inhibit all or part of the defence mechanisms discussed in Chapter III and illustrated in Figure 9.1. These agents are called *"immunosuppressant"* drugs, and in addition most inhibit the reactions of inflammation. In the transplant situation, it appears that the most important part of the immune response to the foreign graft is the cellular one involving lymphocytes. The immunosuppressive agents most commonly used are:

Azathioprine (Imuran) This drug was originally synthesized as an anti-cancer agent. It inhibits synthesis of purines (and hence of DNA and protein) and is most effective in rapidly dividing cells such as lymphocytes. It is given immediately before the graft and thereafter. Usually its dose is kept constant around the level of 2 mg/kg/day. It is a marrow depressant drug, and may cause leucopenia and low platelet count.

Corticosteroid drugs Prednisone is usually employed. This inhibits lymphocytes, and in combination with azathioprine will lower the amount of antibody in the blood. In addition, corticosteroid drugs are powerful anti-inflammatory drugs and stabilize platelets. The doses of corticosteroid drugs may be varied, high immediately after the graft and reducing thereafter, and increased during rejection episodes. Very large doses may also be given intravenously for rejection (up to several grams of Prednisone).

Irradiation was used alone as immunosuppression in the early days of transplantation, and proved inadequate. It is still frequently given during acute rejection episodes but we do not know if this improves results.

Actinomycin is also given by some surgeons during the acute rejection episode but again its value has not been determined. It interferes with the division of DNA during cell replication.

Antilymphocyte globulin (ALG) This is still under investigation. At one time it seemed that this would produce really effective immuno-suppression and that its use was associated with an increased survival of kidneys and transplanted patients. It now seems that its action is much more complicated than at first supposed, and the results are not so strikingly better with its use. Lymphocytes, obtained from a culture or from drainage of the thoracic duct, are injected into horses or goats and the immunoglobulin fraction of their serum prepared, contained anti-bodies to the antigens of the lymphocytes. This is purified, antibodies to other cells are absorbed out, and the product is sterilized. The prepa-ration is injected for 10 - 14 days after transplantation, by which time allergic reactions are usually observed.

Unfortunately, the body's defences against infection by bacteria, viruses, yeasts, fungi and protozoa are the same as those which destroy transplanted organs. Any successful immunosuppressive regime will therefore render the recipient more susceptible to colonization by one or more organisms — often organisms which are living as commensals in his gut or on his skin. The result is that at least one quarter of all patients given cadaver grafts are dead from infections by the time three years have passed following their graft. The infections tend to be with unusual bacteria, yeasts, viruses or protozoa for two reasons. First, we can treat many common bacterial infections successfully, and this leaves the way open for organisms that we cannot treat so successfully; and second, the body's defences against some of the less common agents involves cells more than antibodies, just as in transplant rejection.

PRACTICAL TRANSPLANTATION

Cadaver donors and the donor kidney

Ideally, if the results of cadaver transplantation could be improved use would only be made of cadaver donors. For the moment, however, the results with cadaver donor kidneys are much poorer than those with live donors; much of this depends upon the problems of compatibility outlined above, but much also results from the problems of obtaining cadaver kidneys. The kidneys should be removed as soon as possible after death (the definition of death and the ethical problems related to this decision are discussed in Chapter XVII). The time the kidney spends in the body at 37° C or just below, is called the "warm ischaemia time". Warm ischaemia longer than one hour results in a fall-off in viability of the kidneys, and ideally it should not be longer than half an hour. If the operative time is included, then this can only be achieved when using kidneys from donors with "brain death" maintained on a ventilator. Kidneys from this situation nearly always function immediately, but present laws and professional attitudes in the United Kingdom result in there being only a minority of the cadaver kidneys used (see Chapter XVII).

Usually the kidney is flushed through with an electrolyte or colloid-containing solutions at 4° C; a number of different solutions have their advocates. It is still not clear what the ideal fluid should consist of. The kidney is then placed, sterile, in a plastic bag on ice and transported to the recipient. Cooling is used because the metabolic activity of the kidney is much less at low temperatures, and the isolated organ can survive longer under these conditions. The time at low temperature is called the "cold ischaemia time" and is much less critical than the warm ischaemia time. Up to about ten hours of cold ischaemia the results of cadaver transplantation are about the same.

More use is now being made of *machines* by which the kidney can be perfused after removal. This has proved surprisingly difficult to achieve, and the best solutions, temperatures and perfusion conditions are still not decided. Two machines most used at the moment are the Belzer machine and the Gambro system. These allow a planned operation at a time decided by the surgeon, and more time to carry out the immunological tests on the donor tissue needed for tissue matching.

Most cadaver transplants, however, are done when the opportunity presents. The donor must be tissue typed, and a "cross-match" of recipient's serum and donor cells performed to check whether the recipient already carries any dangerous antibodies against the tissue type of the donor, as a result of previous transfusion, transplantation or pregnancy. If the cross-match is positive and the donor cells are killed, the transplant will not normally be done. These tests must be done very carefully and take time. It is best, therefore, if preparations can be begun before the donor is actually dead, and this is made easier if the donor is maintained by artificial ventilation. The ethical problems are discussed in Chapter XVII. Patients who have malignant disease (apart from some intracerebral tumours which do not spread beyond the central nervous system) are unsuitable as donors. So also are patients with septicaemias, and obviously those with kidney disease. There is no absolute bar so far as advancing age is concerned but it has recently been shown that grafts function less well overall with advancing age of the donor, starting as early as 40 years of age. Most surgeons will not accept kidneys from donors above the age of 65 or so.

Living related donors

Some grafts are performed from close relatives of the recipient. Although in the early days of transplantation volunteer live donors were used, the results were so poor (worse in fact than cadaver donors) that now only close family members are considered. For practical purposes this means immediate family members: father, mother, brother, sister, son or daughter. The chances of a good HL-A match are obviously very much higher than a random donor, in view of the inheritance of two HL-A types in pairs from each parent to a child; but more important than this seems to be the similarity close relatives have in the types they possess at the locus revealed on mixed lymphocyte culture. With sibling grafts, the possibility of identity in all types arises, and these grafts between HL-A and MLC-identical siblings hardly ever fail. Most surgeons therefore welcome the chance to do live donor grafts, despite reservations with regard to performing an operation on a normal individual (the donor) which must carry some risk, however small; this is considered in Chapter XVII.

Before a live donor graft can be undertaken, however, a number of conditions must be satisfied:

(i) the prospective donor must have an ABO blood group compatible with the recipient's.

(ii) preferably the HL-A and MLC compatibility must be adequate; but results are good irrespective of these tests.

(iii) the prospective donor must be in good health with normal blood pressure and good renal function.

(iv) the IVU must be normal.

(i)-(iv) can be done with the prospective donor as an outpatient)

(v) renal arteriograms must show at least one kidney with a renal artery which is single and can be used for grafting. This requires overnight admission to hospital and it is at this stage the nurse may first meet the donor.

(vi) the motives of the donor must be beyond question.

In practice the last is the most difficult to assess. Immediately the question of kidney donation is mentioned, pressures are generated, which may not be apparent to the medical and nursing staff, within the family. In many units, the doctors wait for the family to raise the question of kidney donation, and never suggest the possibility themselves. Even when someone does volunteer, the problems are stressed to allow the prospective donor to withdraw, and the final discussion should be private between the surgeon and the donor.

Rarely, as a result of an operation on a patient's ureter, a good kidney must be sacrificed by the urological surgeon. This is usually referred to as a "free" kidney, and may be used for transplant action.

The recipient

The recipient can be any patient who has renal failure, and who has been returned to health by regular haemodialysis or peritoneal dialysis. It usually takes two to three months before tissues return to normal, after the many problems which may appear in terminal renal failure. As with other situations of regular dialysis, the best time to begin treatment is before complications present a serious barrier to early transplantation. Patients with abnormal urinary tracts will need preliminary operations to correct their bladder abnormality, and even patients in whom the bladder is useless have been transplanted successfully into ileal loop bladders created by the surgeon. This is a matter to be judged very carefully by the transplant surgeon. Some patients such as those with infected polycystic kidneys, or those with pyelonephritic kidneys and urinary reflux up the ureters, will need to have their kidneys, or kidneys and ureters, removed before transplantation. In some units the kidneys are removed routinely before transplantation, but this is now less popular. Sometimes patients will be transplanted without any dialysis at all, rather earlier in their renal failure than if dialysis is used first. This is done when it can be seen that transplantation offers the patient his only hope and a dialysis place is impossible. Results with these "snatch" grafts are surprisingly good, especially since these tactics are often adopted in patients who are less than ideal recipients.

Some doubt exists concerning forms of glomerulonephritis which may attack the new kidney as well as being responsible for the patient's primary disease: "transmissible" nephritis. This can take place in patients with lupus nephritis and polyarteritis, as well as in patients whose nephritis is characterized by many epithelial crescents, or is a mesangiocapillary glomerulonephritis with a low serum complement level (see Chapter IV). Some sclerosing forms of glomerulonephritis also seem to transmit to the grafted kidney on occasion. The decision whether to transplant such patients is a difficult one, but the frequency of severe disease in the grafted kidney is not high enough to make the presence of these forms of nephritis a firm contra-indication to transplantation.

During the period waiting for a kidney the patient's blood group, HL-A tissue type, and lymphocyte type will be determined, and this information kept locally and at the National Organ Matching Service.

Preparation of the recipient

The patient may be at home or at work, when a suitable kidney presents and there may be very little time or a long wait after he or she is called. Obviously the whereabouts of all transplant recipients must be known to members of the transplant team at all times. This puts a great strain upon the potential recipient, especially if he waits some time for a suitable kidney, and above all if he is called in several times for "false alarms" when no kidney is finally obtained.

(1) On arrival the blood is taken for haemoglobin, packed cell volume, blood urea and electrolytes and for cross-matching blood. A sample of clotted blood may also be taken for mixed lymphocyte culture.

(2) The recipient may need a brief haemodialysis (a) to remove fluid and (b) to lower his plasma potassium. If the patient has been on haemodialysis on a shunt he will need protamine 1% to reverse the heparin given on dialysis. The amount of protamine to be given intravenously (but *not* into the shunt) will be assessed by the laboratory. Patients on haemodialysis on a fistula will already have been given a routine dose of protamine 1% 5 ml.

(3) The patient should have nothing by mouth.

(4) The anaesthetist will be informed by the doctor as soon as possible because patients on maintenance haemodialysis present special anaesthetic problems.

(5) If possible pre-operative physiotherapy is given in the form of deep breathing and leg exercises.

(6) The recipient's relatives may need to be informed if he has come in from work, or was already on dialysis in the hospital when the donor presented.

(7) The consent form is signed.

(8) The patient is weighed and his height measured.

(9) Temperature, pulse, respiration and a lying and standing blood pressure is recorded.

(10) The patient is shaved from nipples to mid-thigh and given a Savlon bath.

(11) The patient is placed on a stretcher canvas, gowned and identified for theatres.

(12) The premedication is given.

Preparation of the room for transplant recipient

(1) The patient is nursed in a side ward for the first 12 - 24 hours, *not* for barrier nursing reasons but because the frequent observations required disturb the other patients in the ward.

(2)   Postoperative bed with fracture board and drip stand.
(3)   Anaesthetic tray.
(4)   Vomit bowl.
(5)   Bed elevator.
(6)   Spirit level or spirit level arm and drip stand for CVP line (see Chapter XIII).
(7)   Sphygmomanometer and stethoscope.
(8)   Oxygen
(9)   Suction.
(10)   Infant giving set (for IV normal saline to keep the CVP line open)
(11)   Venous pressure set.
(12)   Urine testing equipment for sugar, blood, pH and albumin. Urimeter and Winchester.
(13)   Intensive care chart.
(14)   *Drugs*: IV Lasix 200 ml bottle, hydrocortisone, potassium chloride.
(15)   Needles and syringes.

The operation

The *removal of the kidneys* from the donor is a skilled procedure, and many units send an experienced doctor with packs containing everything he may need to the hospital where the donor is. Since techniques differ from unit to unit, and individual surgeon's preferences differ, there is little point in enumerating these. The removal is performed under sterile conditions, preferably in theatres but failing that a side ward or treatment room. Most surgeons now use the "monoblock" dissection in which both kidneys and their attached vessels, together with a length of aorta and inferior vena cava bearing these, are removed *en bloc*. The two kidneys can then be separated by dividing the aorta and IVC outside the body, providing a vascular cuff for the anastomosis is on the end of the renal vessels. As much ureter as possible is taken — about 15 cm is usual. This is not dissected free since it may impair its blood supply. The kidneys are then perfused and cooled as discussed above. The doctor provides the perfusing solutions. The kidneys are then transported on ice in a vacuum flask to the recipients.

In the case of *living donors*, the donor will be anaesthetized in a second operating theatre adjacent to that in which the recipient is placed. It is usual to ensure that kidney's well-perfused and passing large quantities of urine at the time of removal by an intravenous infusion of dextrose, with or without mannitol. The donor will be catheterized in the ward or the anaesthetic room. When the surgeon operating on the donor con-

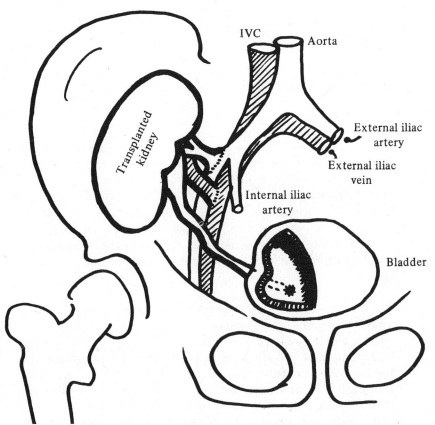

Fig. 9.2 Diagram of a transplanted kidney *in situ*. The donor renal
artery, which divides just outside the kidney, has been anastomosed
end-to-side onto the external iliac artery, using a cuff of aorta
removed with the kidney. When this cuff is not available (for example in the case of a live donor graft) then the surgeon may bring up
the cut end of the internal iliac artery and anastomose it end-to-end
to the donor artery. The donor vein is also anastomosed end-to-side
on to the external iliac vein, so that the kidney lies comfortably in
the iliac fossa – in this case the right. It is usually necessary to place
the donor's left kidney in the right iliac fossa, and vice versa, because
of the relationship of the vessels and ureter in the hilus of the kidney.
Finally, the ureter is brought through a tunnel made by the surgeon
in the bladder wall and anastomosed to the mucosa lining the bladder (a Leadbetter-Politano anastomosis). Other forms of anastomosis may be used, including the use of the recipient's own ureter, if
available. The whole operation is conducted extraperitoneally in
adults, although in placing adult kidneys in small children a trans-
peritoneal approach may have to be used.

firms that the removal is safe and feasible, the surgeon operating on the recipient will begin. Usually the recipient will already be anaesthetized and prepared on the operating table.

Speed is essential, so that the detailed organization of the operation such as the availability of theatres and theatre staff is very important. These difficulties are enhanced by the fact that transplantation is not yet an elective procedure.

The kidney is not usually placed in the natural site in the loin but in the pelvis. The main reason for this lies in the precarious blood supply to the ureter, which must be kept as short as possible. One can also avoid operating on the recipient's aorta and inferior vena cava by placing the kidney in the pelvis. If the left kidney of the donor is available, then it is placed in the right iliac fossa of the recipient, so that vessels and ureter lie properly. This may be important if only one kidney is available, or if the recipient has already had one unsuccessful transplant into one iliac fossa.

The surgeon makes an oblique lower lateral abdominal incision and proceeds, extraperitoneally, to expose the iliac vessels. The donor renal artery is anastomosed end-to-side onto the external iliac vein in a similar fashion, using the cuff of aorta and inferior vena cava attached to the donor vessels already mentioned (see Figure 9.2). Less commonly, with cadaver grafts (but in all living donor grafts), the surgeon will anastomose the internal iliac artery, end-to-end, onto the donor artery. This may be done because there is no cuff of donor artery available, such as in living-donor transplants. After completing the anastomoses, the vascular clamps are removed and the kidney fills with the recipient's blood. The kidney becomes pink and changes from flaccid to turgid.

Some urine may emerge from the cut end of the ureter almost immediately if the kidney is fresh or from a live donor. The bladder is then opened and the ureter is anastomosed to it. The surgeon creates a tunnel in the bladder wall and passes the ureter through it to prevent subsequent reflux of urine up the ureter, and then sews the end of the ureter into the inside of the bladder. Clips may be placed or sewn onto the upper and lower poles of the kidney so that its position can be determined on X-rays without the necessity of injecting contrast medium. The wound is closed over drains into the perirenal space and a catheter is left in the bladder. Usually, the ureter is not splinted with a ureteric catheter but this may be necessary when the ureteric anastomosis has been toublesome.

Postoperative nursing care

Immediate and for the first 12 - 24 hours.

(1)   When recovery from anaesthetics is complete the patient is usually nursed in the supine position with one or two pillows as is comfortable.

(2)   Half hourly observations of: blood pressure, pulse and respirations and level of consciousness.

(3)   The central venous pressure is measured half hourly, a chest X-ray is taken to check the position of the line.

(4)   Care of the peripheral line.

(5)   Temperature is taken 4 hourly.

(6)   The urine volume is measured hourly and tested for sugar, pH, albumin and blood. Continuous 24 hour urine collections.

(7)   Weight should be done twice daily.

(8)   'Lasix drive' i.e. continuous iv frusemide may be started in the operating theatre. Lasix IV is commenced and is infused at the rate of 4 drops per minute for 24 hours.

(9)   The arteriovenous shunt (if *in situ*) should be observed hourly.

(10)   Care of the catheter and any drainage apparatus.

(11)   Care of the mouth and pressure areas 2 hourly.

(12)   Passive exercises to the limbs and physiotherapy to the chest 4 hourly

Subsequent nursing care.

(1)   The observations are reduced to four hourly. After instilling 2·5% 'Noxyflex' solution into the bladder the catheter is removed on the first day, and the patient should be offered frequent bed pans or urinals if passing urine.

(2)   If the patient is anuric, the catheter should be removed after 2·5% Noxyflex or other antiseptic has been instilled into the bladder. Leaving a catheter in an anuric bladder causes infection. If the transplant is functioning the catheter will be left in for 5 - 10 days to allow the bladder incision to heal.

(3)   Haemodialysis if necessary.

(4)   Commence oral fluids and a light diet, fluid and diet restrictions as ordered.

(5)   Discontinue intravenous fluids as soon as ordered.

(6)   Ambulate patient and sit out in a chair the following day.

(7)   Expose and spray wound with antibiotic spray as soon as possible

(8)   Mouth care 4 hourly.

(9)   Careful recording of intake and urine output.

(10)   Drugs (such as Prednisone, azathiprine, frusemide and Aludrox) given as ordered.

Laboratory estimation of blood and urine

(1)   Blood will be taken postoperatively and then daily for:
    (i)   Urea and electrolytes
    (ii)   White blood count and platelets
    (iii)   Haemoglobin and packed cell volume
    (iv)   Creatinine
    (v)   Glucose

(2)   All urine will be saved 12 or 24 hour specimens sent regularly for laboratory estimations of:
    (i)   Urine protein
    (ii)   Electrolytes and urea
    (iii)   Osmolarity
    (iv)   Microscopy and culture
    (v)   Creatinine (for clearance).

The patient will also have portable X-rays of chest and investigations of the transplanted kidney, as ordered. Dialysis will be avoided in the case of a transplant which does not function immediately in the first 24 hours after transplantation unless a rapid rise in the plasma potassium or inadvertent fluid overload makes this essential. The dangers of heparinizing a patient for dialysis when he has just been submitted to vascular surgery need not be emphasized. If dialysis is necessary during the first week after transplantation, then "tight" heparinization will be employed with the object of keeping the clotting times about 20 - 30 minutes at most. Because a rise in potassium is to be avoided at all costs, stored blood may be transfused through bags of resin which remove the excess of plasma potassium always present in this fluid.

Preparing the patient for discharge

The patient is taught to take his own temperature, blood pressure and weight and to record them in a note book. The patient must also learn to record his own fluid intake and output, and to test his urine for albumin, pH and sugar.

It is important that he understands and is able to recognize the signs and symptoms of rejection. In the case of living donor, the *donor* will be managed postoperatively as for nephrectomy under other circumstances.

Immunosuppressive regime

This varies somewhat between transplant units and is of course given as the doctor directs. All or some of the agents discussed on page 124 may be employed and this page should be consulted for details. The nurse should always keep in mind the fact that these drugs and treatments all increase the susceptibility of the patient to infection, and meticulous care is necessary in the immunosuppressed patient of the potential portals of entry through which organisms may gain access. They are:

(i)   the shunt
(ii) the bladder catheter
(iii) the intravenous infusion
(iv) the drains
(v)   the wound(s)
(vi) the respiratory tract

This is especially important during rejection episodes, when immuno-suppressive agents are at their maximum dosage. Many units attempt to reduce the immunosuppression to a maintenance level as soon as possible, usually within two to four months of the transplant, since rejection episodes are commonest in the early months. Whether this is possible depends upon the tissue compatibility and the number of rejection episodes. The white cell count and platelet count are carefully watched and the azathioprine dosage reduced or even stopped altogether if a leucopenia develops.

FUNCTION OF THE KIDNEY

Some kidneys never function. A few for technical reasons, such as blockage of the renal artery or vein; a few because, despite adequate matching, severe immediate rejection sets in which may be apparent even on the operating table; a few because they were irreversibly damaged by the time they were transplanted and some for reasons at present obscure. Most cadaver kidneys have a period of a few days to several weeks before function is sufficient to support the recipient. This is very similar to the course of acute renal failure (Chapter II) and as in this condition, an occasional transplant may take two or even three months before function appears. Arteriography or dynamic scintillography using the gamma camera may be performed to visualize the renal vessels and detect whether obstruction is present. Renography is also useful because, unlike the other techniques, the apparatus can be taken to the bedside. It is particularly good at detecting obstruction (see Chapter XI). A high-dose IVU may also be performed, or a renal biopsy, which presents special problems in the transplanted patient (Chapter IV).

Until function of the kidney appears dialysis is continued as before transplant, with the reservations about heparin already discussed. Live donor kidneys usually function immediately, and a considerable diuresis may be seen. This is usually smaller if the patient is well dialysed pre-operatively so that the amount of urea and sodium to be excreted is small.

Complications

There are many complications of the transplanted state with which the doctor and nurse may have to deal. They may be divided into complications of the transplant itself, the far more numerous complications of the present unsatisfactory immunosuppressive regime and a miscellaneous group.

(i)   The transplant itself

(a) Rejection   This is the event most feared after organ transplantation. The real problem is that to be treated successfully, rejection must be diagnosed before the organ has been irreversibly damaged. As soon as the kidney is the subject of the immune attack, platelet thrombi are formed. Once these thrombi have organized and scar tissue (collagen) is deposited, the vessels will be permanently narrowed or obliterated, and the kidney damaged or even destroyed. So that at any event, especially in the first few days or weeks, will be nervously examined by the doctors to decide whether rejection is taking place. The nurse is frequently in the position of observing the earliest signs of rejection. These signs are numerous, but rather non-specific. The following observations may be made during rejection:

(i)   General signs of inflammation: anorexia, malaise, fever, tachycardia, raised white cell count, ("flu-like" syndrome), fall in platelet count.

(ii)   Raised blood pressure.

(iii) Local signs of inflammation: tender kidney, increased in size on X-ray judged by the clips inserted at operation

(iv)   Reduced function (if function is present): fall in urine volume, fall in GFR rise in plasma creatinine and blood urea.

(v)   Appearance of abnormal constituents in urine: protein, lymphocytes, renal enzymes.

The conditions which may look very much like rejection are:

(i)   Infection, especially in or around the kidney itself.

(ii)   Blockage of the ureter.

(iii) Blockage of the arterial or venous anastomosis.

(iv)   haematoma.

The doctor will have special difficulty in diagnosing rejection in the period following a cadaver transplant when the kidney is still in renal failure and is only producing small quantities of urine containing protein, cells and debris from the renal tubules. Most units, if there is any real doubt whether rejection is present or not, will proceed to treat the patient as though rejection is taking place and to see whether the suspicious signs improve. Even so, one may miss rejection episodes completely, and find evidence of them later when the kidney is biopsied to determine why it has failed to function.

(b)   Infarction of the kidney   This may come about by blockage of the artery. It may be difficult to diagnose and the patient will usually need various radiological investigations such as a high dose IVU and an arteriogram, as well as renogram or scan (see Chapter XI) to determine whether this is so. Occasionally there is blockage of the renal vein rather than the artery.

(c)   Urinary infection   is common after transplantation and the nurse should endeavour to see that contamination of the bladder does not take place. The signs are those of urinary infection of an orthotopic kidney. Treatment will be vigorous.

(d)   Sloughing of the ureter   This can arise from several causes but is fortunately rare with good matching and good surgery. The ureter may be rejected, just as the kidney; its blood supply may have been impaired at operation; infection may be present. A urinary leak develops into the perirenal tissues and is usually followed by fistula formation and infection. The patient's life may be lost as well as the kidney.

(e)   Haemorrhage   Gross haemorrhage from the arterial anastomosis is rarer than trouble with the ureter. Clearly an arterial bleed from a vessel of the size of the iliac artery is a serious matter. More usually there is a steady ooze from the operative bed. Heparinization for dialysis may contribute in the immediate post-transplant period, as may infection a week or more later. Haematuria is common in the first 24 hours after transplantation, which is not surprising since the bladder has two wounds in it. This will give rise to no anxiety unless heavy or prolonged.

(ii)   The immunosuppression

(a)   Infection   This problem has already been mentioned above, where the frequent occurrence of unusual and difficult organisms in transplanted patients was discussed. Systemic infection may occur in any patient maintained on high doses of immunosuppressive agent, and the doctor may well consider removing an otherwise good kidney if an

unacceptable level of immunosuppression is required, just because of the fear of complications. It is wrong to say that until recently many transplanted patients died of infection; they died as a result of excess immunosuppression. Hopefully, better tissue typing will allow less immunosuppression, until we have solved the problem of making patients tolerant of foreign tissue without destroying their ability to fight infection.

At present, infection with gram negative bacteria is the major bacterial problem, particularly resistant strains of E. coli, proteus and the ubiquitous pseudomonas aeruguinosa (pyocyanea). This is a weak pathogen but is deadly in debilitated or immunosuppressed patients because until recently there were no antibiotics which could treat it. Now colomycin, gentamycin and carbenicillin are available and although still feared, systemic infection with pseudomonas is no longer the almost invariably fatal condition it was.

Many immunosuppressed patients become infected with a number of other types of organisms besides bacteria. The commonest seen are:

Viruses:
cytomegalovirus (CMV). This is a commensal in the respiratory system but may cause pneumonia in immunosuppressed individuals. Also a cause of jaundice.
herpes viruses, particularly varicella (chicken pox, shingles) and herpes simplex (cold sores) which may become systemic hepatitis virus

Fungi:
aspergillus, in the chest and then systemically; nocardia

Yeasts:
candida, from the mouth or vagina
cryptococcus

Protozoa:
pneumocystis carinii, in the chest

The great number of these that gain access via the lungs should be noted. "Transplant pneumonia" or "transplant lung" has been described and is an infective complication of the immunosuppression used for the rejection. The organisms found are pneumocystis and a variety of other organisms, particularly the cytomegalovirus. The patients have only a little dry cough, their pulse, temperature and respiration rate rise, they become cyanosed although the amount of CO_2 in the blood remains the same or even falls. The condition carries a very high mortality indeed. The only drugs of any use against pneumocystis at present are the rarely used pentamidine isethionate, or trimethoprim-sulphonamide (cotrimoxazole).

(b) Cushing's Syndrome Most transplanted patients have the appearance of patients on corticosteroid therapy — a fat, rather hairy face, sometimes with a red complexion and acne. More serious, however, are the underlying metabolic abnormalities, such as depletion of protein from bone leading to osteoporosis, necrosis of the femoral head and fractures; the increased risk of peptic ulceration, thrombosis, hypertension and other disorders. Changes of mood and personality may be seen.

(c) Tumours In the early days of transplantation, several malignant tumours were unwittingly transplanted from patients dying of various carcinomata. Now the presence of such a tumour would be a contraindication to using the donor. However, it has become apparent that the immunosuppressive agents themselves may occasionally lead to malignancies. These have been lymphosarcomata for the most part, and although tragic, their importance should not be exaggerated; much less than 1% of patients transplanted have been affected.

(iii) Miscellaneous

(a) Hypertension after transplantation may have many causes, amongst them rejection (acute and chronic), corticosteroids, renal artery stenosis in the graft, ureteral obstruction or the recipient's own kidneys. Hypertension in the immediate postoperative period is common and is probably mostly due to the ischaemic damage to the graft before its insertion into the recipient. It may also arise from overfilling of the circulation in the patient who requires transfusion and was already overloaded at operation: for example, if no preoperative dialysis was possible.

(b) Hyperparathyroidism If the hyperparathyroidism brought about by the chronic renal failure (Chapter VI) is severe it may be autonomous and not reversed by either adequate maintenance haemodialysis or transplantation. In this case, removal of all or almost all the parathyroid tissue may be necessary. Most doctors prefer to wait if at all possible following transplantation, since the condition settles in the majority of patients, especially if the tendency to a low phosphate is corrected by giving oral phosphate.

(c) Defective tubular function persists for some time after transplantation, as after renal failure. The transplanted kidney even when working well cannot concentrate or acidify the urine as well as normal, and this may lead to an acidosis with a low bicarbonate concentration

in the blood. It also loses phosphate, as noted above, and this is made worse by the fact that the level of parathyroid hormone is very high immediately after transplantation, because of the prolonged uraemia.

Patients whose transplants survive the technical problems (and these form the great majority today) are then subject to the problems outlined. A number of kidneys are lost in the first four or six months after transplantation, but loss of kidney thereafter is a relatively uncommon event, at least for several years. With tissue typing, recipients made fit by haemodialysis, and careful control of immunosuppression, survival of 70-85% of kidneys transplanted between close relatives can be expected. Survival of cadaver kidneys is poorer at present — between 40 and 60% — at two to three years following the graft. We do not know how long a successful transplant may last; the longest surviving graft at the time of writing is fifteen years, in a patient who received it from a living close relative. It seems that we can offer at least five years, and probably ten years, of useful life to patients successfully grafted using cadaver donors. Occasional patients who received cadaver grafts have now reached ten years, but overall about 5% of grafts are lost for each year following the first.

TRANSPLANTATION IN CHILDREN

Transplantation in children has been more frequent from living closely-related donors. This arises from parents' natural wishes to help their child in every way possible, and to the facts that a good tissue match is very likely within a family, and that parents of children are rarely over 50. They therefore form a good group of potential donors. Usually the parent will raise the question of kidney donation himself, and it is important that should a transplant not be possible, or should fail, that the parent is left without guilt. It is important also that no parent should give a kidney under pressure, conscious or unconscious, because it is expected of him. Usually the doctor will be able to avoid this situation by being aware of the possibility, and by discussing the situation with the prospective donor, alone.

The operation is identical to that in adult-adult transplantations, except that the adult donor kidney is much larger in relation to the small pelvis of the child. It is usual to place the kidney outside the peritoneum in very small children. This may become important later if it is wished to perform a biopsy of the graft, since a needle biopsy may be impossible across the peritoneal cavity, if this remains in the vicinity of the graft.

Children are, of course, likely to suffer growth arrest from corticosteroids used as part of the immunosuppressive regime. The doctor will therefore try to reduce these as much as possible. Usually it is possible to gain some height after a transplant, but if the child is already stunted from chronic renal failure it is rare for him to "catch up" with his predicted height.

As with dialysis, both graft survival and patient survival are higher in children aged five to fifteen years than in any older age group, both for cadaver and for living donor grafts. Below the age of five years there are many problems, but successful grafts have been placed in children right down to less than one year of age. Adult kidneys cannot be used in children weighing less than about 10 kg, and childhood donors are needed for most small children. These are, of course, not frequent. In most units living donors below the legal age of consent are not used.

Suggestions for further reading:

Baldwin, J. (1973). Dialysis or transplantation? *Nursing Times*, 29.11.73.

Calne, R. Y. (1971). *Renal Transplantation*. 3rd Ed. London: Arnold.

Calne, R. Y. (Ed.) (1973). *Immunological Aspects of Transplantation Survery*. London: M.T.P. Books.

Dialysis and Transplantation (Journal) published from 15300 Ventura Boulevard, Los Angeles, California.

Harrington, J. de L., Brener, E. R. (1973). *Patient Care in Renal Failure*. Philadelphia: Saunders.

Longmore, D. B. (1971). *Spare Part Surgery*. London: Aldus Books.

Proceedings of the European Dialysis and Transplant Association. Published by Pitman Medical, Bath. (annual 1964 -).

Proceedings of the European Dialysis and Transplant Nurses Association (annual 1973 -).

Russell, P. S., Winn, H. J. (1970). Transplantation (3 parts). *New Eng. J. Med.*, **280**, 786, 848, 896.

Transactions of the American Society for Artificial Internal Organs. Published by the University of Georgetown Press (annual 1962 -).

CHAPTER X

Miscellaneous renal diseases

I POLYCYSTIC KIDNEYS

Adult polycystic renal disease is an inherited disease transmitted by a dominant gene, so that a family history of kidney trouble or high blood pressure is frequently obtained, perhaps affecting several consecutive generations. Both kidneys are involved but one may be damaged earlier and more severely than the other, so that the disease at first appears unilateral. The kidneys are covered on their outer surfaces, and throughout their substance, by cysts of varying size; most of these contain clear fluid but some may be filled with fresh or altered blood. The exact origin of these cysts is unknown, but they appear to result from disordered maturation of nephrons, and may be in fact grossly dilated tubules. Early in life both renal function and blood pressure are normal, but usually between the ages of 20 and 40 both become abnormal. Death occurs most frequently about the age of fifty, earlier if there is severe hypertension. Why some patients develop hypertension and others do not is unknown, but those that do not are often those who maintain a high excretion of sodium in spite of declining renal function. Again, why function should decline is not clear; the cysts usually enlarge gradually throughout life and with them the kidneys. At postmortem they may be huge, weighing several kilograms and extending over into the opposite iliac fossa.

The presence of polycystic kidneys may become apparent for a variety of reasons:

(1)   screening because of a family history
(2)   haematuria
(3)   loin pain
(4)   urinary tract infections
(5)   a mass in the loin found incidentally
(6)   hypertension
(7)   chronic renal failure

The nurse may be confused by references to other, less common cystic diseases of the kidney. Sometimes very large multiple cystic kidneys are found at birth ("juvenile polycystic kidney"). This condition is distinct from the adult form and is usually fatal in the first few days of life. Very occasionally, "adult" polycystic kidneys are found in a child, representing a more rapid progression than usual of the condition. Mention is sometimes found of *medullary cystic disease* ("sponge kidney"). This is fairly common, but the cysts are in the medulla as the name suggests, the surface of the kidneys being smooth, and the organs of normal size. This does not normally lead to either renal failure or hypertension, but gives rise to repeated infections and to stone formation since the cysts may communicate with the calyces. *Nephronophthisis* is a rare cystic disease of the medulla, leading to renal failure in childhood.

II ANALGESIC NEPHROPATHY

For twenty years it has been known that the prolonged, excessive intake of mixed analgesic tablets and powders may lead to both necrosis and sloughing of the papillae of the kidney (*papillary necrosis*) and an *interstitial nephritis* which may lead to renal failure. It is still being debated whether this occurs only with mixtures of analgesics, with phenacetin alone, or from aspirin. At the moment, metabolic breakdown products of phenacetin seem the likely main culprit, but their toxicity may well be increased by concomitant intake of aspirin. Aspirin itself, although toxic to the kidney in several ways, does not appear to cause renal failure on its own in man, although it can cause papillary necrosis in rats. The other important feature of analgesic nephropathy is that the effects of the drugs are increased by chronic dehydration. This may account for the frequency with which renal failure is seen from analgesic nephropathy in Australia and South Africa. In Australia, about one fifth of all renal transplants are done for renal failure from analgesics although in the United Kingdom the figure is only about one or two per cent. Undoubtedly, however, social factors determine how much analgesics patients take, and it is only when huge quantities are taken that damage appears. For example, the equivalent of about 1 - 2 *kilograms* of phenacetin must be taken before damage appears. These huge quantities are rarely taken for strictly medical reasons such as arthritis, but more commonly as a form of dependence on the drugs. It is important to remember that these patients rarely volunteer their analgesic consumption, and may even conceal it actively.

It is also important to diagnose the condition, because it is progressive, and the renal damage can usually be arrested if the patient can be persuaded of the danger in continuing the tablets or transferred to some less harmful form of support. Short of uraemia, the main features of the condition are an inability to concentrate and acidify the urine, because of papillary loss and tubular damage.

III DIABETES MELLITUS

The kidneys of diabetics may suffer from a variety of diseases.

(i)   The specific diabetic nephropathy affecting the afferent arteriole and glomerulus, which gives rise to proteinuria, sometimes a nephrotic syndrome (as discussed in Chapter IV) and finally chronic renal failure. Patients with this type of disease nearly always have diabetic retinopathy in addition and may be blind. Renal failure is the commonest cause of death in juvenile-onset diabetes (under 25) but not in older maturity-onset diabetes, who more frequently suffer from vascular disease.

(ii)   Diabetics are more than usually prone to hypertension and vascular disease, and these may also damage the kidney and accelerate renal failure.

(iii) Diabetics are not more prone, of themselves, to pyelonephritis and urinary tract infections but both conditions are more common in the diabetic population because diabetics are more frequently catheterized and because diabetic neuropathy may affect bladder drainage.

(iv)   Diabetics suffer from a curious tendency to infarction and separation of the renal papillae (papillary necrosis) which is also seen in patients suffering from chronic analgesic abuse.

This emphasizes the meticulous attention needed when catheterizing diabetics, and urinary tract infections will be treated energetically. There is little one can do to stem the advance of the specific diabetic lesion, but hypertension can and should be controlled, and the amount of fat in the blood may be controlled by diet and insulin, thus helping to prevent vascular disease. Patients with diabetes do badly on regular dialysis, largely because of vascular and infective problems. Transplantation opens up the possibility of giving pancreatic tissue as well as a kidney, but this will not solve the problem of the patient who is already blind as well as in renal failure.

IV GOUT

Gout, as mentioned in Chapter VI, is a rather rare cause of renal failure. It may also bring about less dramatic scarring of the medulla leading to proteinuria and pyelonephritis with or without organisms in the urine. These changes seem to be brought about by the deposition of uric acid within and around the renal tubules. The doctor will usually opt for treatment with allopurinol, which prevents uric acid formation, rather than one of the drugs which increases the urinary excretion of uric acid. If allopurinol is still being given when the patient receives a transplant, it enhances the effects of azathioprine and the dosage of this drug may have to be reduced.

V MYELOMATOSIS

Myelomatosis is a malignant proliferation of plasma cells within and occasionally outside the bone marrow. Since plasma cells produce a variety of protein including antibodies, these appear in the blood in excess and also appear in the urine. Albuminuria may also be noticed, which, unlike the globulin antibodies, will give a positive reaction with "Albustix". The protein may coagulate in the renal tubules, giving rise to acute renal failure. This may also be brought about by the saline depletion or calcium deposition in the kidney brought about in turn by hypercalcaemia; the rise in the serum calcium comes about by erosion of the bone with the plasma cells from the marrow. Less commonly, the loss of albumin is large and a nephrotic syndrome may appear.

Uncomplicated myelomatosis can be treated fairly successfully with a number of drugs, including cyclophosphamide, corticosteroids and melphalan but if renal failure is present the outlook is bleak.

VI TUBULAR DISORDERS

Tubular damage may, of course, occur in adults or children as part of a number of renal diseases, particularly pyelonephritis. A number of substances which are normally reabsorbed almost completely may then appear in the urine in large quantities. If chronic renal failure is also present this effect of tubular damage is aggravated by the osmotic diuresis (Chapter VI). An example of this "non-specific" tubular damage is the loss of large quantities of salt into the urine in patients with pyelonephritis and reflux of urine up the ureters. However, there are a number of rather rare inherited disorders in which specific enzymes are missing from the renal tubules, and loss of particular substances into the urine occur even when the glomerular filtration rate is normal. These occur particularly in children, but may be found in adults.

Defects in proximal tubule

(i) Renal glycosuria In this harmless condition there is a defect in re-absorption of glucose with all other functions remaining normal. It is important that it may be confused with diabetes mellitus until a glucose tolerance test is done. The "renal threshold" for glucose is low in renal glycosuria, and normal in diabetes mellitus (Chapter I).

(ii) Phospho-gluco-aminoaciduria (The "Fanconi Syndrome") In this condition the enzymes responsible for reabsorption of some or all of these compounds are defective, and all three may leak into the urine in excess. The aminoaciduria is a "generalized" aminoaciduria (Chapter XI). The loss of glucose and amino-acids is usually not important but the loss of phosphate in the urine may lead to *rickets*; this is resistant to Vitamin D in ordinary doses, and is often therefore called "Vitamin D-resistant rickets". Because of the bone disease, children with this condition may be dwarfed. If a child showed rickets or dwarfing, therefore, the doctor will assess him to see whether he has chronic renal failure, an inherited tubular disorder or renal tubular acidosis (see below).

(iii) Cystinuria In this condition there is a defect in a specific enzyme responsible for the reabsorption of cystine and three other specific amino-acids. Only these amino-acids are found in excess in the urine. Cystine is insoluble in acid urine and children with this condition form renal stones at an early age. The condition is usually treated by keeping up a good urine flow throughout the 24 hours, and rendering the urine alkaline.

Defects in the distal tubule

(i) Renal tubular acidosis Here hydrogen is kept in the body in excess because the enzyme responsible for its secretion is defective. The result is acidosis, which has a number of effects. The retained hydrogen ion goes into bone, and calcium is lost from the bones into the urine. Deposition of calcium in the kidney may occur (nephrocalcinosis) and the urine is alkaline because of the lack of hydrogen ion secretion. Bone disease appears, usually rickets. Finally, because there is little hydrogen ion in the urine, potassium is lost in excess. The condition is usually treated with alkalis containing potassium as well as sodium, and fairly large doses of Vitamin D.

(ii) "Nephrogenic" diabetes insipidus In this rare condition there is an inherited insensitivity of the distal tubule to ADH. It only affects male children. It must be distinguished from the other conditions giving rise to a large urine volume listed in Chapter XI. The commonest cause of polyuria in children is chronic renal failure, but the urine volume in diabetes insipidus, whether from pituitary failure or inherited tubular insensitivity, is usually much larger.

VII AMYLOIDOSIS

Amyloidosis is a rather rare condition affecting blood vessels throughout the body, and it is therefore not surprising that the kidney is affected. Amyloid is a fibrous protein deriving from the deposition of part of the gamma globulin antibody molecule in the vessel wall. It is found as a complication of chronic infections, particularly tuberculosis, bronchiectasis and osteomyelitis. It may also complicate rheumatoid arthritis and myelomatosis. All these are conditions in which there are high concentrations of antibody in the blood for long periods. Amyloidosis may also be seen without apparent cause: this is usually called *primary amyloidosis* to distinguish it from the *secondary* causes just mentioned. There is no means of arresting amyloidosis other than removing the primary cause if this is septic. Patients with renal amyloidosis usually present as proteinuria or as a nephrotic syndrome, less usually in chronic renal failure.

VIII RENAL STONES

Stones in the urinary tract are usually dealt with by the urologist, or in cooperation with him, and for a full coverage of this subject textbooks of urological nursing should be consulted. However, there are some medical aspects of stones, and you may meet such patients in medical or nephrological wards.

Stones are rarely a problem in themselves: they cause problems because of the infection and obstruction they may bring about, or be associated with. Stones may form in any part of the urinary tract. In the upper tract, they may be very large, filling the pelvi-calyceal system of the kidney completely: these are called "staghorn calculi" because of their shape. However, stones in the pelvis or the calyces may be small and rounded, as may those more commonly found in the ureter. At this site, they commonly cause pain if they move, the pain being very severe (ureteric (*not* renal) colic). Alternatively, they may block the ureter and give rise to a sterile hydronephrosis or an infected pyonephrosis.

Finally, stones may form in the bladder and become very large. For reasons which are not yet clear, bladder stones are now rare in the United Kingdom although they were formerly quite common as they are still in the Middle East.

Some stones are radio-opaque, and are therefore visible on straight X-rays of the abdomen. Others are transradiant (radiolucent) and require the injection of radiocontrast medium to show their position. Uric acid calculi are the only common transradiant calculi, and even they may have a coating of calcium deposited later in their course which renders them visible.

Stones are formed from different substances crystallising out from the urine. Our understanding of this process is still incomplete. The commonest form of stones are those formed from *calcium oxalate*. Urine is often "supersaturated" with regard to calcium; that is, it contains in solution more calcium than can be dissolved in pure water. Urine contains substances, not yet identified in detail, which render the calcium more soluble, and it is a deficiency of these substances, rather than an excess of calcium, which leads to precipitation and stone formation in most patients with calcium oxalate stones. However, in a minority there is excess calcium in the urine. Some of these patients simply eat and absorb more calcium than usual, and are generally referred to as having "idiopathic hypercalciuria". A very small proportion have, in addition, a raised plasma calcium as the cause of their hypercalciuria and stones. In patients with calcium stones the calcium and phosphate levels in blood and urine will be estimated carefully. If hypercalcaemia is found, then evidence of hyperparathyroidism, or of neoplasia affecting bone will be looked for.

Usually calcium oxalate stones are small and present with pain with or without urinary infection. Staghorn calculi, in contrast, are usually formed from *calcium phosphate* or *ammonium magnesium phosphate*. Phosphate is insoluble in alkaline urine, and usually there is infection with a urea splitting organism such as proteus, which causes the large amounts of ammonium. Often, the kidney is shown by an acid-loading test to be incapable of producing an acid urine.

Uric acid stones are much more common in patients, with or without overt gout, who have high blood and urine uric acid concentrations. They form best in acid, concentrated urines in which uric acid is most insoluble. Finally, a rare cause of stones is *cystinuria* (see VII) and all stone forming patients are screened for this disease because it is treatable.

Treatment is beyond the scope of this section, but for all patients with stones, after the acute problem has been dealt with, increasing the urine output will decrease the likelihood of precipitation and further stones. If the patient takes a large amount of calcium in the diet then the dietician may need to discuss with him cutting down on milk and milk products and changing to a low calcium bread. The infection in patients with staghorn calculi *in situ* is often impossible to treat, since the bacteria live within the stone substance. In uric acid stones, treatment with allopurinol may be used to reduce the amount of urate in the urine, together with alkalis and again a high fluid intake. The same treatment is successful in cystinuria, where quite large stones may be dissolved.

Suggestions for further reading:

British Medical Journal editorial (1974). Analgesic nephropathy or phenacetin poisoning? *British Medical Journal*, 1, 558.

Cameron, J. S., Ireland, J., Watkins, P. (1975). Diabetic nephropathy. *Complications of Diabetes Mellitus*. (Eds.) Jarrett, J., Keen, H. London: Arnold.

Dalgaard, O. Z. (1973). Polycystic disease of the kidneys. *Diseases of the Kidney*. 2nd. Ed. Vol. II, 1223. (Eds.) Strauss, M. B., Welt, L. Boston: Little Brown.

Diabetic Nephropathy. Supplement No. 6. *Kidney International* (December 1974). Proceedings of a conference at the University of Minnesota. Berlin: Springer.

Martinez-Maldonado, M., Yium, J., Suki, W. N., Eknoyan, G. (1971). Renal complications of multiple myeloma: pathophysiology and some aspects of clinical management. *Journal of Chronic Diseases*, 24, 221.

Milne, M. H. (1973). Renal tubular dysfunction. *Disease of the Kidney* Vol. II, p. 1071. (Eds.) Strauss, M. B., Welt, L. Boston: Little Brown.

Murray, R. M., Lawson, D. H. Linton, A. L. (1971). Analgesic nephropathy: clinical syndrome and prognosis. *British Medical Journal*, 1, 479.

Simmonds, H. A., Cameron, J. S. (1976). *Uric acid and the kidney*. In *Advanced Medicine* Vol. 12. (Ed.) Peters, D. K. Bath: Pitman Medical.

Triger, D. R., Joekes, A. M. (1973). Renal amyloidosis – a fourteen year follow-up. *Quarterly Journal of Medicine*, 42, 15.

CHAPTER XI

Investigation in patients with renal disease

In studying and treating renal disease we are particularly dependent upon investigations other than simple physical examination. Often decisions whether to treat a patient or not, and with which drug, agent or operation, will depend upon the results of the investigations. In these investigations, the nurse has an important role in carrying out some, in the collection of specimens for others, and in preparing the patient for the more complex procedures. It will also improve her understanding of the patient's condition if she is aware of when the various investigative techniques may be employed, and the influence the results obtained may have upon his management.

Investigations of the kidneys fall under a number of headings:

(I)   tests on urine
(II)   tests on blood
(III) tests of renal function
(IV) morphology of the kidneys
(V)   renal biopsy (dealt with in Chapter IV)

These may be considered in order.

I URINE TESTS

(i) Urine volume

This most basic aspect of renal function is surprisingly difficult to assess.

Timed urine collections

This plan applies to any timed collection of urine.

(1)   Ask the patient to empty his bladder and discard this urine. This

ensures that only the urine produced during the allotted span is collected and not that already in the bladder.

(2) Note the time.

(3) Collect every subsequent specimen passed until the end of the collection, when

(4) the patient again empties his bladder. This sample is included in the collection.

(5) Again note the time.

The exact length of the collection is not usually critical, provided that the duration is precisely known. For example, an accurate $13\frac{1}{2}$ hour collection is preferable to an inaccurate 12 hour collection where the patient was actually unable to pass urine exactly at the twelve hour point. The urine will usually be collected into a clean but not sterile two-litre glass or polythene bottle.

Absolute accuracy is essential since the excretion rates of substances such as electrolytes, proteins, etc., are based on timed specimens; if the volume of urine is not correct, nor will the final result be. Where possible the patient should always be told that all his urine is required for a specified length of time, so that he may cooperate and not be found coming out of the toilet bottle-less and unaware of the consternation of the nursing staff.

The 24 hour urine volume is most often employed because of the variation in the rate of urine flow at different times. This may vary from about 2 ml/min down to 0·5 ml/min at night. Normally urine volumes depend a great deal upon fluid intake and the amount of water lost as sweat and from the lungs. However, in a 70 kg adult on a normal diet (say 70 g protein) the products of metabolism cannot be excreted in less than 0·5 ml/min urine; that is, 30 ml/hour or 720 ml/day. This figure will be correspondingly less for smaller individuals and lower protein intakes. Unless the patient is catheterized, short time observations of urine volume over an hour or two are quite unreliable because many patients find it difficult to empty their bladders, particularly men and above all when they are recumbent in bed.

Timed specimens of urine in children

Once the child no longer needs nappies (i.e. over the age of 3 or 4) the instructions given above are satisfactory, provided that either the full cooperation of the child is obtained or supervision is continuous. If the child wets the bed or any accident happens during the collection there is no need to abandon the collection and start again. Provided that the times of previous voidings have been noted, an accurately timed collection will have been made and the fact that it is a $16\frac{1}{2}$ hour sample up to the time the urine was lost, rather than a 24 hour sample, does not matter too much for most tests. For infants and young children some form of collecting apparatus has to be attached to the child. The commonest are:

(i)   an adhesive collecting bag which fits over the whole perineum but excludes the anus

(ii)   Paul's tubing for older male children

With either method a young child may unfortunately have to be restrained in a harness in the cot, or strapped in a chair to prevent the bag being dislodged. Leakage and loss are best prevented by immediate emptying of the bag once urine has been passed.

If the parents are there, explain what is happening and above all, USE them; they are anxious to help and will supervize a urine collection in a more obsessional and often more efficient way than a nurse who has many other duties.

In disease, urine volume may be altered by factors other than intake, insensible loss and diet:

Pathological causes of larger volumes of urine than usual (polyuria)

1 Patients in *chronic renal failure* tend to pass large volumes of dilute urine, which is produced evenly throughout the 24 hours so that the patient has to get up at night to pass urine (nocturia).
2 If ADH secretion fails in the condition of *diabetes insipidus* then very large volumes may be passed (up to 20 litres or more per day).
3 An occasional patient with emotional disturbance may equal this output by *compulsive water* (or occasionally milk) *drinking*.
4 Any large solute load will cause an increase in urine volume by carrying out water (*osmotic diuresis* – Chapter XVI).
5 *Diuretics*, by interfering with tubular reabsorption of sodium, cause an increase in urine flow.

Pathological causes of a lower volume of urine than normal (oliguria)

1 Inability to pass urine (urinary retention). Obstruction to urine flow may also occur further up the urinary tract, where bladder catheterization will not help; for example, by stones in the ureters or involvement of the ureters by tumour.
2 Acute renal failure.
3 Acute glomerulonephritis.
4 The nephrotic syndrome, especially when oedema is being formed.

Total absence of urine is called *anuria*. Urine output is much more frequently underestimated than overestimated because of the ease with which urine specimens can be lost.

(ii) Constituents of the urine

Urine testing

(1) Observation Much may be learnt from merely looking at the urine and the nurse is often the first person to do this. A specimen should be saved daily for inspection and colour, sediment, smell, etc. noted before the routine tests are carried out.

Colour:Dark urine may indicate disease but is usually the result of passing small quantities of concentrated urine. Dark urine may also be seen in jaundice (from bile pigments) and also if a small amount of blood is present. Green, blue or other exotic colours may be imparted to the urine by substances taken as drugs or foods. Methylene blue may turn the urine blue-green, or beetroot to a reddish colour (beeturia). In haemoglobinuria the urine is a rather bright cherry or wine colour.

Turbid urine may be the result of bacteria and leucocytes (pyuria) arising from infection; more commonly, turbid urine results from the precipitation of phosphates as the urine cools, particularly if it is alkaline. Rarely there may be enough fat in the urine to render it turbid (chyluria) resulting from communication between the lymphatics and the bladder.

Frothy urines may be the result of proteinuria or of bile salts in jaundice; the persistence of the froth is more important than the amount.

Foul urine is usually the result of infection, if the urine is fresh. Old urines smell sharply of ammonia produced by urea breakdown, but the ammonium produced normally by the kidney is in solution and is odourless. Some drugs impart a characteristic odour to the urine, e.g. ampicillin.

(2) Chemical tests Ames Co. have produced a range of products that are by now almost universally used and have superseded in part many of the older and more time consuming methods.

(a) Proteinuria Normally about 30–100 mg of protein is excreted per day, about one-third of which is albumin. The rest is fragments of plasma protein and protein added by the glands and epithelium of the urinary tract.

Exercise and an upright posture increase the amount of protein so that even in normal people the afternoon urine contains more protein than that passed during the night. Violent exercise may cause it to increase to levels that would be considered abnormal if they persisted. A number of young people, particularly men, have easily detectable quantities in urine passed during the day, while the early morning urine formed during the night has quantities too small to detect. This is sometimes called "postural" proteinuria and is regarded as benign. However, some conditions give rise to slight proteinuria which is not detectable in the morning specimen, and the doctor may wish to investigate even a patient with this intermittent proteinuria.

The normal small amount of protein may be increased in a variety of diseases. These may be divided into those conditions which lead to the excretion of up to one or two grams of protein per day, and those which lead to losses of large quantities of protein. Small quantities of protein in the urine may be the result of either glomerular or tubular damage, and usually contain globulins as well as some albumin; large quantities are almost always the result of glomerular damage (see Chapters III and IV) and are principally albumin. The only visible sign of proteinuria is that the patient's urine is more frothy than usual; some patients describe this as like soapy water. There are several methods for detecting and measuring protein in the urine and we must distinguish those tests we use on untimed "spot" urine samples to determine whether protein is present or not, and very crudely its concentration; and those tests which are used to measure the amount of protein in an accurately timed specimen of urine. Most of the latter are laboratory procedures.

(i) "Albustix"   Albustix reacts only when *albumin* is present in the urine. The test depends upon the fact that certain indicators which change colour at a particular acidity are affected by the presence of protein, particularly albumin. The stick has upon it a paper containing a buffer (to keep the acidity of the stick constant even in urines of various acidities) and the indicator dye. After dipping the stick in the urine for just long enough to moisten it, its colour is immediately compared with the scale on the bottle. The concentrations of albumin which correspond to the colours on the scale opposite.

These figures are approximate only. Note that the reading of "trace" proteinuria can mean anything from an almost normal amount of protein to a definitely abnormal amount. The "trace" reading is commonly obtained in normal individuals and is therefore of little significance. The multipurpose "Labstix" incorporates a strip of "Albustix" paper.

Colour		*Approximate Concentration of Protein*
Yellow	Nil	Less than 30 mg/100 ml
Just Green	Trace	4 - 40 mg/100 ml
	+	about 30 mg/100 ml
	++	about 100 mg/100 ml
	+++	about 400 mg/100 ml
Dark Green	++++	about 1000 mg/100 ml

Several problems may arise from using "Albustix".

(1) If the stick is kept in the urine for more than the minimum period, the buffer may be washed out from the paper and the acidity may change, and with it the colour.

(2) In urines containing a great deal of ammonia – usually those that are infected or not fresh – the stick shows froth and turns à blue-green colour quite different from the normal yellow-green. This may be falsely reported as proteinuria.

(3) A good light is necessary in reading the scale, and some individuals are much poorer than others at recognizing the colours.

A positive test with "Albustix" should always be confirmed with a heat or SSA test, and the urine tested for blood.

(ii) Heat Heating acidified urine is the classical ward test for protein. The urine (10 ml) is placed in a test tube and 10% acetic acid added dropwise till acid. Heat from a bunsen flame is then applied and the flocculent precipitate of protein appears. This may range from a slight opalescence to a dense curdy precipitate; the urine may even set completely solid in very heavy proteinuria, like the white of an egg.

(iii) Sulphosalicylic acid (salicylsulphonic acid, SSA) This is the most convenient chemical test. Other acids such as trichloracetic and picric may be employed but have no particular advantage. 5 ml of urine is placed in a test tube, 6 drops of 20% SSA are added and *shaken*. The protein is precipitated as a white cloud, as with heat.

These simple tests can give a great deal of information about the actual amount of protein in the urine as well as its presence, especially if they are performed on specimens collected at the same time each day, such as the early morning urine. The Esbach picric acid test on casual specimens of urine has no advantage over a careful "Albustix" reading on a daily early morning urine and is being abandoned in most hospitals.

To measure the quantity of protein excreted a 24-hour collection of urine will be sent to the laboratory. Some information can be gained by measuring the protein output over shorter periods, but because of the variation in protein excretion throughout the day this is not so valuable. Many laboratories employ a rather more refined SSA test for measuring protein excretion, or it may be done by automatic chemical analysis using dyes which bind on to the proteins. Protein excretion rates (in g/day) are used for

(1)   the diagnosis of glomerular and tubular disease
(2)   assessing treatment in patients with proteinuria
(3)   adjusting dietary intake of protein

(iv) Postural proteinuria   If protein is found in the urine of an otherwise healthy individual it will often be necessary to see if protein is also present in the urine passed while recumbent. The easiest way to do this is to collect the first urine passed after rising in the morning. With children, it may be necessary to put them to bed to ensure that the appropriate collection is obtained. "Postural proteinuria" is the name given when the day-time urine contains protein but that passed at night does not. The implication is that the condition represents merely an exaggeration of the normal tendency for the urine to contain more urine when the subject is up and about, or taking exercise. This is often the case in the young adults who frequently show a tiny amount of protein in their daytime urine, but the doctor will want to be satisfied that no underlying renal disease is being missed and this will lead him to investigate a proportion of such individuals further.

(v) Proteins other than albumin in the urine   80 - 95% of the protein in the urine is albumin in heavier proteinurias, with only one exception: *myelomatosis*, where large quantities of globulins or globulin fragments are excreted. These do not react with "Albustix" and may be missed if only this test is employed. Some of the globulin fragments (light chains) have the peculiar property of precipitating out at moderate temperatures and then redissolving on boiling. These are called Bence Jones "proteins" after an early description of them by Henry Bence Jones. 50 ml of an early morning specimen of urine will be required.

Proteinurias of between 0·3 and 1·0 g/day contain more globulins than do heavier proteinurias and this is particularly so in tubular diseases and pyelonephritis. Nowadays the pattern of protein excretion is usually studied by separating the proteins by *electrophoresis*, and demonstrating them by staining the bands obtained, or by reacting them with antisera (*immunoelectrophoresis*). In heavy proteinurias, *differential protein clearances* may be measured by comparing the clearances into the urine of proteins of different molecular weights. When the proteinuria is mostly of low molecular weight proteins, the proteinuria is referred to as "selective" proteinuria; when there are appreciable quantities of larger proteins, as "poorly selective". This in general occurs in patients with more severely damaged glomeruli.

(b) Blood in the urine (haematuria) Blood in the urine may be readily visible (macroscopic haematuria), intimately mixed with the urine if the source is in the upper urinary tract, streakily present if from the lower urinary tract. If bleeding is profuse clots may be present, and in passing through the ureter may cause ureteric colic. Occasionally retention of urine may occur from clotting of blood in the bladder. Much more frequently, however, in medical conditions the macroscopic haematuria is slight and the urine gives an appearance which is variously described as rusty, smoky, like tea or Coca Cola. Often the red cells are visible only under microscopic examination (microscopic haematuria). Haemoglobinuria gives a clear, cherry or wine coloured tint to the urine quite unlike the smoky appearance of haematuria, but it must be remembered that if the urine is kept, the red cells will break down and release their haemoglobin. Haematuria, both microscopic and macroscopic, may come from a variety of lesions anywhere in the urinary tract from the kidney to the urethra.

Many of these are conditions such as tumours of the kidney or the urinary tract, stones or inflammatory disease of the urinary tract, and are dealt with principally by the urologist; clearly the full investigation of a patient with haematuria will often require cooperation between urologist and physician. The common medical conditions which give rise to haematuria are:

(1) disorders of coagulation, either primary or produced by anti-coagulant drugs.
(2) renal disease, principally
   (i)   acute glomerulonephritis
   (ii) recurrent haematuria
   (iii) amyloidosis
   (iv) "connective tissue" disorders, e.g. polyarteritis

Testing the urine for blood The simplest test is one of the stick tests ("Hemastix, Ames). "Haemacombistix" and "Labstix" contain a strip which is identical to that in "Haemastix". These detect the haemoglobin from the blood cells and therefore rely on some haemolysis of the blood taking place in the urine. The reaction produces a blue-green colour which is read 30 seconds after dipping the stick in the urine against the chart provided on the bottle. A more sensitive method is to microscope the urine, using a Fuchs-Rosenthal counting chamber ("Crystalite" 4-chamber; Hawksley) on uncentrifuged fresh urine. More than one red cell/cubic mm is an abnormal finding.

(c) **Glucose**   Glycosuria may result from a normal kidney being overwhelmed by an abnormally large amount of glucose in the blood; this is usually described as a normal renal threshold (Chapter I) being exceeded. The commonest causes of this situation are diabetes mellitus and intravenous infusion of strong glucose solutions. Sometimes, however, glycosuria results from abnormal tubular function, that is the renal threshold for glucose is abnormally low and glucose may appear in the urine at relatively normal blood sugar concentrations. This may arise in a variety of inherited tubular disorders (Chapter X) or as the result of tubular damage from nephrotoxic substances, or of renal diseases such as glomerulonephritis or pyelonephritis.

Testing the urine for glucose   This may be done by dipping "Clinistix" (Ames) into the urine sample and reading immediately. The stick will turn blue if positive. This test is specific for glucose. The amount of *sugar* may be ascertained by putting five drops of urine, then ten drops of water into a clean test tube and then adding a "Clinitest" (Ames) tablet. When the boiling has stopped it may change colour from blue through to orange, indicating 0 – 2% glucose. With higher concentrations the urine may be diluted before reading.

This test depends upon the reducing power of glucose and will react with other reducing substances in the urine, such as other sugars (e.g. fructose, lactose, galactose) and some drugs (e.g. aspirin).

(d) **Glycosuria**   from renal disease is frequently associated with *aminoaciduria*, because they are reabsorbed from the glomerular filtrate at approximately the same site. Small quantities of amino-acids are normally present in the urine, but in tubular damage they all spill into the urine. This is called a *generalized aminoaciduria*. However, there are a number of diseases (mostly rare) which lead to particular amino-acids being lost in the urine. The best known example of this is *cystinuria*, where along with cystine three other specific amino-acids are lost in the urine, and cystine stones may form. The chemical pathologist can determine individual amino-acids in the urine (and plasma) by a variety of techniques, but the commonest screening method is by chromatographic separation on paper.

(e) Concentration of urine The concentration of urine depends upon

(1) the amount of water available for the excretion of the body's waste products. Provided that ADH can be secreted and the kidney is in a position to respond to it as outlined in Chapter I, the urine concentration will depend upon the amount of water taken in and the amount lost through the lungs and skin. The less water available for excretion of metabolites, the more concentrated the urine will be and *vice versa*.

(2) Renal perfusion If the kidney is not receiving a normal amount of blood, then renin will be secreted, angiotensin and aldosterone produced in excess (Chapter I) and the tubule is receiving less blood than usual. The net result of all these changes is a highly concentrated urine which is almost devoid of sodium. Poor renal perfusion may result from

  (i) heart failure, due to valvular or myocardial disease
  (ii) hypovolaemia (low blood volume) from haemorrhage, salt depletion or a low serum albumin as in the nephrotic syndrome
  (iii) renal arterial disease.

Measuring the concentration of urine All these tests measure the total amount of solute in the urine.

(1) *Specific gravity* is measured by a *Urinometer* (hydrometer) placed in a cylinder of urine and read at eye level. In plain water the urinometer reads 1000 and the normal range of sp. gr. in urine is 1002 – 1030. It determines roughly the amount of solute (salts, urea etc.) in the urine. Patients with chronic renal disease have a fixed sp. gr. of about 1010 (see Chapter VI).

The specific gravity often gives less information than it can because of errors in its measurement.

(a) if a small amount of urine is available and a narrow vessel used, the surface tension of the urine may cause a false high reading or the hydrometer stick to the side of the vessel.

(b) Most hydrometers are calibrated at $22°$ C, and fresh warm urines should not be used since they will give a low reading. The readings may be corrected by adding 0001 per $3°$ C difference above $22°$ C i.e. a urine at $37°$ C will read 0005 too low.

(c) The hydrometer should be tested against plain water from time to time to ensure it is still accurate.

Specific gravity beads   The problem with small children is that there is insufficient urine to enable a hydrometer to float freely without touching the bottom or sides of the container, so that beads are often employed to measure the sp. gr. The beads are supplied in a series of different weights so that they just sink in urine of the specific gravity inscribed on them:- 1000, 1005, 1010, etc. Unfortunately these are easily lost and their chief difficulty is keeping the set complete. A minimum of 10 ml of urine is required.

(2)   *Osmolarity*   Total solute (the sum of all the substances dissolved in the solution) is expressed as *osmolarity* and the units employed are milliosmoles/l (sometimes osmola*l*ity is used, mOsm/kilogram of water; for clinical purposes there is no difference). This is assessed by measuring the freezing point of the urine on an osmometer, and reading off the osmolarity which corresponds to the amount the observed freezing point of the solution is depressed below the freezing point of pure water. The osmolarity corresponds rather roughly to the total of milliequivalents and millimoles of the substance dissolved in the solution; usually it is rather less. For example, normal plasma osmolarity is about 285 mOs/l. The osmolarity of the urine varies from 100 – 1,000 mOs/l sp. gr. 1002 – 1035) in health.

(3)   *Refractometry*   The concentration of total solutes may be determined by viewing a drop of urine in a refractometer. Several simple hand models are now available and may find increasing use, especially in paediatric wards.

(4)   *Concentration test*   The ability to concentrate the urine is impaired early in many progressive renal conditions, especially those involving the tubules such as pyelonephritis. It is therefore sometimes useful to test the patient's ability to produce a concentrated urine. The patient is deprived of fluid for 16 hours or overnight, or for such a period as produces a 3% fall in bodyweight. This is a good check that fluid has not been taken surreptitiously. The urine osmolarity should rise to at least 900 mOsm/l and the sp. gr. to 1025 or more. Alternatively, pitressin (ADH) tannate in oil, 5 units may be given i.m. without fluid restriction. The urine concentration achieved after six hours is usually rather less than can be achieved by thirsting. Care must be taken to dissolve or suspend the pitressin, which tends to collect as a scum at the bottom of the ampoule before injection. Some doctors also test the kidney's ability to dilute the urine although the test is more unpleasant for the patient and it gives relatively little information.

(5)   *Dilution test*   This may follow on from the concentration test. 1·5 litres of water are given to the patient at say 10 a.m. to be drunk in

half an hour. The bladder is emptied one, two, three and four hours later and the volume and sp. gr. of the urine recorded. The sp. gr. should fall to 1002 and all 1·5 litres excreted in the four hours if normal function is present.

(f) The reaction of the urine Litmus paper is still used in many hospitals to test whether the urine is acid or alkaline (more or less than pH 7). It is a very crude test and provides little information. More accurate and useful estimation can be made by using specially prepared strips (BDH universal indicator paper) which indicate the hydrogen ion concentration (pH) by colour change; they register to the nearest pH unit from pH 3 to pH 10; normal urine may vary in pH from 4·8 to 8·0 but usually lies between pH 5 – 7. Accurate measure of the hydrogen ion in the urine can only be made by measuring the pH on a pH meter in a laboratory and, if necessary, the ammonia concentration (see Chapter I).

Tests of acid secretion Sometimes it is necessary to test the ability of the kidney to secrete hydrogen ions. This may most conveniently be done by the so-called "short" ammonium chloride loading test. 0·1 g/ kg bodyweight of ammonium chloride are given as the salt in gelatine capsules; enteric-coated tablets should not be used since they are unreliably absorbed. The capsules should be given over half to one hour on a full stomach to avoid vomiting (in which case the test is void); urine is collected at four, five and six hours later and its pH measured immediately on a pH meter; if this is not possible, then the samples must be refrigerated in sealed containers or under paraffin. Normal individuals will produce urine of pH 5·3 or less in one of the samples. One may check that the dose has been absorbed by taking a blood sample before and during the urine samples and checking the bicarbonate concentration.

(g) Urinary electrolytes These may be measured as concentrations on 'spot" samples of urine or as excretion rates on timed urine samples.

Sodium and *potassium* are measured on a flame photometer in the laboratory. The measurements are useful.

(i)   in renal disease, especially chronic renal failure, in determining how much sodium and potassium the diet should contain if balance is to be maintained.

(ii)   the urine sodium concentration is very low (less than 10 mmol/l) when the kidneys are poorly perfused whether from valvular or myocardial disease of the heart, loss of circulating volume, from saline depletion, haemorrhage or a low serum albumin such as in the nephrotic syndrome. The sodium concentration or excretion is very useful in the diagnosis of these states and in following the progress of treatment.

In many patients the urinary *chloride* is not required, since it usually reflects closely the sodium excretion; however, in some patients, especially those with gastrointestinal disorders, the urinary chloride may be important.

Urea is a major constituent of the urine, and is the major end product of protein metabolism in man. Urea is usually measured by automatic chemical analysis in the laboratory. The urea *concentration* gives a good guide to the concentration of total solutes in the urine and the specific gravity. Concentrated urines may contain up to 600 mmol/l urea or even more. This may come about because

(i)   little water is available for the excretion of the urea and ADH secretion is maximum

(ii)   the kidneys are being very poorly perfused with blood for the reasons listed above

(iii)   there is a great deal of tissue breakdown, leading to protein breakdown and the production of a large amount of urea.

Urines dilute with respect to urea may obviously come about if the patient is excreting a water load, but pathologically dilute urines also occur in renal failure. Most patients in chronic renal failure pass urines containing only 100 – 180 mmol/l of urea and cannot concentrate it any further. In acute renal failure the urea concentration of the urine is very low, being 35 – 100 mmol/l. The *rate of excretion of urea* per day will give some indication of tissue breakdown, provided that the kidneys are working normally. It is also of great use in chronic renal failure, once the patient is stable, in determining how much protein should be in the diet (see Chapters VI and XII).

The *calcium* and *phosphate* concentration or excretion are most frequently measured in patients with renal stones, to determine whether an excess of these substances may be contributing to the tendency of the patient to form stones. The excretion of both is reduced in chronic renal failure, and increased in hyperparathyroidism. The passage of large amounts of calcium through the kidneys may lead to calcification of the kidney (nephrocalcinosis) and this may be seen in many conditions with a high urine calcium. Some doctors also measure the urine *magnesium* because it may be that the lower the magnesium in the urine the more likely it is that calcium stones will form.

(h) Microscopy of urine Much can be learned from microscoping a *fresh* sample of urine. The essential point is that the urine must be examined *less than half an hour* after it is passed. This is often difficult, and in some instances the doctor will collect the urine himself to ensure its freshness. If, however, the nurse is responsible for the urine collection and knows it is to be microscoped (or cultured) she should endeavour as far as possible to see that it reaches the person performing the microscopy (or culture) within half an hour. The reason for this haste is that the cells and structures described below dissolve in the urine after its passage; this process begins in the bladder even before the urine is passed. Breakdown is faster in dilute alkaline urines (such as those passed during the day) and slower in concentrated acid urines (such as those passed overnight and early morning). It follows that the best specimen for examining cells etc. in the urine is that passed first after rising, *after* the stale overnight urine has been voided and *before* the dilute urine of the day. This urine is usually available about 10 a.m. and should be supplied where possible.

Cells Red cells have already been discussed above. White cells (sometimes called "pus" cells) may also be seen in the urine and are an important indicator of infection. Again, the best way of counting is in a counting chamber (such as the Fuchs-Rosenthal) under the microscope, using uncentrifuged urine. Some doctors prefer to centrifuge the urine and resuspend the precipitate but this procedure introduces errors. Unfortunately, unless the specimen is a clean MSU (see below) the number of leucocytes is of little use. On a clean specimen more than 5 white cells/μl in men and more than 10/μl in women is abnormal. Many other cells, such as those lining the urinary tract, may also be seen in the urine, and must be distinguished from leucocytes. In patients with malignant growths in the urinary tract malignant cells may also be seen in the urine.

Tubular casts The name indicates their site of origin and nature. They are casts of the renal tubules, formed from protein filtered at the glomerulus and a peculiar protein secreted by the distal tubules, together with any cell debris that are present from diseased tubules. They may contain white cells (white cell casts) particularly (but not exclusively) if there is infection within the kidney. Red cell casts are particularly valuable because if found in the presence of haematuria they indicate that the blood in the urine must be coming from the kidney and not further down the urinary tract. The commonest forms of casts are clear casts containing only protein and no visible debris (hyaline casts) and those containing fragments of degenerating tubular cells or red cells (granular casts). Obviously the latter indicates rather more severe damage to the kidney than the hyaline cast, which may be seen in any patient with proteinuria or in the concentrated early morning urine of normal individuals.

Crystals   Crystals of the various normal constituents of the urine (such as phosphate, oxalate) are frequently seen if the urine is examined under the microscope, but the examination is particularly valuable if unusual crystals are present in excess; for example, in cystinuria.

Bacteria   Often, motile or dead bacteria may be seen and the urinary deposit may be Gram-stained after centrifuging to identify the organisms as with any bacteriological preparation. Again, this investigation is relatively useless unless the specimen used is fresh and uncontaminated.

(i) Bacteriological examination of the urine   Bacteria may multiply in the kidney substance and in the urine (bacteriuria). The urine is incubated at 37° C in the bladder and even a few bacteria may become many millions over several hours. The problem of determining whether bacteriuria is truly present arises from two circumstances:

(i)   in passing through the urethral meatus, especially in the female, it is contaminated by meatal organisms

(ii)   after passage, both the organisms present in the bladder urine (if any) and the contaminants continue to multiply.

A casual specimen kept at room temperature for some hours may only reflect, when cultured, those organisms added to it during passage. Our efforts are directed at:

(i)   minimizing contamination of the urine during passage

(ii)   ensuring that the urine is cultured as soon as possible, after passage, as well as being examined microscopically.

To these ends a fresh, mid-stream urine specimen is examined, or in children suprapubic aspiration of urine may be employed (see below).

Mid-stream urine (MSU)

The patient is asked to clean the external urinary meatus by gently swabbing with saline from front to back in females. It is important not to exceed this concentration or the saline may contaminate the urine and prevent bacterial growth, and some doctors prefer for this reason simple sterile saline. A few mls of urine are then passed into a receiver (either bed-pan or urinal) and the stream then directed into a sterile container. Women must be instructed to keep the labia apart to avoid contamination of the urine, using one hand while the other holds the receiver. The first mls are discarded as they may contain bacteria found around the external meatus. The second, sterile specimen is transferred to the labelled specimen jar and sent to the laboratory. Clear detailed instructions are necessary, for patients have great difficulty in passing urine with another person present, however well-intentioned; the success of the venture depends upon the nurses' explanation. If the specimen is inadvertently contaminated the procedure must be repeated.

Clean, uncontaminated urines from children

Older children will be able to cooperate in the production of a mid-stream specimen suitable for bacteriological culture and microscopy. Infants present considerable problems. Three approaches are available:-

(i)   Adhesive bag collection, the perineum having been cleaned and dried before the bag is applied. The urine must be drained from the bag promptly, as it becomes infected if it slops about the perineum for long.

(ii) Clean catch. After cleaning the perineum the infant is suspended over one hand; two fingers of the other hand are stroked down either side of the lower spine. Micturition usually begins within five minutes. Exposure of the infant, or its lower half, to a cool environment when its bladder is full may initiate micturition. Placing the baby on a cold surface may have the same effect; therefore it is worth having a sterile container handy when changing a baby. A fresh clean catch specimen from a baby who has not been specially cleaned is more useful than a specimen which has stagnated in a collecting bag on a baby's "cleaned" perineum.

(iii) Suprapubic aspiration (SPA). The infant's bladder lies higher in the abdomen than the adult's (see Figure 11.1) and so is easier to puncture. In children over the age of a year it is best to ensure that the bladder can be palpated, percussed or seen before attempting aspiration. The suprapubic area is cleaned with an antiseptic swab as for a venepuncture. The doctor selects a point in the midline about one finger's breadth above the symphysis pubis and inserts a 2 ml or 5 ml sterile syringe carrying a no. 1 needle. The needle is directed a little towards the baby's feet and aspirated gently as the needle is advanced. When the bladder is entered urine is aspirated into the syringe and the syringe can be withdrawn. This procedure is surprisingly simple, successful and free of side effects. Occasionally, slight haematuria may be noticed afterwards.

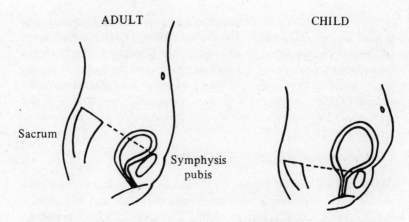

Fig. 11.1 The position of the bladder in the adult and in the child. The bladder is much more within the abdomen in the child than in the adult, even when empty. This makes the procedure of suprapubic aspiration of urine relatively easy in the child; however, it is also used in adults when a clean specimen of urine cannot be obtained otherwise.

Immediate quantitative culture of the urine is performed as soon as possible. This should be within half an hour of voiding but if this is not possible the specimen may be refrigerated at 4° C in its sterile container for up to 24 hours before culture (such a specimen is not, of course, suitable for microscopy). The urine is plated on to nutrient media using a calibrated loop which delivers a known quantity of urine onto plate (often 0·01 or 0·05 ml). The number of bacterial colonies may then be counted after incubation and the result expressed as organisms per ml in the original urine. If the specimen has been collected properly, and if cultured immediately, then almost all infected urines will show more than 100,000 (10^5) organisms/ml, and those contaminated 1000 (10^3) or less. If the culture shows between 10^3 and 10^5 organisms/ml then it must be repeated on a fresh specimen until it falls into one of the clear categories. The presence or absence of leucocytes will also help the doctor to decide whether infection is indeed present, since nearly all urines which are infected contain more than 50 cells/ul.

Dip inoculation media have been introduced which permit immediate culture, and it seems likely that nurses will use these, particularly in District practice. These are slides ("Uricult" Oxoid) coated with media, or small spoons containing media, supplied sterile in sterile screw-top containers. After collection of the MSU into the sterile foil bowl, the dip inoculation spoon or slide is removed from its container, dipped into urine, touched on the side to drain and replaced in its sterile container. This may then be incubated at leisure and read the next day. The number of colonies on the spoon or slide gives an estimate of the number/ml of fresh urine.

To detect acid-alcohol fast bacilli, a complete early morning urine (EMU) is sent to the laboratory, centrifuged and the urinary sediment examined.

II TESTS ON THE BLOOD

Numerous substances may accumulate within or be lost from the blood through abnormal action of the kidneys.

Blood is more difficult to obtain from infants and is available in smaller quantities. Many laboratories use micromethods which need only tiny amounts of blood, such as that available from a heel stab. The disadvantage of such capillary blood is that collection is slow and haemolysis may occur causing a falsely high serum potassium level.

(i) Haemoglobin, packed cell volume (PCV haematocrit)

Patients with chronic renal failure are usually anaemic, the anaemia paralleling their uraemia. The haemoglobin and PCV therefore fall together. Nephrotic patients frequently have a high haemoglobin and PCV because their plasma volume is low.

(ii) White cell count and platelet count

The white cell count may be low in uraemia, and high in nephrotic patients on corticosteroid drugs. The white cell count and the platelet count are of particular importance in patients on immunosuppression after renal transplantation, and in patients with glomerulonephritis of various sorts receiving cytotoxic drugs.

(iii) Blood electrolytes

These will be measured frequently in renal patients. The plasma sodium may vary in a variety of renal disorders, particularly falling in some patients with chronic renal failure. The plasma potassium is of more immediate interest because of its effect upon the heart. Diuretics, and occasionally chronic renal failure may lower it, and acute renal failure and terminal renal failure raise it to lethal levels.

(iv) Nitrogenous metabolites

Since the excretory function is one of the kidney's vital roles, we are often concerned with measuring the concentrations of nitrogenous metabolites in the blood. Those most commonly assessed are urea, creatinine and uric acid. The blood urea tends to vary with diet and hydration, so that the plasma creatinine gives a better overall idea of the kidney's ability to excrete nitrogen than the blood urea. It is worth remembering that in children, particularly infants, the blood urea may rise more spectacularly than in an adult in response to water (or salt and water) losses with consequent hypotension, poor renal blood flow and concentrated urine. It must also be remembered that there is little rise in either the blood urea or the plasma creatinine until renal function has been considerably impaired.

Uric acid rises along with the urea and creatinine, and it is of interest for the understanding of gout that very few patients with renal failure develop gout even though their plasma uric acid is very high from *retention* of uric acid. It seems that *overproduction* of uric acid is necessary before clinical gout arises.

(v) Calcium and phosphate

These are frequently measured in patients with renal disease because both may be lost in excess in renal tubular diseases (see Chapter X) and phosphate is retained in chronic renal failure. Bone disease, as discussed in Chapters VI and X, may arise in both of these states and so the level of the bone enzyme *alkaline phosphatase*[1] is usually measured at the same time as the calcium and phosphate. This enzyme is excreted through the liver so that the concentration in the blood may also rise in liver disease. The plasma *magnesium* rises in both acute and chronic renal failure, but rarely to levels where it produces clinical effects and it is not often measured. Similarly, plasma magnesium may rarely fall during intense diuresis.

(vi) Serum proteins

The laboratory is frequently asked to measure serum proteins in patients with renal disease, usually for two reasons:
(i)   as an index of nutrition
(ii) to assess the derangement produced by proteinuria

The serum albumin provides quite a sensitive index of protein nutrition and patients on protein restricted diets, or during protein depleting pro-

---

[1]   not to be confused with acid phosphatase, which comes from the prostate.

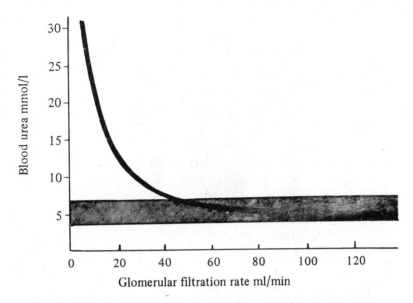

Fig.11.2   The relation between blood urea and the level of renal function, judged by the glomerular filtration rate. Notice that the blood urea does not rise above the normal limits (the shaded area) until two-thirds of the renal function has been lost. Notice also how steeply the blood urea rises with small decreases in renal function after this point.

cedures, such as peritoneal dialysis, will need to have their serum protein estimated. This can be done crudely as total protein, but it is usually important to know the serum albumin concentration since in many renal disorders (the nephrotic syndrome, for example) the serum globulin concentration rises and masks the fall in albumin to some extent if only the total protein is assessed. In general, heavy proteinuria produces a similar pattern of abnormal plasma proteins whatever the particular disease causing the heavy proteinuria may be. This is best shown by *electrcphoresis* of the serum proteins. A small amount of serum is placed on paper or similar medium, soaked in a buffered electrolyte solution, and a current is passed through the paper. The proteins separate according to the charges they possess at the particular acidity selected for the test, which is the one producing the best separation. The paper is then stained giving the appearance shown in Figure 11.3.

The paper strip may also be scanned, as in the figure. The characteristic derangement of serum proteins in heavy proteinuria is a fall in those bands mostly composed of small molecular weight proteins.

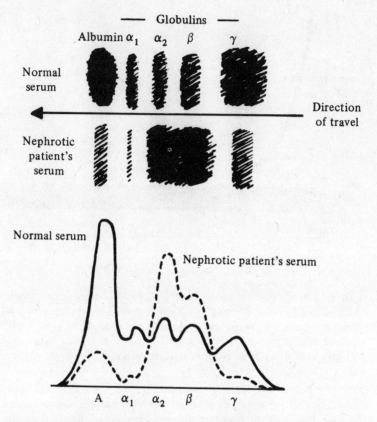

Fig. 11.3 Electrophoresis of serum. Above, the pattern is shown which
appears after staining the paper on which the serum is electrophore-
sed. Current is passed so that the proteins migrate from right to left
in the solution used to soak the paper. The normal serum shows a
densely stained albumin band, and a considerable amount of gamma
globulin. The nephrotic serum, in contrast, has very little albumin,
an excess of alpha-2 and beta globulin and a diminished gamma
globulin.

If the stained paper is scanned to plot the density of staining, a more
accurate idea of quantities may be obtained. The type of pattern
obtained is shown below. The normal serum (continuous line) again
shows the predominant albumin peak. The nephrotic serum (interrupted line) has very little albumin, but the excess of alpha-2 and
beta globulins is shown by the fact that the interrupted line exceeds
that of the normal serum. The gamma globulin is low.

(vi) Erythrocyte sedimentation rate (ESR)

This is frequently deranged in renal disease but provides relatively little information because it is so regularly abnormal. This is because

(i)   the plasma fibrinogen is very high, especially in those patients with heavy proteinuria
(ii) the patients are frequently anaemic
(iii) patients with disturbed plasma proteins have high ESRs.

III TESTS OF RENAL FUNCTION

Tests to determine the ability of the kidney to make a concentrated or acid urine have already been described.

(i) Tests of the glomular filtration rate

Clearances   The glomerular filtration rate (GFR) is one of the most important measurements of the kidneys performance. Measurements of GFR are made by the *clearance* into the urine of certain substances. The clearance of any substance is given by the formula:

$$\frac{\text{Urine concentration} \times \text{volume of urine/time}}{\text{plasma concentration}}$$

usually abbreviated to UV/P. The clearance is really the amount in the urine, corrected for two things: the amount in the plasma and the rate of urine flow. By dividing the amount in the urine in a given time (UV) by the plasma concentration (P) we get a volume, which has no real existence but is the volume of plasma from which the amount in the urine *would* have been taken if *the plasma had been completely cleared of the substance* in its passage through the kidney. The importance of this idea is that if the substance measured is freely filtered, and is not broken down in the kidney or reabsorbed by the tubules, then its clearance will equal the amount of water filtered at the glomerules – the GFR.

Inulin clearance

The prototype substance is a sugar derived from Dahlia tubers, *inulin*. However, to perform a clearance, one must fill up the patient's extracellular water with an injected priming dose of inulin, and keep this level constant with an intravenous infusion of inulin. Because this cannot be continued indefinitely, the urine collection periods must be short and either considerable error in the measurement accepted, or a bladder catheter passed. Because of these limitations the inulin method is only performed in investigational units and not in routine ward work. Fortunately, the clearance of one naturally occurring substance, creatinine, approximates to the glomerular filtration rate. It is handled by the kidney in a complex fashion but the bulk is filtered freely and not reabsorbed. However, in some circumstances (particularly terminal renal failure) the creatinine clearance exceeds the GFR.

Creatinine clearance

The blood level of creatinine is rather constant so that performance of creatinine clearance is simple in principle. A timed urine sample is collected over a fairly long period (24 hours being the most popular) during which time a single heparinized sample of blood is taken. The creatinine content of both urine and plasma is estimated in the laboratory, and the figure UV/P calculated expressing the urine volume (V) in ml/min so that this is the unit in which the clearance is expressed. The normal value for an adult man is about 100 – 120 ml/min, rather lower for women. By far the greatest variable in doing a creatinine clearance, as in any clearance, is the accuracy and completeness of the urine collection. Here the nurse can play a vital part in making this crucial measurement an accurate one; without accurate urine collection the performance of any clearance is useless.

Urea clearance

A urea clearance can be performed just as described, over a six to twenty-four hour period. However, the urine flow should be kept up to 2 ml/min by pushing the patient's fluid intake during the period of the urine collection. The urea clearance is then calculated just as before, but under these circumstances will represent 60% of the GFR, which can be calculated from the urea clearance on this assumption. Many doctors prefer to perform the urea clearance because the estimation of plasma creatinine is difficult and inaccurate if automatic chemistry is not available. Also at very low GFRs (sometimes below 10 ml/min and certainly below 5 ml/min) the urea clearance may provide a better measurement of the GFR than the creatinine clearance.

"Single shot" clearances

Because all these methods depend upon accurate urine collections, and because this is so difficult in practice in a general ward, methods for measuring the GFR without using urine collections at all have been sought. If a substance like inulin is injected, after it has mixed with the extra-cellular fluid its rate of removal from the blood will depend only upon the GFR since it is removed or destroyed by no other route. If we take a number of blood samples and measure the concentration of the substance in each sample we can draw a line which describes the fall-off in concentration of the substance in the blood. The slope of this line will be a measure of the GFR. For example, if the patient had no kidneys at all, after mixing there would be no decline in concentration at all, i.e. a slope (and a GFR) of zero.

Inulin is not very easy to measure, but a number of compounds have become available, labelled with radioactive tracers which can be measured easily on blood samples. Some can even be measured simply by pointing an external counter at the heart. Several compounds are in use but the most popular are metal chelates such as ^{51}Cr edetate (EDTA) and ^{125}I iothalamate and other labelled X-ray contrast media.

No special preparation is necessary. An intravenous injection of the compound is given, and at least three heparinized blood samples (5 – 10 ml) are collected. The exact timing of these will depend upon the doctor's estimate of the likely GFR, but will generally be between 3 – 12 hours after the injection. The bloods, and a proportion of the material injected, are sent for counting to the radioisotope laboratory.

The glomerular filtration rate in children

Any of the techniques described may be used, but in young children the difficulty of obtaining timed urine collections interferes with creatinine and urea clearance estimations, and the difficulty of venepuncture interferes with "single shot" clearances. Clearances are usually corrected to the "normal" adult surface area of 1.73 m^2, the child's actual surface area being calculated from its height and weight.

Tests of renal blood flow

Renal plasma flow can be obtained by measuring the clearance of the dye PAH (sodium para-aminohippurate), which is almost all removed in each passage of blood through the kidney. If a catheter is placed in the renal vein, then the measurement is very accurate indeed but this is clearly unsuitable for routine ward use. Some doctors make use of the excretion of the similar dye PSP (phenolsulphthalein) into the urine, but this is so crude that it is better to measure the GFR by one of the techniques outlined above.

Some idea of renal blood flow can be obtained, however, by the radioactive renogram.

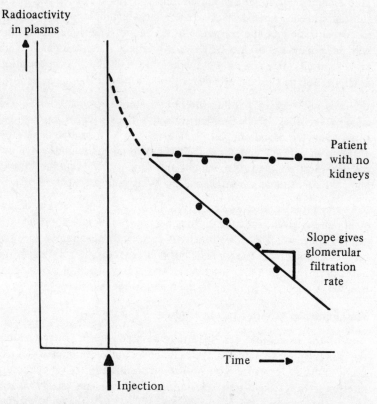

Fig. 11.4 Principle of the "single shot" measurement of glomerular filtration rate. After the injection of the radioactive compound into the plasma, it is rapidly distributed throughout the plasma and then the extracellular fluid; this phase is represented by the interrupted line. The compound must be one not broken down in the body, or cleared from the kidney other than by filtration. If this is true, then the slope of the decline in concentration in the plasma of the compound will be proportional to the glomerular filtration rate. The less the GFR, the slower the decline; if there is no filtration at all, then, as shown in the diagram, the slope of the decline will be zero and there is no fall-off in counts at all. Conversely, if the GFR is high then the fall-off in counts will be rapid.

Radio-active renogram (Figure 11.5)

The patient should preferably be off all hypotensive therapy for 48 hours prior to the test. The usual diet may be given, and the patient encouraged to drink half a litre of fluid before the test. In the radio-isotope department 1 ml of hippuran (orthoiodohippurate) labelled with I^{131} is given intravenously. The patient is seated in front of two counters which are placed over his kidneys. These counters pick up and plot on a graph the blood flow up to, and the excretion of the compound from the kidney. No urine collection is needed and the whole test takes less than one hour. Some doctors attempt to calculate the actual renal blood flow from the tracings obtained, but because the positioning of the counters over the kidneys is crucial many do not believe this accurate enough to be worthwhile. Radioactive renograms are most used in comparing the rate of entry of blood into the kidneys in patients suspected of having unilateral renal disease (Chapter VII).

This occurs most frequently when screening patients with hypertension. Another use is in picking out obstructed kidneys, because the radio-activity will leave the obstructed kidney slowly or not at all, whilst the other will show a normal tracing. It is also useful in patients with acute renal failure or non-functioning transplants, in determining whether the organ has a blood supply at all or is obstructed.

IV MORPHOLOGY OF THE KIDNEYS

Renal radiology

Radiological investigation of the urinary tract has now developed to the point where the morphology of the kidneys and outflow tract is possible in nearly every patient should it be required.

IVU and straight X-ray of abdomen

This is commonest, and properly performed one of the most valuable investigations. The term intravenous urogram (IVU) is preferable to the older, and to many more familiar intravenous pyelogram (IVP) since we are at least as interested in the pictures obtained from the lower urinary tract.

General preparation In order to obtain a good view of the renal tract there must be little or no intestinal obscuration, whether by faeces or by gas. Aperients such as the vegetable preparation Senokot, or the mild peristaltic Dulcolax are usually given as ordered before the IVU.

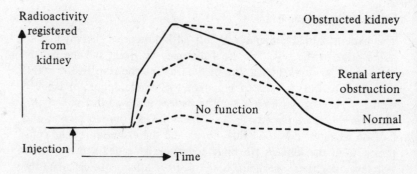

Fig. 11.5 A radioisotope renogram, obtained by injecting I^{131} labelled hippuran intravenously and placing a counter over the kidney externally. In practice, tracings are obtained from both kidneys simultaneously, with carefully matched counters. The continuous line shows the tracing obtained from a normal kidney, the height of the line representing the counts received and hence the amount of radioactivity within the kidney at that time. If the kidney is obstructed, it will show radioactivity entering the kidney, but failing to leave it (upper interrupted line), when compared with the opposite side. If there is renal artery stenosis, the entry phase (the initial upstroke) will be slower, the peak counts lower as the dye is secreted, and the dye persists longer in the kidney (middle interrupted line). If there is no renal function, the dye does not enter the kidney, the counts merely reflecting the blood flow in the tissues around the kidney.

Low residue diet, containing no vegetables, brown bread or cereals may be requested for one or two days prior to the X-ray. Patients troubled by flatus may find comfort by moving around as much as possible, by taking Aqua Menth. Pip., or charcoal biscuits. If all these fail, passing a flatus tube may prove necessary. Any bismuth preparation, Mist. Mag. Trisil. etc. should be avoided for 48 hours prior to X-ray as they show up on the film and obscure renal detail. Enemas before radiography are not generally given. Fluids will usually be restricted according to the radiologist's preference, the day and night before the IVU.

IT MUST BE EMPHASIZED STRONGLY, HOWEVER, THAT FLUID RESTRICTION, APERIENTS, OR ENEMAS MUST NOT BE GIVEN TO PATIENTS WITH RAISED BLOOD UREAS WHO HAVE CHRONIC RENAL FAILURE. The resulting saline depletion may lower their renal blood flow to a point where their renal failure may worsen, and if they are precariously balanced already, may even precipitate acute on chronic renal failure (Chapter II). In these patients — and in those whom the preparation has failed to clear intestinal shadows — the radiologist will give a larger dose of contrast media than usual, and take nephrotomograms just as one can tomogram a tuberculous cavity in the lung. In small children who are especially vulnerable to fluid restriction and whose abdomen usually contains a great deal of air, it may be useful to give, deliberately, a very fizzy drink just before the IVU and to take the pictures of the kidneys through the very large gastric gas shadow obtained. The X-ray machine may be terrifying to children, who may think it is going to fall on them. Here, explanation is more important than sedation. When a high dose of modern contrast medium is employed together with nephrotomography, it is possible to obtain at least an outline (nephrogram) of even a kidney virtually devoid of function.

The amount of information gained from a good IVU may be very great. The presence or absence, functional ability, and position of the kidneys is revealed. Scars of pyelonephritis may be seen in the renal outline (Figure 5.2) as well as distortion of the calyceal pattern. Growths, detached papillae or radiotranslucent stones may be seen in the pelvis. The position of the ureters may be distorted by growths or fibrosis, or the ureter obstructed. The bladder may be abnormally muscular, show diverticula, the indentation of an enlarged prostate, or filling defects due to new growths. Finally, one can see whether the patient can empty his bladder of the excreted dye or not.

Micturating cystogram

No special preparation is needed beyond explanation and reassurance. Many patients find a cystogram an unpleasant and embarrassing experience, and it is wise to forestall some of their apprehension. The patient is catheterized in the ward (Chapter VI) and the urine obtained will usually be sent immediately for microscopy and culture, since most patients who have cystograms are suspected of having, or actually suffer from, recurrent infection of the urinary tract. Then in the X-ray department the radiologist fills the patient's bladder with contrast medium, noting the capacity of the bladder, whether the patient experiences the usual sensations of bladder filling, and above all, whether dye refluxes up the ureters. This may happen when the patient is asked to void the contrast after removal of the catheter and during this pictures are also taken of the urethra. Abnormalities of the urethra such as obstructions or diverticula may be seen, as well as incoordination of the muscles surrounding the bladder neck. The doctor will usually order a sulphonomide or antibiotic to cover the procedure.

This is a common investigation in children because of the frequency of vesicoureteric reflux associated with urine infection, and also the need to detect obstructive urinary tract abnormalities. Once again, it will be a great help if the mother and a nurse who knows the child can be there when the X-rays are taken, as satisfactory pictures are more likely to be obtained if the child is calm and cooperative.

Renal arteriogram

Renal arteriograms are useful in outlining renal cysts or confirming the presence of tumours; and in diagnosing renal arterial abnormalities, such as renal artery stenosis or renal arterial embolism. The arteriogram may be done under heavy sedation, or general anaesthetic, and the anaesthetist or radiologist will order the premedication. The patient's permission will be required and he or she should be gowned and placed on a stretcher as for a surgical operation. The contrast is usually injected through a catheter inserted in the femoral artery, and this area may need to be shaved and prepared. Postoperatively the femoral artery should be observed for bleeding or swelling.

Cystoscopy and retrograde pyelography

A full description of these is outside the scope of this text, and a book on urological nursing should be consulted. Frequently the investigation of the renal patient involves collaboration between urologist and physician, and between urological and medical nursing staff.

Renal scanning

This has something in common with both renal radiology and the radioactive renogram. A compound which is concentrated in the kidney, and which can be labelled radioactively, is injected intravenously. The renal areas are then "scanned" by a device sensitive to the gamma rays being emitted from the compound in the kidney. The radioactivity from each small portion of kidney which is "seen" by the scanner as it moves over the area is plotted out, usually in the form of marks on a paper, whose density corresponds to the intensity of the radiation. Thus a "map" of the kidney may be obtained, and areas which do not concentrate the compound (such as cysts or tumours) may be seen. In renal artery disease the scan on the affected side is later and fainter than on the other. The absence of a kidney may be seen, or a gross alteration in outline. The scan is still present (like the nephrogram of an IVU) even if no excretion of urine is taking place, and this technique may be useful in acute renal failure, or in a non-functioning transplant, to determine whether the renal artery is patent or not.

A number of different compounds have been used for renal scanning, the most common being DMSA, ^{99m}Tc DPTA or ^{131}I Hippuran.

Dynamic scintillography (the gamma camera)

Scanning has the disadvantage that it is slow and can give only a single static picture of the kidney. It is possible to take a rapid series of "pictures" of the passage of radio actively labelled substances through the kidney, using the *gamma camera*. This has a very large crystal capable of detecting gamma emissions over an area at least a foot square, and often much greater. It also has a system of integrating and recording the information received, which allows great flexibility. The combination of crystal and data processor records the entry of the radionuclide into the kidney in both space (i.e. position) and time. In this way it is possible to "playback" from the store of information a series of pictures at different times; or the time course of the compound through a given area of the kidney (rather analogous to a renogram, but for an area specified exactly rather than a blind external localization of the counter); or to calculate rates of entry into various parts of the kidney, when compared with its passage down the vessels leading to it. If appropriate material is used, then the ureter may also be visualized and the entry of the compound into the bladder timed. Various agents can be injected, which label the blood within the kidney only, which are filtered and excreted, or which are taken up by the tubules. Examples of these in use at the moment are ^{51}Cr red cells, ^{99m}Tc DPTA (a compound resembling ^{51}Cr EDTA) and DMSA respectively. Clearly the gamma camera has great use, combining both renogram and IVU information, but capable of more precise analysis than either. The resolution, however, is at the moment less than that of an IVU.

A note on units

Throughout this book the metric system is adhered to for conventional measures of weight, length, volume, etc.

Nurses are often puzzled by the different units in which concentrations or quantities of urine or plasma constituents are expressed. At the time of writing there is some general agreement but no consistency about this. The following points may be of help:

At the moment, units are again in a state of change as the *système internationale* (SI) units are introduced into clinical medicine. In this, all units are ultimately derived from a limited number of "base" units: length, mass, time etc. The main changes with regard to medicine are that in future many substances present in body fluids will have their concentrations expressed in *molar* quantities, rather than the mixture of mg/100 ml (g/l in some continental countries), mEq/l or mmol/l as at present. This includes both ionized substances such as Na^+, K^+, HPO_4'' HCO_3' and so on, as well as un-ionized substances such as urea, creatinine, glucose, bilirubin, uric acid and cholesterol.

Milliequivalents are being phased out, but fortunately the concentrations in *millimoles* are the same, at least for ions with a single charge such as sodium, potassium and bicarbonate. The figures in the new system for the substances formerly expressed as mg/100 ml are however very different[2].

The base of this new concentration system is the *mole*. A mole is the molecular weight of the substance in grams, which means that a mole of any substance will contain the *same number of molecules* as that of any other. This is an advantage in biology, since in many situations it is the *number of molecules in solution* that is important, not the weight of the substance. We have met this already in considering the osmotic pressure of a solution. This may be expressed as the *total* number of molecules in a given solution.

The mole is too large a unit for most uses in medicine, and for general purposes the *millimole*, which is one thousandth of a mole, is the base. Since the unit of volume used in the SI system is the litre (l), most concentrations will be expressed as *millimoles per litre* (mmol/l). Some substances present in very small concentrations will be expressed in micromoles (μmol/l) and one, hydrogen ion, in the even smaller unit the *nanomole* (nmol/l) which is one thousandth of a μmole (10^{-9} mole).

Fortunately, nurses will be glad to know that the SI system will not be applied rigidly throughout medicine. For a changeover period, the mg/100 ml figures will be retained but will change slightly to mg/dl, or

---

[2]   Normal concentrations of substances commonly measured in renal patients using the new (SI) system:

substance	normal range in plasma (mmol/l*)
urea	2·5 – 6·5
creatinine	50 – 90 (μmol/l)
uric acid	0·1 – 0·4
glucose	3 – 5
phosphate	0·8 – 1·4
cholesterol	3·6 – 7·8
Ca^{++}	2·1 – 2·6
PO_4''	0·8 – 1·4
Total protein	62 – 82 (g/l)
Albumin	36 – 52 (g/l)
	*unless otherwise stated

milligrams per decilitre. The decilitre is simply another name for one tenth of a litre and will be familiar to many from drinking wine in restaurants abroad. Blood pressure, also, will *not* be changed to the SI pressure system of kiloPascals per square metre, but will remain in mmHg as before. The other change, that of energy from calories to joules, is considered in the next section on diet (Chapter XII).

Acid The concentration of hydrogen ions in the blood and urine is at present expressed in the confusing pH scale. The pH of the urine will go as low as 4·8 (very acid) and as high as pH 8·0 (very alkaline). Blood usually has a pH of between 7·30 and 7·40. Gradual use is being made of the hydrogen ion concentration itself; the millimole is far too large a unit, so we use nanomoles (one millionth of a millimole, 10^{-9} mole, nmol/l), or *nano* equivalents (nEq/l). The normal plasma hydrogen ion concentration is about 40 nmol/l, pH 7 being 100, and pH8 10 nmol/l.

Suggestions for further reading:

Black, D. A. K., Cameron, J. S. (1976). Renal Disease. *The Chemical Diagnosis of Disease.* (Eds.) Brown, S. S., Mitchell, F. L., Young, D. S. Amsterdam: Elsevier.

British Medical Bulletin (1972). Radiology of the kidney. Volume 28, No. 3.

Hampson, P. G. (1974). Some less common investigations of the urinary tract. *Radiography*, June 1974.

Hodson, C. J. (1973). Radiology of the kidney. *Renal Disease.* p. 218. (Ed.) Black, D. A. K. Oxford: Blackwell.

Kerr, D. N. S., Davison, J. M. The assessment of renal function. *British Journal of Hospital Medicine*, October 1975, p. 360.

Morrison, R. B. I. (1973). Urinalysis and assessment of renal function. *Renal Disease.* p. 251. (Ed.) Black, D. A. K. Oxford: Blackwell.

Saxton, H. M. (1969). Urography. *British Journal of Radiology*, **42**, 321.

CHAPTER XII

Diet in renal disease

With MISS J BRICE, BSc Nut, SRD and H BROWN BSc Nut

I INTRODUCTION

The part played by special diets in renal disease is always a palliative one, that is, the diet is aimed at the alleviation of symptoms rather than the cure of the disease. For example, in chronic renal failure a low protein diet is used to reduce the uraemia, and hence the feeling of nausea and general malaise. All the diets described are used to help restore the balance that in health is maintained by the normal kidneys. In many states a well controlled diet forms a central part of the management.

The use of diet in the treatment of renal disorders depends therefore upon the clinical signs and symptoms rather than the nature of the underlying disease. The following groups will be discussed in turn:

Acute renal failure
Acute nephritis
The nephrotic syndrome
Chronic renal failure
Regular haemodialysis

The preparation, serving and eating of food is a vital part of day to day life. Food is not only a necessity for life but is also an important symbol socially, emotionally and ritually. For example, a children's tea party, a picnic, a formal banquet, or a wedding anniversary dinner. When a special diet is planned for a patient, three major factors must be considered:

(i)   the medical requirements;
(ii)   the patient's background: age, race, sex, occupation, financial resources, way of life;
(iii) whether nutritionally adequate with respect to other requirements not being specifically modified.

182

As long as the patient is in hospital it is generally easier to ensure that the diet is suitable for the pattern of meals served, and patients in general adapt to the ward routine of meals. In the stricter diets it is generally impossible to fulfil all the patient's wishes and he must be shown *why* and *how* to change his pattern of eating to fit the new dietetic requirements. On admission to hospital, many patients are too ill and too worried to understand much that is explained to them, and it is important to spend several sessions with the patient and the "cook" of the family to inform and help with specific culinary problems. Usually, many of the ideas will be completely new to the patient and his family, and written instructions for future reference should always be given to the patient on discharge.

The nurse's role

Even in a hospital where the diet is constructed by a trained dietician, the nurse is the person who sees the food eaten or rejected, and she may be able to help the patient adapt to new eating habits. She may be able to modify the basic diet by individual additions in the ward, but obviously to do this she must know what foods or savouries can and cannot be given. For example, in chronic renal failure or other situations where a high energy intake is important she can endeavour to give the patient extra high energy drinks. She will also be the person who sees that the dietary instructions are adhered to, and to report to the doctor difficulties or deviations from instructions.

Many hospitals, however, do not have a dietician and the construction as well as the administration of diets falls on the medical and nursing staff. This chapter therefore endeavours not only to provide information on the principles upon which diets used in patients with renal diseases may be constructed but also brief practical instructions on how to put the various diets into operation.

Factors important in constructing diets

The age, size, sex and occupation of the patient will determine the energy and protein needs. The following figures are these recommended (NOT minimum) intakes for various groups (Table I).

Religion and race

It is usually possible to adapt the English hospital menu to suit people of various racial and religious backgrounds, particularly if there is a selective menu. Relatives may be able to provide special items, with the reservations discussed below.

Table I   ENERGY AND PROTEIN REQUIREMENTS

		MJ/day	k calories/ day	Protein (g/day)
Children				
0 – 1 yrs.		3·4	800	20
1 – 2 yrs.		5·0	1200	30
2 – 3 yrs.		5·9	1400	35
3 – 5 yrs.		6·7	1600	40
5 – 7 yrs.		7·6	1800	45
7 – 9 yrs.		8·8	2100	53
Boys				
9 – 12 yrs.		10·5	2500	63
12 – 15 yrs.		11·8	2800	70
15 – 18 yrs.		12·6	3000	75
Girls				
9 – 12 yrs.		9·7	2300	58
12 – 15 yrs.		9·7	2300	58
15 – 18 yrs.		9·7	2300	58
Men				
18 – 35	sedentary	11·3	2700	68
	active	12·6	3000	75
	very active	15·1	3600	90
35 – 65	sedentary	10·9	2600	65
	active	12·2	2900	73
	very active	15·1	3600	90
65 – 75 }		9·9	2350	59
75+ }	sedentary	8·8	2100	53
Women				
18 – 55	most occupations	9·2	2200	55
55 – 75 }	sedentary	10·5	2500	51
75+ }		9·0	1900	48
Pregnancy		10·1	2400	60
Lactation		11·3	2700	68

Muslims take no meat unless it is "ritually" killed and, in hosptial, may prefer a vegan (no animal products) menu.

Hindus are generally vegetarian, but some will take any meat except pig or cow. Both Muslims and Hindus make extensive use of milk and curds, and in some instances cheese.

The majority of *Orthodox Jews* can obtain a dispensation from the strictest rules of eating whilst in hospital, but many dislike the normally forbidden foods such as pork, because of unfamiliarity. Frequently a vegetarian diet is the best compromise, since many will prefer not to eat meat killed by the usual methods. Very strict Jews cannot eat meals prepared by non-Jews and this may present a considerable problem.

Some *Roman Catholics* and some Christians of other denominations prefer to abstain from meat on Friday, but this presents little difficulty.

Vegans will not eat anything that involves killing an animal, but will accept milk and milk products. *Vegetarians* will generally take eggs as well as milk, cheese and sometimes fish. Strict vegans take most of their protein from vegetable sources and make extensive use of pulses such as peas, beans, lentils, etc., together with rice and nuts.

The majority of patients with special dietary habits will explain them when requested to do so and will often be prepared to accept simple meals to replace the special foods their religion or habit forbids. When a special diet is to be continued at home then special care is need to adapt the standard foods.

Non-British cuisine may have to be accommodated to diets, particularly in hospitals serving large towns, the commonest cuisines which differ significantly from British foods being Italian, West Indian, West African, Pakistani and Cypriot. A frequent problem is a request from a patient to include a particular food in the diet when its sodium, protein or potassium content are not available. It may be necessary to get the hospital laboratory to estimate the electrolyte content, after homogenizing the food. Highly seasoned foods from the Indian sub-continent may be a particular problem since they contain large amounts of both salt and potassium.

Financial resources and social habits

Foods given in hospital should as far as possible be similar, although often not the same as that to which the patient is accustomed. Hospitals with larger dietetic departments or good selective menus will experience less difficulty. Instructions for home must take the normal way of life, their accepted meal pattern and food habits, as well as the financial resources, into consideration. There is no point in telling a labourer to have fillet steak and salmon for his high protein diet. It has often been said that to change a person's food habits, even when they know it is for their own health, is one of the most difficult things to achieve. Thus the world of dietetics must bring together as far as is humanly possible the medical requirements and the patient's wishes.

Children

Children in hospital may be a problem, particularly if the diet is very restrictive. Children tend to want either what they have at home or what the other children are having in the ward. In many cases their diets can be simple modifications of the other children's e.g. if supper is fried egg, bacon and chips, the nephrotic child on restricted salt can be given extra fried eggs but no bacon.

The majority of young children dislike strong flavours and unfamiliar foods. Discussion with the parents will quickly establish the child's preferences. Some children, however, enjoy curries or Italian and Spanish foods, particularly if they have visited these countries during the holidays. In these cases, the very restricted low protein dishes can be introduced with relative ease.

The visual aspect of any meal is important to a child. They tend to dislike sloppy meals and like to be able to distinguish the various foods on the plate. Contrasting colours (e.g. carrots and peas) often encourage the child. For the younger child, small pieces should be served, e.g. chopped meats and vegetables.

Timing is important to children and they become upset if the routine is broken. When it is especially important that food is taken, punctuality should be aimed for at all times.

II   ACUTE RENAL FAILURE

There are now the two main methods of management of the patient in acute renal failure (Chapter II) and the dietary regime used depends on which of these methods is employed.

(1)   Conservative methods
(2)   Dialysis
    (a)   peritoneal
    (b)   haemodialysis

1 Conservative methods

(a) In the *oliguric phase* the aims of dietary management are
(i) reduce the endogenous protein breakdown to a minimum;
(ii) fulfil energy needs;
(iii) avoid overloading the patient with fluids or electrolytes.

Carbohydrates are know to have a protein sparing action in the body and in normal circumstances 120 g carbohydrate per day is sufficient for this purpose. In renal failure more is necessary and at least 300 g carbohydrate should be given daily. A *total* energy intake of 12·5 to 17·0 MJ (3000 - 4000 kcal) for an adult at rest should be aimed at but cannot usually be achieved. Since the conservative method of treatment is not used in patients who are catabolic (i.e. breaking down tissue very rapidly) an intake of less than this is probably satisfactory.

A totally protein-free regime may be given for up to seven to fifteen days if necessary, that is if no remission of the renal failure occurs. After this time body protein reserves are reduced to a minimum and 20 g protein in the form of eggs and milk must be given (e.g. two eggs plus 200 ml ($\frac{1}{3}$ pint) milk as egg flip) to supply essential protein needs. Some doctors prefer to give this type of diet from the start.

Initially high energy electrolyte-free fluids should be given. Hycal (Beechams) (see Section V) and Caloreen (Milner Scientific) are probably tolerated the best. Sucrose, glucose or other sugars may be used but these tend, in high concentrations, to be very sweet and may produce nausea and/or diarrhoea because the osmotic pressure of the solution formed is high which attracts large volumes of water into the gut. Hycal is a mixture of glucose and glucose chains ("liquid glucose"), needs no preparation and is supplied in 175 ml bottles, each containing 1700 kJ (425 kcal). It may be given neat or, if fluid volumes allow, dilute, and in the concentrated form it is more acceptable when chilled. If fluids allow, it may be diluted, 2 Hycal:1 water, and deep frozen. As such, it is far less sweet. This form is very popular with children as it may be served as "ice lollies". Hycal is supplied in six flavours: lime, lemon, strawberry, raspberry, pineapple and blackcurrant. Caloreen, in contrast to the sweet Hycal, is a non-sweet compound consisting of chains of glucose molecules, averaging about five glucose units in each chain. It is supplied in a powder form and in appearance resembles icing sugar. It may be prepared by gently *warming* equal weights of Caloreen and water until dissolved. It is then cooled and used when desired. Care must be taken never to allow the mixture to boil as a very sticky, sweet mixture will result. This solution will contain 1670 kJ (400 kcal) for every 100 ml water. Even at this concentration the solution looks like slightly yellowed water, appears no thicker and tastes virtually like water. It is very suitable for nauseated patients. Caloreen may be flavoured with suitable low-electrolyte flavours, chilled or frozen if desired. Both these products are pure carbohydrates, virtually electrolyte-free and protein-free.

All these sugars may be given orally or via an intragastric drip. The total volume allowed per 24 hours will depend on individual requirements but 500 ml plus the previous day's urine output is a rough guide for the patient without fever. If fever is present more may need to be given to compensate for additional losses.

In all cases care must be taken to avoid using high potassium fruit juices as a base for sugar or glucose in the initial stages, since hyperkalaemia is often present. For this reason the use of low electrolyte Hycal, which is flavoured, or Caloreen, which is non-sweet, is often preferred. Vitamin supplements should be given; vitamin B_1 is particularly important since the body's stores may be depleted after only a few days.

If other dietary variations are requested by the patient during the oliguric phase, tea and coffee may be used with caution. Both contain potassium and instant coffee is particularly hazardous since it is generally available, easy to use and has a high potassium content.

The table gives potassium values of tea and coffee.

Potassium contents of drinks   *Potassium*

1 cup tea		1·5 mmol
1 cup ground coffee	with 30 ml (1 oz) milk	4 mmol
1 cup instant coffee	contains	6 mmol
(1 tsp dry weight coffee)		

Barley sugar or other boiled sweets are often enjoyed and if the patient becomes hungry sugar, salt-free butter, honey, jams and sugared salt-free rice may all be given (see Chronic Renal Failure for details of protein-free products). All fats and some fatty foods may be given but tend to be nauseating at this stage.

(b)   When *diuresis* sets in fluid volumes are increased, and electrolytes may now need to be given or else depletion can occur. Great care is needed since sodium and potassium must be replaced *only* as necessary. Caution must be taken when giving foods at this stage. As the renal failure permits so the patient may be given a low protein diet (20 - 40 g protein) and this gradually increased to normal (see Chronic Renal

Failure, Low Protein Diets). Potassium losses may be great, will usually be measured, and high potassium fruit juice, such as orange or blackcurrant, may be very useful.

2 Dialysis

Dialysis is now often performed before the patient has become severely uraemic or may be started if diuresis has not occurred within a few days. Whether peritoneal dialysis or haemodialysis is used will depend on the patient's condition and facilities available.

(a) Diet in peritoneal dialysis Peritoneal dialysis permits a more liberal intake of fluids, electrolytes and protein. The removal of the severe dietary restrictions necessary in the conservative management not only helps prevent tissue wasting but does much to improve the patient's morale and feeling of well-being.

Depending on the volume and strength of the peritoneal dialysis solution used, the patient will receive quite a considerable amount of energy from the peritoneal dialysis fluid itself. These solutions are hypertonic to body fluid and thus glucose passes from the dialysis fluid to the body fluids.

1 litre of peritoneal dialysis fluid
  of 1·36 g% strength glucose gives approx. 200 kJ (50 kcal).
  of 6·36 g% strength glucose gives approx. 500 kJ (120 kcal).

This has obvious advantages as it lessens the need to force energy into an often reluctant patient. This does *not* mean that no attention need be paid to the patient's nutrition, but merely reduces the necessity of forcing carbohydrate energy. This considerable carbohydrate load in an easily assimilated form may precipitate an acute carbohydrate intolerance especially in diabetics or pre-diabetics. Dialysate fluids prepared with sorbitol or fructose are available for use with such cases. Sorbitol and fructose, like glucose, supply a considerable amount of energy to the patient, but do not require insulin to enter cells.

During 24 hours of peritoneal dialysis between 10 g and 40 g protein are lost from body fluids via the peritoneum into the dialysate. Allowing for essential daily protein requirements, patients need about 60 g protein a day. Similarly, in general about 60 mmol of both sodium and potassium is required per day. Most patients will be maintained adequately on the ordinary ward diet (provided foods with obvious high sodium and potassium content are avoided). An example is given below:

60 g Protein, 60 mmol Sodium, 60 mmol Potassium
8·5 MJ (2000 kcal)
1000 ml Fluid allowance (= 6 cups)

Avoiding high sodium and high potassium fruits and vegetables.

Early morning   Tea as desired. Milk from daily allowance.

Breakfast   Grapefruit (tinned or fresh) with sugar, if desired.
30 g (1 oz) Cereals and milk from allowance.
30 g (1 oz) Bread, fried, plain or toasted.
1 egg, cooked as desired.
Butter, marmalade, jam or honey.
Tea or ground coffee.
Sugar as desired.

Mid-morning   Tea or ground coffee.

Lunch   60 g (2 oz) meat or 90 g (3 oz) fish or 2 eggs.
120 g (4 oz) potato or 90 g (3 oz) rice.
Vegetables or salad.
150 g (5 oz) milk pudding or equivalent.
Tea or ground coffee.

Tea   Tea
30 g (1 oz) bread or 30 g (1 oz) (3 – 4) biscuits or 30 g
(1 oz) (small) cake.

Supper   60 g (2 oz) meat or 90 g (3 oz) fish or 2 eggs.
120 g (4 oz) potato or 90 g (3 oz) rice.
Vegetables or salad.
Sweet fruit with 90 g (3 oz) custard and sugar.
Tea or ground coffee.

Bedtime   Tea or ground coffee.

Milk allowance   200 ml (7 oz) (= 1 cup).

Many more severely ill patients are not well enough to manage the full
menu outlined above and the following indicates how 60 g protein may
be given with a higher energy intake.

Semi-solid
60 g Protein, less than 60 mmol Sodium and Potassium, 8·5 MJ
(2000 kcal)

Breakfast   Porridge or cereal with 110 ml (4 oz) milk and 15 g
($\frac{1}{2}$ oz, 3 tsp) sugar.

Egg flip [60 g (1 large) egg + 140 ml (5 oz) milk + 15 g ($\frac{1}{2}$ oz, 3 tsp) sugar + 30 g (1 oz) Caloreen]
Tea, with 30 ml (1 oz) milk and 10 g ($\frac{1}{3}$ oz, 2 tsp) sugar.

Mid-morning   Cup of milk, 170 ml (6 oz)

Lunch   Sweet milk pudding, 140 g (5 oz) with 30 g (1 oz) Caloreen or 30 g (1 oz) Hycal.

Tea   Cup of tea and egg flip, as at breakfast.

Supper   As lunch.

Bedtime   Egg flip as breakfast.

Soups may be employed if there is no sodium problem. As the patient improves, eggs may be cooked and meat offered at main meals. The total protein is kept similar by increasing tea and Hycal, etc. and reducing milk intake. When main courses are introduced the sodium will increase because of salt in cooking and with the addition of vegetables and fruit the potassium will rise also (see potassium explanation in Chronic Renal Failure).

Peritoneal dialysis is generally continued until diuresis sets in; the patient should then be encouraged to take high energy fluids and as the renal function improves to take a more normal diet, including those high sodium and potassium foods.

(b) Diets in haemodialysis This is similar to that used in peritoneal dialysis except that there is usually a somewhat stricter fluid restriction, and energy intake must be encouraged. This is discussed in detail under Chronic Renal Failure.

III ACUTE NEPHRITIS

The treatment of acute nephritis in its oliguric phase is similar to that of acute renal failure (see above). That is, a high carbohydrate diet, at least 300 g for adults, low fluid, protein and electrolytes. In children the amount of energy required depends on age but in general an unlimited carbohydrate intake can be allowed together with restricted fluid and little else (see the Table in the Introduction).

In the oliguric stage only fluid foods are generally tolerated. In severe cases with uraemia treatment should be protein free, as for acute renal failure. If the uraemia is mild the essential protein requirements, that is 20 g per day, should be given in the form of milk and/or eggs. Three eggs or one pint of milk are equivalent and sufficient but the milk contains more salt. Energy should again be supplied by Hycal or Caloreen as they may be administered in small volumes. Caloreen may of course be added direct to the milk or egg/milk mixture. Again, it is necessary to watch potassium levels and if these rise eggs should be given in preference to milk and all fruit juices which are high in potassium should be eliminated.

As diuresis sets in and the blood pressure returns to normal a low salt/ low protein (40 g protein) diet may be immediately tried (see Chronic Renal Failure). As normal function improves so may the protein and electrolytes be increased to the normal levels.

When diuresis begins patients generally start requesting solid foods. It is probably safest to start with lightly cooked eggs, fish or meat (not high sodium – see list), together with a little bread and butter, or if potassium is not a problem, creamed potato. If the blood pressure is still very high all foods should be prepared without salt. Too severe salt restriction, however, tends to make the patient anorexic.

IV   THE NEPHROTIC SYNDROME

As outlined in Chapter IV, the principal problems of the nephrotic syndrome are protein loss in the urine, leading to protein depletion and endogenous tissue breakdown and indirectly to sodium retention. The dietary treatment therefore involves:

(1)   A high protein intake
(2)   Restricted sodium and fluid intake
(3)   Adequate energy intake

1   Protein

It is usually possible to raise the plasma albumin concentration, even in the face of continuing heavy proteinuria, by feeding a high protein intake. Provided that there is no renal functional impairment, particularly with a raised blood urea to begin with, this should be about 90 – 100 g of protein per day. Some patients will achieve intakes of 150 g per day but this is usually poorly tolerated for long periods. In children the quantity must be adjusted for age and size; this presents a problem because the nephrotic child may be at the same time wasted, stunted and oedematous, so that neither the height, weight nor surface area gives a good basis for adjustment. In practice the age is probably the most useful, the age/15 times the adult level of intake (say 100 g) being a rough guide.

The protein intake is normally made up from protein sources such as meat, fish, eggs, milk and milk products, apart from cheese, which is rich in salt; from cereals and cereal products such as bread, biscuits, cakes, pasta and rice; from pulses, such as beans, peas and lentils; and finally from potatoes (Table III).

When designing a high protein diet, foods should be selected from the first group of animal protein sources (Table II). Eggs are particularly useful because the quantity of protein is simple to calculate, they can be prepared easily in a variety of ways, and are generally palatable. Use may also be made of low-salt protein supplements such as Edosol, Casilan and K-Lo (see below).

Table II   ANIMAL PROTEIN SOURCES

The following each contain about 7 g of animal protein, and can be used interchangeably in diets:

> 1 large egg (60 g, 2 oz)
> 30 g (1 oz) cooked meat
> 45 g (1½ oz) cooked fish
> 200 ml (7 oz) milk
> 30 g (1 oz) cheese
> 200 ml (7 oz) milk pudding or custard
> 150 g (5 oz) egg custard

Table III   VEGETABLE PROTEIN SOURCES

Exchanges for 1 oz BREAD (equals 2 g PROTEIN)
Instead of 1 oz of ordinary bread (one thin slice from an ordinary loaf) you may have one of the following:

BISCUITS, etc.

*Biscuits, plain, mixed or sweet,	3 or 4	1 oz
*Cream crackers	3	1 oz
*Flour	1 heaped tblsp	1 oz
*Ryvita	3	1 oz
*Vita-Wheat	4	1 oz

*If the patient's sodium intake is restricted to 30 mmol/day then no more than three 2 g "slice equivalents" should come from foods marked.

Table III (continued)

CAKES
If bought or made with salt*

Cakes, made with eggs	1 small piece	1 oz
Pastry, scones, shortbread, home-made plain biscuits		1 oz
Jam tarts, or cakes with heavy cream and/or icing or rich fruit cakes	2 oz	2 oz

BREAKFAST CEREALS
This does *not* include any milk taken with the cereal

*Cornflakes	6 heaped tblsp	1 oz
*Porridge, made with water	6 level tblsp	6 oz
Puffed Wheat		$\frac{1}{2}$ oz
Rice Krispies		1 oz
Shredded Wheat	1 biscuit	1 oz
*Weetabix	$1\frac{1}{2}$ biscuits	$\frac{3}{4}$ oz

PUDDINGS
If bought or made with salt*

Short, flaky or puff pastry, crumble (plus fruit, jam, etc.)		1 oz
Suet pastry as pudding or dumpling		2 oz
Sponge pudding ($\frac{1}{3}$ normal serving) or jam roll, baked		$1\frac{1}{2}$ oz
Ice cream		$1\frac{1}{2}$ oz

SAVOURIES
*only if cooked with salt

Macaroni, boiled	$\frac{1}{2}$ cup, 2 heaped tblsp	2 oz
Macaroni, dry, raw	1 heaped tblsp	$\frac{2}{3}$ oz
Rice, boiled	$\frac{3}{4}$ cup, 3 rounded tblsp	3 oz
Rice, dry, raw	2 level tblsp	1 oz
Spaghetti, boiled	3 rounded tblsp	3 oz
Spaghetti, dry, raw	2 level tblsp	1 oz
Potatoes, cooked as desired	2 small (egg-sized)	4 oz
*Yorkshire Pudding		1 oz

---

*If the patient's sodium intake is restricted to 30 mmol/day then no more than three 2 g "slice equivalents" should come from foods marked.

2 Salt

Confusion sometimes arises as to the units the doctor wishes to employ when asking for a salt restricted diet. Various terms are also used to describe diets – "low salt", "restricted salt", etc. Conventionally, these have the following meanings (Table IV):

Table IV SODIUM INTAKES

	mmol Na⁺/day
Normal free salt, according to choice	60 – 300
Restricted (no salty foods, no salt added at table)	60 – 80
Low (no salt used in cooking, or at table, salty foods avoided)	40 – 50
Very low (as above, but with use of salt-free bread and salt-free butter)	15 – 30
Minimal or ultra low; requires the use of formulae and special foods	less than 15

(1 g NaCl = 17 mmol Na^+; 1 g Na^+ = 40 mmol)

When the diet is high in protein, the sodium content will be at the higher end of the range indicated, so that it is difficult for the nephrotic patient eating 100 g of protein per day to take less than 30 mmol of sodium per day, whatever restrictions are imposed.

It is usual to start with the *restricted sodium diet* because too intensive salt restriction leads to anorexia. This consists of no salt added at the table and salty foods should be avoided (Table V).

With a high protein intake this will give a sodium intake of 60 – 80 mmol Na^+ for 100 g protein.

Next, a *low sodium diet* may be tried; this should give 40 – 50 mmol Na^+ per day. Here, in addition to the above precautions, no salt is used in cooking. Bread and flour products, such as cakes and biscuits, should be kept to no more than five slices per day of bread or their equivalent (see protein exchange list, Table III). If sodium intake must be restricted even further then salt-free bread and butter must be used

Table V FOODS HIGH IN SALT AND TO BE AVOIDED IN ALL SALT RESTRICTED DIETS

(1)   Cheese, except unsalted cream cheese.

(2)   Tinned, pickled, smoked or salt meats and fishes e.g. sausages, luncheon meat, bacon, ham, salt beef, pilchards, smoked haddock.

(3)   Meat and fish pastes.

(4)   Shellfish.

(5)   Tinned vegetables and tinned or packet soups.

(6)   Pickles, salad cream, sauces, chutney, Bovril, Oxo, Marmite and gravy cubes and mixes.

(7)   Dehydrated, pre-packed meals.

(8)   Salted nuts.

(9)   All breakfast cereals, EXCEPT unsalted porridge, Shredded Wheat, Puffed Wheat and Sugar Smacks.

(10) Bread, cakes and biscuits in excess of stated amounts.

(11) Horlicks, Bournvita, Ovaltine, chocolate, cocoa and other flavourings.

(*very low sodium diet*). Salt-free bread is obtainable from most large bakeries, or may be made by local bakers. The bread may be made more palatable by toasting and serving with tasty preserves.

Low salt protein supplements   When a very low sodium intake is required, and when the patient is either too small or unable to take a high protein intake from ordinary foods, then use may be made of special foods. Edosol (Trufoods) salt-free milk has the same content when made up as a 12·5% solution as cows' milk but only 1 mmol of sodium per 500 ml instead of the 12 mmol in cows' milk. It may be given double strength, or used in puddings, if fluid restriction is severe or when large quantities must be given. Casilan (Glaxo) is calcium casei-nate, and gives 26 g protein per 30 g (1 oz) dry weight. The sodium and potassium content are virtually nil. Like Edosol, Casilan has a distinc-tive, rather unpleasant taste which most patients prefer masked. Casilan is most easily taken as a water/milk mixture, well-flavoured and blended in a liquidizer or mixer. Care must be taken to avoid high salt flavourings such as "Horlicks", "Bournvita" and "Ovaltine". A useful set of flavours are those sold under the brand name "Nesquick" (Nestles), or strong coffee (not instant if potassium is restricted) may be used. Casilan may also be used in puddings, egg custards, sauces and soups.

Salt substitutes Most patients with the nephrotic syndrome are on diuretics, which frequently leads to potassium depletion (Chapter IV). Potassium supplements may be prescribed by the doctor to minimize this, and therefore it is usually safe to allow salt substitutes, which are potassium salts. However, this should be discussed with the doctor in case the patient has renal functional impairment, and they should never be used indiscriminately. Salt substitutes are most satisfactory when added after cooking, since they are more bitter than salt and this bitterness may be imparted to the food if used in cooking.

3 Fluids

When oedema is present, the fluid intake will generally be restricted, although it is more important to control the salt intake. Fluid produced by metabolism, and in "solid" foods, approximately balances that lost in the faeces, breath and through the skin. This allows one to balance the fluid given as such in cup or glass, against the urine output. If oedema is to be lost, the urine output must exceed the input; the doctor will, of course, at the same time be trying to increase the urine output with diuretics. Usually intake is restricted to one litre per day in an adult nephrotic patient; further restriction is poorly tolerated over long periods.

4 Fat

Some doctors feel that a low fat diet should be given in an attempt to lower the fat and cholesterol levels in the blood of nephrotic patients whose condition persists. The value of dietary measures in reducing the cardiovascular complications attributed to high fat levels is doubtful and this only imposes yet another restriction on the patient. Most doctors do not therefore ask for fat to be restricted, unless the patient has actual evidence of coronary artery insufficiency, such as angina or myocardial infarct. Some doctors give anti-hyperlipidaemic drugs to patients with persistent nephrotic syndromes and marked increase in serum lipids.

Constructing the diet

The doctor will indicate the amounts of protein, sodium and fluid he would like the patient to take daily. Using the general principles outlined a diet can then be constructed for each patient, taking into account their personal preferences and ethnic background. If the patient is to continue the diet at home, as frequently happens, then the intelligence of the patient, the home cooking facilities and who will actually prepare the food must all be taken into consideration as discussed in the Introduction. For example, two basic diets are shown, if more rigid sodium restriction is required then salt must be removed from cooking, bread and biscuit intake limited or salt-free bread and butter used, as indicated above.

Diet for a nephrotic patient
100 g Protein, 60-80 mmol Sodium, 1 litre Fluids (105 MJ (2500 kcal))

Breakfast	Fresh, tinned or stewed fruit with sugar if desired 2 eggs cooked as desired 2 slices bread, butter, marmalade
Mid-morning	1 cup milk
Lunch	120 g (4 oz) meat or 180 g (6 oz) fish 2 small (egg-sized) potatoes Vegetables as desired 210 ml (7 oz) milk pudding, or other protein-containing pudding
Tea	1 slice bread, or small cake, or 3-4 sweet biscuits
Supper	120 g (4 oz) meat or 180 g (6 oz) fish or 4 large eggs 2 small potatoes or 1 slice bread Vegetables or salad as desired Sweet fruit or jelly with cream if desired
Drinks	210 ml (7 oz) milk per day, in tea, coffee, etc. Fruit squash or fruit juice may also be taken. Six cups to be taken over whole day.

Other foods allowed as desired:
Jam, honey, marmalade, sugar, glucose and Caloreen.
All fats including butter, margarine, cooking oils, fat and cream.
All fruits and vegetables.
Boiled sweets and peppermints.
Fruit drinks, lemonade, Lucozade, Hycal, tea and coffee.

Salt allowed in cooking. Foods listed as high in sodium (see Table V) to be avoided.

Diet for patient restricted to one litre fluid per day and with a poor appetite
100 g Protein; 60 - 80 mmol Sodium; 1 litre fluids

Breakfast	Fresh, stewed or tinned fruit or fruit juices 1 egg cooked as desired 1 slice bread, butter, marmalade
Mid-morning	1 cup milk mixture* 1 - 2 sweet biscuits
Lunch	60 g (2 oz) meat, or 90 g (3 oz) fish or 2 eggs 120 g (4 oz) potatoes (2 small) Vegetables as desired 150 g (5 oz) milk pudding + 10 g Casilan
Tea	1 slice bread, or small cake, or 3 - 4 biscuits
Supper	60 g (2 oz) meat, or 90 g (3 oz) fish or 2 eggs 120 g (4 oz) potatoes (2 small) Vegetables or salad as desired Sweet fruit or jelly, with cream if desired
Bedtime	1 cup (200 ml, 7 oz) milk mixture* 1 - 2 sweet biscuits
Drinks	*Milk mixture:- 280 ml ($\frac{1}{2}$ pint) milk + 30 g (1 oz) Casilan + 280 ml ($\frac{1}{2}$ pint) water. Mix well. Flavour as desired.

6 cups of fluid to be taken in whole day, from tea, coffee, fruit drinks.

Other foods allowed:
Jam, honey, marmalade, sugar, glucose, Caloreen, boiled sweets, peppermints.
All fats including butter, margarine, cooking fat oils and cream.
All fruit and vegetables, fruit drinks, Lucozade, Hycal, tea, coffee.

Salt allowed in cooking. Foods listed as rich in sodium (Table V) to be avoided.

V CHRONIC RENAL FAILURE

The diet for patients in chronic renal failure is at best palliative rather than therapeutic, but administered well can do much to improve the well-being of the patient. A well controlled diet is one of the major ways in which these patients can be helped. They have an accumulation of urea in the blood, and control of the uraemia has obvious advantages since by achieving this many of the symptoms are decreased (Chapter VI). It must not be forgotten, however, that like all medical treatments dietary manipulation can do harm as well as good. This is particularly true for the more extreme forms of diet used in patients in advanced renal failure. Here, protein restriction is easy to achieve in most patients, but unless this is accompanied by a considerable increase in energy intake the result is starvation: protein-energy malnutrition. It is often forgotten just how much the energy intake must be increased in a uraemic patient on maximum protein restriction (18 – 20 g/day), before nitrogen balance can be achieved. In a normal-sized adult, *at least 0·25 MJ (60 kcal)/kg/day must be taken to remain in balance; that is a daily energy intake of no less than 18 MJ (4200 kcal)* for a 70 kg man. If this energy intake cannot be achieved, then maximum protein restriction can only do harm, and accentuate the nutritional and metabolic problems of the uraemia. With less strict diets and milder renal failure the situation is less critical, and outside special units with extra dietetic help, it is in this group that most can be achieved.

The dietetic management may be considered under three headings, depending on the severity of the condition:

(1)   Mild renal impairment
(2)   Moderate renal impairment
(3)   Severe renal impairment

1   Mild renal impairment

At this stage there is usually little or no rise in blood urea and the patient generally feels relatively fit. Dietetic instruction probably only needs to be in general terms. The patient should be advised to take small helpings of the protein dish at each main meal (that is meat, fish, egg and cheese), to limit milk to about 280 ml ($\frac{1}{2}$ pint) a day and to eat plenty of high energy foods. Most will benefit by being advised to drink large volumes of fluid.

2   Moderate renal impairment

As the kidneys progressively fail, so the blood urea will begin to rise and symptoms will begin to increase (Chapter VI). At this stage a traditional 40 g protein diet (for adults) is probably sufficient and this will include ordinary bread and flour products. A high proportion of the protein should come from animal sources; that is, meat, fish, eggs, cheese and milk. In many cases it is difficult to maintain a high energy intake on this restricted diet since limited bread and potatoes means reduced butter, fats and jams, and hence a reduced intake. It may be very useful to include some of the protein-free products at this stage (see next section – Giovannetti-Giordano Diet – for details). Protein-free biscuits. Hycal and Caloreen are often especially useful. A typical 40 g protein diet is as follows:

40 g Protein Diet for Chronic Renal Failure

		Protein (g)
Breakfast	Half grapefruit, fresh fruit or fruit with sugar	
	1 egg OR 30 g (1 oz) bacon, OR 30 g (1 oz) ham	7·0
	Bread 60 g (2 oz), butter and marmalade as desired	4·0
	Milk (from allowance) in tea or coffee	
	Sugar as desired	
Mid-morning	Milk (from allowance) in tea or coffee	
Dinner	Meat or chicken, 30 g (1 oz) OR fish 45 g (1½ oz)	7·0
	Potato 120 g (4 oz) OR bread 30 g (1 oz)	2·0
	(NOT peas, beans, lentils or spinach)	
	Fresh or stewed fruit OR jelly OR protein-free pudding (see pudding list)	
Tea	Bread 30 g (1 oz) and butter	2·0
	Jam, honey or syrup as desired	
	Milk (from allowance) in tea	
	Sugar as desired	
Supper	Meat or chicken or cheese 30 g (1 oz) OR fish 45 g (1½ oz) OR 1 large egg	7·0
	Salad or vegetables as at dinner	
	Potato 120 g (4 oz) OR bread 30 g (1 oz)	2·0
	Fresh or stewed fruit OR jelly OR protein-free pudding (see pudding list)	
	Milk (from allowance) in tea or coffee	
Bedtime	Milk (from allowance) in tea or coffee	

Foods allowed without restriction:

        Fruit, fruit juice, sugar, boiled sweets.
        Jam, marmalade, honey, syrup
        Protein-free products
        Double cream, butter, margarine, cooking
          fats and oils

MILK   Daily allowance 280 ml (10 oz,
        $\frac{1}{2}$ pint)   9·0

                                       40·0

The ratio of animal protein: vegetable protein in the above diet is 3:1 and this is generally suitable. The basic menu is between 5 and 6·8 MJ (1200 and 1500 kcal) and additional energy must either be obtained by eating sweets, jams, cream and sugar in reasonable quantities or by making use of the protein-free products. Most patients enjoy a variety of all these foods. Patients who take sugar in beverages are less likely to encounter problems of energy insufficiency. It is especially important to ensure that young, active adult patients receive sufficient energy (Table I).

3   Severe renal impairment

The Giovannetti-Giordano diet   At this point in the progress of chronic renal disease the dietetic aims are to preserve as far as possible the well-being of the patient. The Giovannetti diet or a modified version is designed to decrease the uraemia and/or hold it at reasonable levels, such that the symptoms are reduced and held in abeyance.

The important components of this dietary regime are protein, energy, sodium, potassium, fluids and vitamins; these will be discussed in turn.

(a) Protein   It is logical to restrict the protein in the diet still further in order to decrease the production of urea, since urea is formed from essential protein turnover and surplus dietary protein. To reduce the anaemia quickly a protein-free diet would appear to be suitable, but in fact this leads to breakdown of the patient's own body muscle to cover essential daily requirements of protein and this in turn increases the blood urea.

Rose and others have determined the minimum quantities per day of all the essential amino-acids that are necessary for an average adult man. This reference pattern of amino-acids is given a score of 100, and other proteins may be compared with these quantities of essential amino-acids. Thus by comparing the quantity of each amino-acid in the given protein food to this reference pattern, they may be given a protein score out of 100. The amino-acid which *least* satisfies the reference pattern is called the limiting amino-acid. *For example* – in beef tryptophan is found to be the limiting amino-acid and has a value of 75, as opposed to 90 in the reference pattern; hence the protein score = 75/90 x 100 = 83. Similarly for wheat, lysine is the limiting amino-acid and the protein score is found to be 47. It is not yet clear whether these data derived from studies in normal individuals, can be applied without reservations to patients with uraemia. Some relatively non-essential amino-acids may become essential in uraemia (for example histidine) while on the other hand uraemic patients are more efficient in recycling their nitrogen.

The following Table VI gives protein scores for various foods, together with their limiting amino-acid.

A mixture of the poor protein foods will combine to give the equivalent of the ideal protein, but with many spare amino-acids, e.g. a diet based on pulses (peas etc.) and wheat products for the staple foods is quite adequate for healthy people, provided they are taken in sufficient quantities. All excess amino-acids are deaminated and hence a great deal of urea is formed. In chronic renal failure the aim is to reduce the production of urea to a minimum, and so the patient must be given protein as near as possible in quality to the reference protein, thus covering essential protein needs and, at the same time, keeping the production of urea to a minimum.

An Italian, Giordano, applied these ideas, feeding patients in chronic renal failure diets based on synthetic amino-acids. Giovannetti and his colleagues applied a more practical low-protein diet which is now usually referred to as the Giovannetti diet. Protein was given in the form of eggs and energy supplied using maize, flour and wheat starch, as spaghetti, wafers, puddings and biscuits, fats, oils, sugars, fruits and vegetables. In Manchester Berlyne and his colleagues adapted the Italian diet to suit the English palate with the substitution of $6\frac{1}{2}$ oz milk for one of the eggs and the introduction of protein-free bread as a staple to replace the spaghetti. It is this pattern that is generally used in Great Britain today and the form given below is similar to those in general use.

Table VI DIFFERENT PROTEIN SOURCES AND THEIR PROTEIN SCORES

Item	Protein score	Limiting amino-acid
Animal Proteins:		
Egg	100	–
Beef	83	Tryptophan
Milk	78	Sulphur amino-acids
Fish	70	Sulphur amino-acids
Vegetable Proteins:		
Rice	72	Sulphur amino-acids
Peas	58	Sulphur amino-acids
Potato	56	Tyrosine
White flour	47	Lysine
Cassava	2	Sulphur amino-acids

20 g Protein, Modified Giovannetti Diet

Early morning Tea, if desired. Milk from daily allowance.

Breakfast Fruit or fruit juice with sugar.
Protein-free bread, fried or toasted.
Butter, marmalade, jam or honey (see breakfast list)
Tea or coffee
Sugar as desired

Mid-morning Tea, coffee, or fruit drink
Protein-free biscuits (see biscuit recipes)

Lunch Protein-free soup, vegetables, salad or vegetable dish (see savoury recipes)
Potato or rice from allowance
Protein-free pasta as desired
Fruit or pudding (see pudding recipes)
Tea, coffee or fruit drink

Tea Tea or fruit drink
Protein-free cake or biscuits (see biscuit recipes)

Supper As for lunch

Bedtime Tea or fruit drink
Protein-free biscuits (see biscuit recipes)

The following must be taken daily:

1 large egg, poached, boiled, fried, scrambled, made into an omelette, hard-boiled or used as in the recipes.

200 ml (7 oz) milk = $\frac{1}{3}$ pint, to be used in drinks or cooked dishes.

140 g (5 oz) potato, boiled or mashed OR 90 g (3 oz) roast potato OR 70 g ($2\frac{1}{2}$ oz) chips OR 90 g (3 oz) boiled rice (cooked weight).

Other foods allowed:

Protein-free bread, cakes, pastries and biscuits

Protein-free pasta

All fats, including butter, margarine, lard, vegetable oils and double cream

Salad or vegetables, EXCEPT peas, lentils, broad beans, butter beans, baked beans and haricot beans.

Fruit

Fruit drink, lemonade, Lucozade, Hycal, tea and coffee.

Sugar, glucose, Caloreen, jam, honey, marmalade, syrup and boiled sweets.

Vinegar, spices and herbs.

Unsuitable foods:

Meat, fish and cheese of all kinds

Ordinary bread, biscuits, cakes, pudding, other products containing flour, breakfast cereals and porridge.

Nuts, soya flour, peanut butter, marzipan, chocolate, ice cream, liquorice, Bovril, Oxo, Marmite, etc.

The one large egg and 200 ml ($\frac{1}{3}$ pint) milk provide the essential amino-acids for an adult/day. This is approximately equivalent to 14 g protein. One large egg must be taken daily, milk may be exchanged for a second egg or occasionally for 1 oz meat or $1\frac{1}{2}$ oz fish, or, if the diet is not salt restricted, 1 oz cheese. These protein foods, together with 5 oz potato or equivalent and the traces of protein in fruit and vegetables gives an average total daily intake of 18 – 20 g protein. This is the lowest level at which a 70 kg man can maintain protein equilibrium. Protein restriction is not usually applied to children since it is vital to maintain growth. An intake of 1 g protein/kg/day is the usual minimum, and this should be protein of high biological value as far as possible. Energy intake is even more important in children than in adults, since growth rate is directly related to energy intake. To achieve normal, or near normal growth in uraemic children the already high energy intake of the child (about 400 kJ/kg/day (90 kcal/kg/day)) must be increased still further, to 500 kJ/kg/day (120 kcal/kg/day).

If there is marked proteinuria additional protein must be given to replace that which is lost. For every $3\frac{1}{2}$ g protein lost in the urine/24 hours an additional half a large egg per day must be given.

Similarly at higher glomerular filtration rates, when the body can excrete more than 6 g urea per day, a slightly increased protein intake may be allowed once the urea levels have fallen to reasonable units — say 100 mg/100 ml. The urine excretion/day x 3 may be used as a guide to the protein intake which may be employed, e.g. 10 g urea/day will permit the use of 30 g protein without a rise in blood urea. An increase to 27 or 35 g protein/day greatly improves the palatability and ease of preparation of the diet, as meat and fish may be allowed as exchanges (Table II). At these levels wheat and other vegetable protein should still be excluded and all additional protein given as meat, fish, eggs, milk and, if sodium restrictions allow, cheese (see Nephrotic Syndrome for exchanges). The following diet sheet gives such an example.

Augmented Giovannetti Diet
35 g Protein, including 5 g Protein from vegetable sources

		Protein (g)
Early morning	Tea, if desired (milk from daily allowance)	
Breakfast	Fruit or fruit juice with sugar	
	1 egg (60 g) cooked as desired	7·0
	Protein-free bread, fried or toasted	
	Butter, marmalade, jam or honey	
	Tea or coffee	
	Sugar as desired	
Lunch	Protein-free soup, if desired (see soup recipes)	
	30 g (1 oz) meat OR 45 g ($1\frac{1}{2}$ oz) fish OR 60 g (cooked weights) 1 egg	7·0
	Vegetables, salad or vegetable dish	
	Fruit or pudding	
Tea	Tea or fruit drink	
	Protein-free bread, cake or biscuits	
Supper	30 g (1 oz) meat OR 45 g ($1\frac{1}{2}$ oz) fish OR 60 g, 1 egg	7·0
	Potato or rice from allowance	
	Protein-free pasta as desired	
	Vegetables, salad or vegetable dish	
	Fruit or pudding	

Bedtime	Tea or fruit drink	
	Protein-free biscuits	
Milk allowance	200 ml (7 oz, $\frac{1}{3}$ pint)	7·0
	140 g (5 oz) potato and protein in	
	fruit and vegetables	5·0
		33·0

Ways of using your protein allowance which must be taken daily
> 3 eggs or meat or fish equivalent, cooked as desired
> Eggs may be poached, boiled, fried, scrambled, made into an omelette or used as in recipes.
> 200 ml (7 oz) milk = $\frac{1}{3}$ pint to be used in drinks or cooked dishes. This may be exchanged for 1 large egg if desired.
> 140 g (5 oz) potato, boiled or mashed, OR 90 g (3 oz) roast potato OR 70 g ($2\frac{1}{2}$ oz) chips OR 90 g (3 oz) boiled rice (cooked weight).

Other foods allowed
> Protein-free bread, cakes, pastries and biscuits
> Protein-free pasta
> All fats, including butter, margarine, lard, vegetable oils and double cream.
> Salad or vegetable, EXCEPT peas, lentils, broad beans, butter beans, baked beans and haricot beans.
> Fruit
> Fruit drinks, lemonade, Lucozade, Hycal, tea and coffee.
> Sugar, glucose, Caloreen, jam, honey, marmalade, syrups and boiled sweets.
> Vinegar, spices and herbs.

Unsuitable foods
> Ordinary bread, biscuits, cakes, pudding, other products containing flour, breakfast cereals and porridge.
> Nuts, soya flour, peanut butter, marzipan, chocolate, ice cream, liquorice, Bovril, Oxo, Marmite, etc.

Fluids
> You will be told how much fluid you may take.

(b) Energy Unless sufficient energy is given, the protein foods will be directed to energy needs, nitrogen released, the urea will rise and the benefit of the careful protein restriction lost. Energy must be supplied

at all times from the high energy food allowed. Thus, as well as the essential protein (egg and milk) it is also vital that sufficient energy is eaten every day.

Ordinary bread and wheat products must be excluded owing to their significant protein content and their low protein score. Energy must, therefore, be supplied by fruits, sugars, fats and specialized protein products, such as bread, biscuits and pasta made from wheat starch. This is the principal problem of the diet.

Specialized protein-free products available on prescription to these patients at present include flour, bread, biscuits, pasta and high energy "sugars".

The incorporation of these specialized foods into what is so often a dull diet needs careful planning and a good cook. With these a varied, appetising and high energy diet can be served. In hospital much encouragement must be given to the patient to eat what are generally unfamiliar and unknown foods and, for the patient at home, discussion about the diet with the cook of the family is essential.

Fruits and vegetables are used to give variety, as vehicles for sugars and fats and as the basis of many savoury and sweet dishes.

Protein-free flour may be used to make bread and biscuits, in a wide variety of soups, savoury vegetable sauces, pastries (for example flans and pies, both savoury and sweet) and numerous puddings. High energy, protein-free puddings can easily be adapted from ordinary recipes and may often be enjoyed by the whole family, thus eliminating the necessity for specialized cooking for every dish.

Protein-free bread, which tends to be crumbly and uninteresting, is far more appetizing if served in the following manner:

(1)   Toasted, buttered when hot and spread with liberal amounts of jam, honey, marmalade or other preserve.

(2)   Fried and served with grilled or fried tomatoes or mushrooms, if at breakfast, or with fried vegetables at a main meal.

Various protein-free biscuits may be made using wheat starch, fats and sugar, apart from the manufactured ones. Home made biscuits are more interesting if flavoured before cooking with spices, e.g. cinnamon or fruit flavours, e.g. lemon juice and rind, or topped with whipped double cream, icing or jam before serving.

All protein-free puddings are relatively high in energy and are as such useful in the Giovannetti diet. When extra energy is required plain fruit may be served with Caloreen added, without increasing the sweetness. 30 g (1 oz) Caloreen per serving (120 g, 4 oz) is a suitable amount and this adds 500 kJ (120 kcal). Caloreen may also be added to other sweets and beverages in a similar manner. Caloreen may also be used in protein-free ice creams, water ices, puddings and confectionery items. A very good book of recipes using this product entitled "Caloreen" may be obtained from Milner Scientific (for address see Caloreen details). It contains a collection of recipes devised by Manchester Royal Infirmary Dietetic Department, who did the experimental work on this product.

Table VII COMPOSITION OF ENERGY SUPPLEMENT FOR PATIENTS IN CHRONIC RENAL FAILURE AND ON REGULAR DIALYSIS

	Energy (kJ)	*Protein* (g)	Ca^{++} (mg)	Fe (mg)	Na^+ (nmol)	K^+ (nmol)	PO_4 (mg)
250 ml milk	69	8·5	300	0·20	5	10	244
80 ml Caloreen ®	1510	–	–	–	–	–	–
55 ml double cream	1090	1·0	28	0·12	1	2	12
1 egg	390	6·8	32	1·44	3	2	124
TOTAL in 274 ml	3680	16·3	360	1·76	9	14	380
	(877 kcal)	(add Nesquik ® to flavour)					

OR Minus egg
   Plus Carnation Instant Breakfast Food (Slender ®)

	Energy (kJ)	*Protein* (g)	Ca^{++} (mg)	Fe (mg)	Na^+ (nmol)	K^+ (nmol)	PO_4 (mg)
	55	8·5	313	4·00	5	9	244
TOTAL in 274 ml	3840	18·0	641	4·32	11	21	500
	(915 kcal)						

Hycal makes a very good jelly and is best if diluted with 1 part water 2 parts Hycal. Similarly it may be deep frozen to make lollipops and in this form is popular with children. The concentrated liquid is generally more acceptable if served chilled as it is less sweet. Hycal also make a very good ice cream.

Double cream is a pleasure for these patients and although it contains a trace of protein its high energy value and high acceptability far out-weighs the disadvantages of the small addition of milk protein. It may be used in numerous dishes, apart from the obvious forms of cream on fruit and in coffee. A double cream and water mixture makes an ideal milk substitute for the preparation of milk puddings and custard. Ingenious cooks will be quick to realize its potentialities in savoury dishes also – a vegetable stew cooked slowly in the oven in a cream and stock mixture can be truly delicious.

Alcohol is another good source of energy for these patients and when fluids are not restricted may be enjoyed in the usual manner. However, it can also play an important part in creating variety in savoury and sweet dishes as the addition of wine, beer, spirit or liqueurs can completely alter the flavour of a simple dish.

The menu outlined for the basic Giovannetti is suitable when the patient feels well, but when he is unable to eat solids these foods must be given in other forms. The egg and milk may be given either in a flip or the egg lightly cooked and the milk taken as a drink. Energy must still be supplied and high energy fluids must be given. Hycal and Caloreen are useful – four bottles Hycal or 330 – 420 g (12 – 15 oz) of Caloreen will cover the patient's requirements. It is difficult to achieve the very high energy intakes needed for growth in children. Apart from encouraging the intake of high energy foods which are palatable (such as double cream and boiled sweets) the most practical approach is to allow a relatively normal diet and feed extra energy as an energy supplement which is prescribed and taken as a medicine rather than a food. Surprisingly this does not depress appetite for ordinary foods and energy intake can be supplemented. The composition of such an energy supplement is given in Table VII. So that it can also be used for children on regular haemodialysis, it has been designed as a low-volume and low-electrolyte source of energy; for the child in uraemia and a normal or supranormal urine output, it may be diluted if needed.

3   Salt

Some patients on Giovannetti diets are salt losers and additional salt over and above that used in cooking may be prescribed (Chapter VI).

Alternatively the patient may show oedema with or without hypertension and sodium intake may need to be restricted. On a normal 20 g protein Giovannetti diet no high sodium foods (see Table V) are allowed. The restriction of the intake of sodium therefore may fall on three parts of the diet:

(a)   salt in cooking
(b)   salt in the bread and other flour products
(c)   salt in butter, margarine and other fats

Table IV (in the section on the Nephrotic Syndrome) gives approximate sodium intakes with varying degrees of restriction. On this restricted protein allowance, the sodium intakes will come at the lower end of the ranges given.

Too vigorous salt restriction may cause anorexia, disinclination to eat and a poor energy intake. An intake of 30-34 mmol is often suitable for quite severe hypertension or oedema and unlike 15 mmol a day, can be tolerated for quite long periods.

4 Potassium

Patients with advanced renal failure tend to have high potassium levels in the blood. This may often be controlled by restricting the potassium content of foods eaten. The Giovannetti diet itself tends to raise the plasma potassium. Potassium is found in the majority of foods, but always in association with proteins, of which milk per gram of protein has the most. The other rich sources of potassium include fruits and vegetables, of which potatoes and nuts are particularly high. Certain other products like tomato juice, dried figs, dates, chocolates, dried milk preparations, instant coffee and savoury flavourings are all high in potassium.

In a potassium restricted Giovannetti diet the protein foods are constant, the eggs and milk yielding about 10 mmol potassium. The potatoes in a potassium restricted diet should always be boiled well in large volumes of water for 10 minutes before chipping, frying or roasting, in order to leach out some of the potassium. Similarly, all vegetables should be boiled in large volumes of water and this water discarded; this is of course contrary to all good culinary advice and vitamin C retention techniques, but it does reduce the potassium content of vegetables significantly. For a mild potassium restriction the fruit and vegetables should be taken in normal amounts and those listed below (Table VIII) should be avoided.

Table VIII   HIGH POTASSIUM FOODS (OVER 6 mmol K$^+$/ PORTION)

Apricots
Avocado Pears
Bananas
Cherries
Currants, black or red
Currants, dried
Damsons
Dates
Figs, green or dried
Grapes, black or white
Greengages, fresh
Mangos
Melon
Oranges
Peaches, fresh
Pineapple, fresh
Prunes
Raisins
Raspberries, raw
Rhubarb
Sultanas

Nuts, all types

Artichokes, Jerusalem
Aubergines
Brussel Sprouts
Celery, raw
Leeks
Mushrooms
Spinach
Peppers, red and green

In addition the following should be avoided:

Fruit gums, chocolate, liquorice
Curry
Instant coffee, or ground coffee that has infused for more than 5
    minutes
Ribena, Bournvita, Bovril, Marmite, Nescafe, Ovaltine
Concentrated pure fruit juices, e.g.   Grapefruit
                                        Orange
                                        Pineapple
                                        Tomato
All Bran, Bemax, Grapenuts, Puffed Wheat, Ryvita
Sherries and Wines

Severe potassium restriction The Giovannetti diet, without any fruit or vegetables but including potato, yields about 28 mmol potassium. Hence, to keep the potassium intake to 30 mmol and still have a palatable menu, the potato must be exchanged for rice, which reduces the basic potassium intake to 18 mmol potassium. This leaves 12 mmol potassium for fruit and vegetables and this is equivalent to four (4 oz, 120 g) servings from the "low" list or two servings from the "moderate" list per day (Table IX).

A 4 oz, 120 g serving from the moderate list will have approximately 5 mmol and is approximately equivalent to 2 × 120 g (4 oz) servings from the "low" list.

This can be made tolerable by using non-fruit containing sweets, such as protein-free ice creams, water ices, jellies, cream and water milk puddings, so releasing the available potassium for use in vegetable dishes. This regime is obviously very restrictive and can only be used for short periods.

A more realistic figure for potassium restriction is 60 mmol, as this allows potatoes to be taken and up to ten servings of low fruit and vegetables each day, or the equivalent of "moderates". For example, a patient could have four servings of "low" and three of "moderate" fruits and vegetables. Care must be taken to include the potassium content of soups and sauces. When many different vegetables are used in a serving of soup or stew, it will contain approximately the same amount of potassium as one serving of "low" or "moderate" vegetable, depending on the type of vegetables used.

5 Fluids

In the large majority of patients benefiting from this regime, a large volume of urine of fixed low concentration may still be produced. High energy drinks such as fruit squashes, fizzy pop, Caloreen and Hycal are all useful as energy boosters at this stage. If and when the urine volume decreases, the fluid intake will have to be restricted and it is then that Hycal or concentrated Caloreen solution are most valuable. (Similarly when the patient feels unwell and is unable to take the protein-free high energy dishes previously suggested these two products are most useful).

6 Vitamins

This diet tends to be deficient in certain vitamins, especially those of the B group. It is usual to give vitamins therapeutically to prevent any deficiencies that might occur.

Table IX   POTASSIUM CONTENT OF FOODS

Low Potassium
(up to 4 mmol K/portion, 4 oz,
120 g) (Average 3 mmol K/
portion, 4 oz, 120 g)

Moderate Potassium
(4 - 6 mmol K/portion, 4 oz,
120 g) (Average 5 mmol K/
portion, 4 oz, 120 g)

Fruits

Low Potassium	Moderate Potassium
Apples	Blackberries
Cherries, glacé *only*	Gooseberries
Cranberries	Loganberries, stewed
Fruit salad, canned	Peaches, canned
Grapefruit	Plums
Lemons	Quinces
Loganberries, canned	Raspberries, stewed
Mandarins, canned	Strawberries
Olives	
Pears	
Pineapple, canned	
Tangerines	

Vegetables

Low Potassium	Moderate Potassium
Artichokes, globe	Beetroot
Asparagus	Corn on the cob
Beans, French or runner	Endive
Broccoli tops	Parsnips
Cabbage, raw or boiled	Tomato, 1 average, 60 g (2 oz)
Carrots	Turnips
Cauliflower	
Celery, boiled	
Chicory	
Cucumber	
Lettuce	
Marrow	
Mustard and Cress	
Onions, raw or boiled	
Radishes	
Seakale	
Spring greens	
Swedes	
Turnip tops	
Watercress	

VI THE PATIENT ON REGULAR HAEMODIALYSIS

The exact dietary intake for patients undergoing regular haemodialysis will depend on age, occupation, size, sex and the duration and frequency of dialyses. Patients dialysing in the home usually have three 10-hour dialyses each week and because of the shorter intervals between dialyses can take a fairly free diet. That is, the exact quantity of protein, salt and potassium taken each day are not critical. However, fluid intake must be carefully restricted, and some salty or potassium-rich foods must still be avoided. Some doctors limit the salt intake of all patients on haemodialysis, even when thrice weekly dialysis is performed. Patients having two 14-hour flat bed dialyses each week must take a more strictly controlled diet since the interval between dialyses is longer and the rise in the concentrations of metabolites (such as urea) is correspondingly greater.

A patient on haemodialysis must consider his protein, sodium, potassium, total fluid and energy intake. Each may be slightly varied from patient to patient and from time to time according to circumstances. These will be the same from day to day in the short term, although some dialysis units permit their patients to take any food they wish during the first few hours of each dialysis. This is especially appreciated by those on salt restricted diets, who may choose a meal containing bacon, sausages or baked beans; obviously this liberty must be watched carefully by those looking after the patients.

(i) Protein intake

The aim of protein regulation in the patient on regular haemodialysis is to maintain the products of nitrogen metabolism (such as urea, creatinine and many other compounds) within acceptable limits, and at the same time to maintain nitrogen equilibrium. In the early stages of dialysis a positive nitrogen balance will be aimed for, since many patients come onto dialysis after prolonged illnesses, often involving proteinuria, dietary protein restriction, peritoneal dialysis, inadequate energy intake or other factors associated with protein wasting. Their weight is subnormal and their muscles obviously wasted.

Most patients (adult) can take about 60 g protein per day, of which 14 g at least should be milk or eggs. Blood ureas tend to be lower (other factors being equal) if a higher proportion than this is protein of animal origin, with a high protein score (see Table VI). If the intake of protein is 60 g/day, 45 - 50 g should be of animal origin. The patient's intake can easily be constructed from the 7 g equivalents of eggs, milk, fish, meat, listed in Table II. The remaining 10 - 15 g/day may come from poorer vegetable protein sources such as bread, biscuits, cakes and potatoes. These may be given as equivalents of slices of bread (2 g protein) as in Table III.

This basic diet must be modified to suit special circumstances, e.g. an extra allowance for growth in children; opinions differ as to how much this should be but if 1 g/kg/day is taken as average for an adult, then at least 20% more on a weight for weight basis should be allowed for children. Difficulty may be encountered in the very ill patient, since if fluids or sodium are restricted then the whole protein intake cannot be as milk; egg flips in milk or protein supplements such as Casilan or Edosol may be added.

(ii)   Fluids

Fluid restriction is essential for the patient on haemodialysis, especially if the patient is anuric because of his disease or following nephrectomy. As a general guide three cups (500 ml) of fluid per day may be taken, plus the average value of urine passed per day; this is usually 200 – 500 ml. Juices served with fruit, gravies, sauces and soups MUST be counted as part of the allowance, which will rarely be more than 1000 ml/day and will often be 500 ml. Most patients prefer "dry" food so that they can enjoy all their fluid allowance as water, tea, coffee or fruit juice.

(iii)   Sodium

Almost all patients on regular dialysis require some limitation of their sodium intake. This must be especially strict in those with severe hypertension as part of their final illness before reaching dialysis. An intake of 30 mmol/day of sodium is generally suitable for these patients, and 60 mmol/day for those without initial hypertension. If very severe salt restriction is required, the lowest that can be attained with a protein intake of 60 g/day is 15 mmol, and this at the price of avoiding all salt foods, using no salt in cooking, and salt-free bread with salt-free butter. On a 30 mmol intake up to three slices of ordinary bread may be taken per day, or other salt-free exchanges listed in Table III. All the foods listed in Table IV must be avoided. Monotony may be avoided by the use of spices, herbs and salt-free flavourings. *On no account should salt substitutes be used, since many contain potassium and the patient should specifically be warned about this.* If 60 mmol of sodium per day are permitted then up to five slices of bread per day or equivalent (Table III) are allowed, and salt restricted diets are given in the section on Diet in the Treatment of Nephrotic Syndrome, above.

(iv) Potassium

Unlike salty foods, those high in potassium cannot be distinguished easily by the patient; the effects of potassium overload (cardiac arrest) appear without warning, and suddenly, whereas the overload, hypertension and oedema of sodium and water excess appear more slowly. It is therefore doubly important to emphasize high potassium foods to the patient. When twice weekly dialysis is performed, an intake of 60 mmol/day of potassium is usually suitable. The protein intake discussed above contributes about 45 mmol of potassium per day, leaving 15 mmol for fruit, vegetables and beverages. In presenting the problem of potassium to the patient it is convenient to divide foods into low, moderate and high potassium foods (Tables VIII, IX). This 15 mmol may be taken as five servings of a low potassium food, or three of the moderate potassium foods; the high potassium foods are best avoided. At all times the amount of potassium in vegetables may be reduced by cooking all in large volumes of water, discarding the liquor; this particularly applies to potatoes which should always be treated in this fashion before roasting or frying. If the plasma potassium is already high, Calcium Resonium or other ion exchange resins may be given to remove potassium; these are not routinely necessary if high potassium foods are avoided.

One problem of particular relevance is the celebration of Christmas. Most of the foods commonly taken at this time in Britain are rich in potassium and great care must be exercised. Table X includes some general points about Christmas foods.

(v) Energy

Breakdown of endogenous protein, such as muscle, may take place if the energy intake is too low. For optimum health on dialysis 170 - 210 kJ/kg (40 - 50 kcal/kg) ideal body weight/day has been suggested as the intake to aim for. This is particularly true of the early phase on dialysis, when many patients are still catabolic and are breaking down their own tissue proteins and thus raising their blood ureas still further. Energy can be augmented by taking all forms of sugars — jams, marmalade, honey and sweets (except chocolates) — and fats, such as butter, margarine, double cream or Prosparol. All these foods are rich in energy but are relatively low in protein, and contain little sodium or potassium. The special high energy, electrolyte-free foods mentioned in the section on chronic renal failure may also be used. Caloreen is perhaps the most useful of these. Patients should be encouraged to sprinkle extra sugar on their food, and to spread butter and jams thickly. Double cream may be used in coffee or on puddings. Fried foods are generally more

Table X WHAT TO DO ABOUT CHRISTMAS

Meats	Have turkey or your usual Christmas meat. Go easy on the stuffings and try to avoid sausages, sausage meat, salt meats and fishes.
Vegetables	Keep down the number of roast potatoes. See potassium list for vegetables.
Pudding	Take Christmas pudding (small) instead of your usual fruit or pudding, with brandy or rum butter and/or cream instead of thick sauces.
Mince pies	Can replace your usual fruit or pudding or instead of cake.
Cake	Have one small piece.
Sweets	Take boiled sweets, pastilles, jellied fruits, crystallized fruit, fondants, marshmallows, peppermint creams, *rather than* chocolate.
Nuts	Avoid *all* salted nuts. All nuts are very high in potassium. Walnuts, cob-nuts and peanuts (unsalted) are best.
Savouries	Remember nearly all cocktail savouries contain lots of salt.
Drinks	"Shorts" (i.e. spirits) are better than beer or cider.

tasty than those boiled, and especially on low sodium intakes this may augment energy intake by the fat incorporated in the food. Children on regular haemodialysis present the same problems with regard to energy intake and growth as children in uraemia who still have renal function, with the added restrictions of limited fluid and electrolyte intake. The same strategy as discussed on p. 205 is used, and the energy supplement outlined in Table VII employed.

(vi) Vitamins and minerals

Since fruits and other foods with a high vitamin content may be excluded from the diet by their high potassium content and vegetables preboiled, the intake of many vitamins may be low in patients on dialysis. The dialysis itself also removes quantities of water soluble vitamins. It is therefore usual to give vitamin supplements, including the B vitamins and folic acid.

The minerals which need most consideration are phosphate and iron. Phosphate may be dangerous in some patients in that it leads to metastatic calcification in patients with secondary hyperparathyroidism and a high serum calcium concentration. Other features may be arthritis and itching and sore eyes from deposits of calcium phosphate (see Chapter VI). Aluminium hydroxide gel may therefore be given to diminish the absorption of phosphate, or foods rich in phosphate reduced. Since these are also those rich in protein it is general to use the gel rather than reducing protein intake.

Iron is poorly absorbed by patients in chronic renal failure, both on and off dialysis. It is rarely possible to correct the anaemia by oral iron administration, although some doctors give this as a routine; generally intravenous iron will be needed.

A typical diet for a patient on regular dialysis might be:

DIET FOR A PATIENT ON REGULAR HAEMODIALYSIS

60 g Protein, 30 mmol Sodium, 60 mmol Potassium. No Salt in cooking. (8·8 - 13 MJ (2 - 2·5 kcal)) 500 ml fluid allowance (= 3 cups)

		Protein (g)
Early morning	Tea if desired. Milk from daily allowance	
Breakfast	Grapefruit (tinned or fresh) with sugar	
	1 egg 60 g (2 oz)	7·0
	Bread, fried, plain or toasted 60 g (2 oz)	4·0
	Salt-free butter. Marmalade, jam or honey	
	Tea or ground coffee	
	Sugar as desired	
Mid-morning	Tea or ground coffee	
Lunch	75 g (2½ oz) meat or 105 g (3¾ oz) fish or 150 g, 2½ eggs.	17·5
No salt in cooking	120 g (4 oz) potato or 90 g (3 oz) rice + salt-free butter	2·0
	Vegetables or salad	
	7 oz milk pudding or equivalent (see Animal Protein List)	7·0
	Double cream and sugar	
	Tea or ground coffee	

Tea	Tea 30 g (1 oz) bread or 30 g (1 oz) biscuits or 30 g (1 oz) cake – made without added salt. + Salt-free butter, jam, cream.	2·0
Supper No salt in cooking	⎰ 60 g (2 oz) meat or 90 g (3 oz) ⎱ fish or 120 g (2) eggs. ⎰ 120 g (4 oz) potato or 90 g (3 oz) ⎱ rice + salt-free butter. Vegetables or salad Sweet fruit with double cream and sugar Tea or ground coffee	14·0 2·0
Bedtime	Tea or ground coffee	
Milk allowance	100 ml (3½ oz) (= ½ cup)	

The following must be taken daily

7 oz meat or alternative, as allocated
(see Animal Protein List).
8 oz boiled potato or low-salt alternative
(see Vegetable Exchange List).
3 oz bread as allocated or alternative
(see Vegetable Exchange List).
Five servings of fruit and vegetables per
day if taken from the low group, or
equivalent moderate servings.

———
59·0
———

Other foods allowed

As much as
possible
{

Sugar, glucose, Caloreen, jam, honey, marmalade,
Golden Syrup, boiled sweets, peppermint, fruit
pastilles, home-made toffee.
Arrowroot, cornflour, jelly, sago, tapioca, wheat,
starch.
All fats including butter, margarine, lard, vegetable
oils, suet and double cream.
All protein-free products, e.g. protein-free bread,
biscuits, pastries and pasta.

Mustard, pepper, vinegar, ginger, herbs and spices
(NOT curry).

Tea, ground coffee, home-made lemonade, fruit drinks, and squashes (NOT fruit juices), Hycal, Lucozade.

Schweppes minerals: American Sweet Ginger; Bitter Lemon, Dry Ginger, Lemonade, Orange Sparkling Golden, Tonic water.

Spirits, champagnes, Chianti, port.

Unsuitable foods

Foods which contain large amounts of salt or potassium must be avoided. Lists will be given describing those foods which MUST NOT BE TAKEN.

The following foods should also be avoided:

All-Bran, Bemax, Grapenuts, Ryvita.

Curry, black treacle.

Chocolate, Fruit Gums, ice cream, liquorice.

Bournvita, Barmene, Bovril, Horlicks, instant coffee, Marmite, Nescafe, Ovaltine, Ribena.

Fruit juices, e.g. Schweppes fruit juices – grapefruit, orange, pineapple, tomato.

Also beers, cider, stout, sherry and wine.

Salt substitutes and low sodium preparatory foods generally contain large amounts of potassium and MUST NOT BE USED.

Obviously diets must be varied to suit each patient's tastes. The commonest fault is to reduce intake because the diet is found monotonous with resultant tissue breakdown, weight loss and increase in blood urea. The use of suitable spices and flavours can help a great deal to make the diet acceptable. Especially is this true during periods of relative ill-health.

VII INTRAVENOUS NUTRITION

When the patient is incapable of ingesting food by the normal gastro-intestinal route, because of unconsciousness, local disease of the gut, or because the nutritional requirements for energy are too high to be met with by the ordinary route, then feeding by intravenous drip may be needed. Until relatively recently, only water and electrolytes were given by this route, but it is now possible to feed patients for months on end if necessary, entirely by the intravenous route.

Access to the circulation

Often a central venous line is used (see Chapter XIII) especially if strong glucose is to be infused. However, renal patients often have access to their circulation, such as arteriovenous shunts or fistulae, or feeding may take place during dialysis, when the infusion may be put into the venous line connecting the dialyser to the patient. If the arteriovenous shunt is to be used for feeding, then a T-tube may be inserted into the shunt instead of the usual PTFE connector. The drip for feeding is connected to the side-arm of the tube. T-tubes of this type are commercially available, pre-sterilized. A-V fistulae must be needled for use between dialyses, and a pump will be necessary on the drip to drive the infusion, because of the high pressure in the arterialized veins of the fistula, which approaches that of the arterial system. Pumped intravenous infusions *must* be monitored mechanically or visually.

If a central venous line is used care must be employed if this remains *in situ* longer than about a week. It seems certain that there is a higher incidence of infection of the catheter tip and consequent septicaemia if the right atrial line is used for intravenous feeding. Infections with *candida* may be seen with particular frequency, perhaps because of the glucose infusions used, but bacterial infections can be equally deadly.

Solutions used

The basic requirements for intravenous nutrition are for energy, and for protein (or amino-acids). Vitamins will also need to be given, especially if the patient is very ill or the intravenous feeding prolonged. Patients often become deficient in phosphate during prolonged i.v. feeding. *Energy* is usually supplied in the form of carbohydrate solutions or fat emulsions. Glucose has the advantage of being the physiological sugar requiring no conversion before it can be used by the tissues. It is the only sugar which the brain can utilize. It has several disadvantages, however. First, strong glucose solutions of the type needed to supply enough energy are very irritant and can only be fed into situations of high flow such as AV fistulae, shunts or the right atrium; they cannot be used for prolonged periods into peripheral veins without the risk of thrombosing the vessel. Adding heparin seems to have little effect upon the incidence of thrombosis. Second, the blood glucose is immediately raised during infusion of strong glucose, and even in patients without overt diabetes mellitus the stresses of the illness requiring the intravenous nutrition together with the carbohydrate load may reveal carbohydrate intolerance with a sudden rise in the concentration of glucose in the blood to 50 mmol/l or above, and the need for urgent insulin administration. In patients with known diabetes the glucose will have to be "covered" with insulin.

These disadvantages have led to the use of other sources, such as the sugar, fructose, and the alcohol sorbitol. Ethyl alcohol itself is also a useful energy source, giving more energy per gram than sugars (29 kJ (7 kcal)) compared with 19 kJ (4·5 kcal) per gram. Fructose and sorbitol have the disadvantage that they must be converted to glucose in the body before the tissues (especially the brain) can utilize them. This is a disadvantage when there is any liver dysfunction, because the conversion takes place in the liver; but has the advantage that the changes in blood glucose are less abrupt, and stress insulin production less violently as they are converted to glucose. None are as irritant on peripheral veins as glucose, but this is less of an advantage in renal patients requiring intravenous feeding since so many of them are in acute renal failure and already have access to their circulations, i.e. fistulae or shunts.

Fat emulsions can give greater energy in more concentrated form, since the burning of one gram of fat gives 38 kJ (9 kcal), twice that of one gram of carbohydrate. The early fat emulsions showed many unwanted side-effects, including rigors and platelet consumption, but modern products with controlled size of fat particles have no such disadvantages. These emulsions stress the ability of the liver to clear fat from the blood, just as glucose solutions stress the pancreas, and high levels of triglycerides in the blood are usual during feeding with fat emulsions. However, as much as 8·5 MJ (2000 kcal) may be obtainable from one litre of emulsion, which makes them attractive in situations where fluid intake may be limited, such as in acute renal failure.

Protein and *amino-acids* may be used to supply protein. Whole plasma protein is useful but carries a greater risk of transmitting hepatitis B even when prepared from tested donors, since it is a product which is pooled from many donors. It may be given as single, double or even triple strength plasma although this is rarely necessary for nutritional purposes. More commonly amino-acid solutions are given. These may be hydrolysates of first class proteins such as casein and, in this case, contain non-essential as well as essential amino-acids. Alternatively, mixtures of synthetic amino-acids may be used which allows the mixture to contain only essential amino-acids. There is some evidence that nitrogen balance in patients given only essential amino-acids as a source of nitrogen is better than patients given mixed essential and non-essential amino-acids.

Solutions containing both energy sources and amino-acids are commercially available, the energy source being carbohydrate such as glucose, fructose, alcohol or sorbitol, with added amino-acids. Fat emulsions in contrast, cannot be mixed with other solutions. Care must be taken in adding drugs to intravenous feeding solutions since some are incompatible and will precipitate, whilst others may be wholly or partially inactivated. In general it is better to use aqueous solutions for administering drugs, especially if the rate of the drip must be varied to give different rates of administration.

In general, also, it is better to use single solutions to provide energy and nitrogen, constructing the daily intake to fall within the allowable fluid intake. A typical day's intake might be 8·5 – 13 MJ (2000 – 3000 kcal) as glucose and fat emulsion, and 60 g of nitrogen as amino-acid mixtures, all in a volume of 1500 ml. The choice of individual solutions will be made by the doctor, and what intake may be necessary.

When intravenous solutions are given during dialysis it is better to give them into the bubble trap of the dialyser, or into the venous line, than into the arterial side of the circulation. This applies especially to amino-acids, which being water-soluble are readily dialysable. As usual, suitable precautions to avoid air embolism must be taken whenever any intravenous infusion is attached to a haemodialysis circuit; these will vary according to the system used.

Finally the energy intake obtained by peritoneal dialysis must not be forgotten. Each litre of 1·36 g/dl glucose dialysing fluid is equivalent to an intravenous injection of 10g of glucose while the stronger 6·36 g/dl solutions gives 25 g of glucose approximately.

ACKNOWLEDGEMENTS

Many of the recipes are based upon those given us by patients and other colleagues both at Guy's and elsewhere. We wish to thank in particular

    Miss Cave and the Department at University College Hospital
    Miss Young and the Department at Withington Hospital, Manchester
    Miss Fowell and the Department at St Mary's Hospital, Portsmouth.

Suggestions for further reading:
    Berlyne, G. M. (ed.) (1967). *Nutrition in Renal Disease.* Edinburgh: Churchill Livingstone.
    Betts, P. R., Macgrath, C. (1974). Growth pattern and dietary intake of children with chronic renal insufficiency. *British Medical Journal,* 2, 189.

Chantler, C., Holliday, M. (1973). Growth in children with renal disease with particular reference to the effects of calorie malnutrition. *Clinical Nephrology*, 1, 230.

David, D. S., Hochgelernt, E., Rubin, A., Stenzel, K. H. (1972). Dietary management in renal failure. *Lancet*, ii, 34.

Harries, J. T. (1971). Intravenous feeding in infants. *Archives of Disease in Childhood*, 46, 855.

Lee, H. A. (1974) *Parenteral Nutrition in Acute Metabolic Illness.* New York: Academic Press.

CHAPTER XIII

Electrolytes and fluid balance

As outlined in Chapter I, the kidneys are the most important organ in maintaining the volume and composition of the body fluids constant. It is not surprising that disorders of electrolyte and water metabolism are often the result of renal disease, and this is evident from the discussion of symptoms and signs in Chapters II - VIII. In this Chapter we draw together these different pieces of information and consider them from the point of view of the whole body.

Many people find electrolytes and water metabolism difficult to understand, and the clinical applications in treatment confusing. In fact, the principles and practice are very simple.

In every situation of disease or health, there are two aspects to consider:

(1)   what is the present state? What is the volume and composition of the body fluids at this point in time?

(2)   what is the present balance? How did the abnormalities (if any are present) arise, in terms of input and output?

this leads on to a third:

(3)   what must we do to restore balance, correct the abnormalities and cope with the continuing situation?

I WATER

Normally, about 70% of the body's weight is water. As pointed out at several points in the text, weight in the short term (hours or days) gives a very accurate idea of changes in total body water. For an adult this will be some 40 litres. The fatter the person, the smaller the proportion of the body weight is water. Thus, women have a rather smaller proportion of their total body weight as water, and infants a considerably smaller proportion – perhaps no more than 50 - 55%. In the obese, and in the very young, it is also more difficult to assess hydration clinically because of the excess fat.

Most of this water is within cells (Figure 13.1) the remainder being
extracellular. One special compartment of the extracellular water is the
plasma, which is distinguished by its high protein concentration. This
protein, especially albumin, protects by its osmotic pressure the volume
of this small but vital compartment, by attracting water into the plasma
and keeping it there. This is vital since without volume, the circulation
cannot be maintained (Figure 13.2).

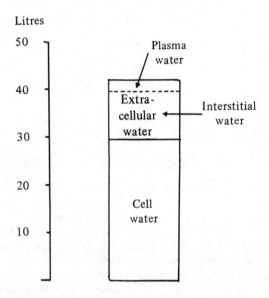

Fig. 13.1   Body water. The body is 70% water so that a 60 kg adult
contains about 42 litres of water. Most of this lies within the cells
(intracellular water) is close association with a high concentration of
protein. The remainder lies outside the cells (extracellular water)
either in the plasma (plasma water) or between the cells (interstitial
water. Note the small proportion of water in the plasma compared
with that inside the cells, and remember that all the cell's input of
metabolic fuel and output of metabolic waste products must first
reach the interstitial water and then be transported in the plasma
water. Although only a small proportion of the extracellular water,
the plasma water is maintained constant even when the interstitial
water volume contracts, because the oncotic pressure of the proteins (especially albumin) present in the plasma water in high concentration attract water into the intravascular space (plasma water).

The cellular water is also vital for metabolism to continue; the water between cells and outside the plasma (the interstitial water) simply acts as a buffer, providing water to plasma and cells, or accepting it from them. It is the volume in this space that we assess clinically when we examine the patient. The body has receptors in vessel walls which provide information on the volume of water within the circulation, and each cell obtains information on the amount of water within it, by the amount of solute in the cell water (osmotic pressure) within the cell compared with that outside the cell. There are *no* receptors in the interstitial water between the cells. Much larger fluctuations can occur in the amount of this interstitial water without changes in circulation and metabolism, which allows it to act as a reserve, to minimize the effects of changes in total body water on plasma water and cell water.

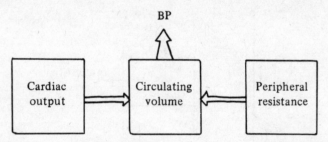

Fig. 13.2 The maintenance of blood pressure. The pressure within the arterial side of the circulation is the product of the action of both the cardiac output and the peripheral vascular resistance upon the circulating volume. If alterations in one of the three components occur, normally the cardiovascular reflexes will operate to minimize the effect on the perfusion pressure (the arterial blood pressure). For example, peripheral dilatation is normally accompanied by an increase in cardiac output, mostly achieved by raising the heart rate. If the circulating volume falls, from saline loss or blood loss, then there will be both tachycardia and peripheral constriction. In heart failure there may be a low blood pressure because of low cardiac output, with constriction of the periphery to maintain the blood pressure. Here, the *total* circulating volume may be normal or even increased; the problem is that the *venous* side of the circulation is overloaded, whilst perfusion of tissues is impaired.

The clinical assessment of volume is very inaccurate: changes of at least 10% must take place before they are detectable by clinical examination, and every nurse should be aware how important serial measurements of body weight are in assessing fluid and electrolyte disorders. Body weight can easily be measured on the same scales with an accuracy of 1% (40 ml = 40 g weight) or better.

Table I WATER BALANCE FOR AN AVERAGE INDIVIDUAL

	Input 1.		*Output 1.*
Oral intake	2·0	Urine	1·5
Metabolic water	0·5	Lungs	0·5
(from oxidation of		Sweat	0·25
fat and glucose)		Faeces	0·25
	2·5		2·5

The assessment of *plasma volume* is best made by assessing the circulation. It is important to remember that because it is so important, changes in circulation as a result of electrolyte disorders occur late and indicate severe gains or losses; also, the circulation obviously depends upon the activity of the heart and the state of constriction of the peripheral vessels (Figure 13.2) both of which may be altered by disease or drugs given for other purposes, as well as by the circulating volume.

The important nursing observations are:

(1)   peripheral temperature (hands, feet, nose)
(2)   arterial blood pressure, lying, *and standing or sitting*
(3)   the central venous pressure, or degree of neck vein filling.

Patients with a low circulating volume generally have a cold periphery, a low arterial pressure which falls 20 – 30 mmHg on standing, and a low central venous pressure (see p. 239). Circulatory volume overload, on the other hand, shows itself by a raised central venous pressure, tachycardia, sometimes a rise in blood pressure and breathlessness from slight, then obvious, pulmonary oedema.

The clinical assessment of the volume of the *interstitial water* is much more crude. Allowing for the amount of body fat, and the loss of tissue turgor with age, the subcutaneous tissues are pinched and the hydration by feel and by eye. Clearly not a very precise observation! The eyeballs tend to sink back into the head as the orbital tissues lose water, but eyeball turgor itself (which is often mentioned as an important sign of volume depletion) is difficult to assess, and changes only with gross dehydration or saline depletion. In overload, following a gain of about 10% of the body weight, oedema will appear, the site depending upon posture and venous drainage.

There is really no way by which changes in *intracellular water* can be assessed, and changes of many litres will go unnoticed except for the changes in body weight.

Assessment of water balance

Measurement of intake and output is of course a part of nursing routine, but many nurses chart patients' fluid balance without realizing what they are doing or why.

Water *balance* is of course the result of water *input* and water *output*. The main routes are summarized in Figure 13.3. It is important to remember from this:

(1)   that the circulation of water through the gut is very large – as large as all the extracellular water, and much larger than the plasma water from which it takes place.

(2)   that all external balance is transmitted through the small plasma water.

This means that very rapid changes in circulating volume take place in gastrointestinal disease associated with fluid losses from the gut – for example, in cholera.

(3)   the only regulation points are the intake and renal excretion. The kidneys must excrete the products of metabolism, and some urine (about 600 ml/day in an average adult on an average diet) is obligatory whatever the intake may be. The normal kidney can concentrate better than the diseased kidney, and in states of renal failure larger volumes of urine must be passed to maintain excretion of even a reduced amount of metabolites. Hence the patient with chronic renal disease is very vulnerable to failure of intake.

(4)   the "insensible" losses from lungs and sweat are very dependent upon ambient temperature and the patient's temperature. In tropical climates or in high fever several litres per day may be lost by this route. These losses are not controllable but must be estimated and replaced.

(5)   some water is produced each day from the burning of fatty acids and sugar to CO_2 and water. This may increase several fold in states where the body is burning fat rapidly e.g. after trauma or operation, or in starvation.

The *regulation* of water balance is normally made by varying intake in response to thirst, which is itself controlled by sensing the *concentra-*

tion of solutes in the blood in the hypothalamus; and by the release or withdrawal of ADH (antidiuretic hormone) release, again from the hypothalamus into the posterior part of the pituitary gland (see Chapter I). The regulation of the *volume* of the body fluids is considered below in connection with sodium and potassium.

Disorders of water or electrolyte balance can occur from increase or decrease in any of the elements listed in Table II. Usually, more than one factor is present. Oral intake may fail because of unavailability of water, because of unconsciousness, or because of vomiting. Metabolic water may increase in catabolic states; obligatory urine volume may be high from renal disease, or urine absent because of acute renal failure;

WATER BALANCE

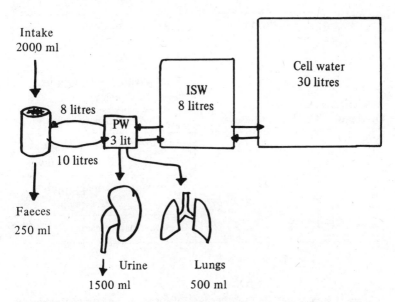

Fig.13.3 Water balance for 24 h in a 60 kg subject under normal circumstances. PW = plasma water, ISW = interstitial water. Again note that the plasma water is small compared with the total body water, and yet all external exchange passes through it. The output of urine can be varied to meet the input, provided the kidneys are healthy. In contrast, losses through the lungs (and skin, not shown) are not under the control of the individual, and must be met by variations in input. The interstitial water acts as a "buffer" between the plasma water and the cell water, being expanded or contracted temporarily while they remain relatively constant. Note also the large exchange between plasma water and the gut.

Table II   THE GENESIS OF ELECTROLYTE AND FLUID
              DISORDERS

Depletion	output up	urinary: chronic renal failure; diuretics
		gastro-intestinal: vomiting diarrhoea fistulae ileus
		insensible losses: fever hyperventilation (water only)
	input down	gastro-instestinal: unconscious vomiting
		intravenous: inappropriate i.v. regime
Overload	output down	urinary: anuria or oliguria
	input up	gastrointestinal: oral gastrostomy
		intravenous: inappropriate i.v. regime
		severe catabolism

insensible losses may be high because of fever, or gastrointestinal losses present because of small bowel disease. In other kidney diseases (such as acute nephritis or a nephrotic syndrome) there may be inappropriate retention of both salt and water with oliguria and oedema.

The most important fact from the point of view of renal disorders that in the short and the long term the kidney normally regulates fluid balance; in states of renal disease, in partial or total renal failure this ability to regulate is lost and so the patient, the nurses and the doctors must see that the input fits within the kidney's capabilities. Failure to do this will result inevitably in under- or over-loading.

II SODIUM AND POTASSIUM

Sodium and potassium balance are intimately related to water balance and the regulation of all three is interdependent. *Sodium* is the predominant positively charged ion of the extracellular space, and potassium that of the intracellular space. Within broad limits the amount of sodium and potassium in the body determines the amount of water in the body, since the concentration is regulated approximately constant (Figure 13.4). In disease situations the body will sometimes sacrifice concentration in order to preserve volume; this is particularly so in states of sodium depletion, where if the volume falls too far the circulation will fail, as outlined in the previous section.

BODY WATER = $Na^+ + K^+$

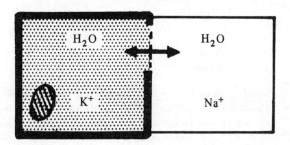

Fig.13.4 The distribution of water within and without the cells is controlled by the amount of cation in these two compartments. Within the cells the principal cation is potassium, and outside the cells the principal cation sodium. The distribution of body water is controlled by the relative amounts, and the total body water by the total amount of these two cations. The water inside the cell is shown stippled to indicate that the cell contains a lot of protein whereas that outside (with the exception of the plasma) does not.

We can look at sodium balance in the same way as we considered water balance a moment ago (Figure 13.5). The contrast is how little sodium there is within the cells – there has been argument as to whether there was any at all, but it now seems certain that there is a little.

Note:

(1)   the circulation of sodium through the gut is large, as with water, exceeding the amount in the plasma. Gastrointestinal diseases may lead to great losses of Na^+ as well as water.

SODIUM BALANCE

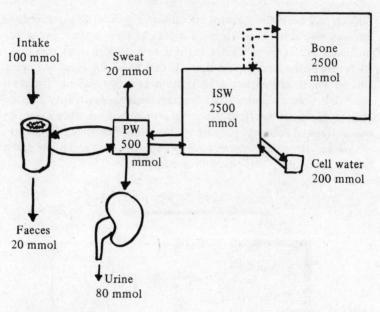

Fig.13.5   Sodium balance for a 60 kg individual for 24 h. Nearly all the body sodium is extracellular, but a considerable amount lies in bone and is not susceptible to rapid change. The exchangeable Na is about 3000 mmol. As with water, a large exchange occurs with the gut, and again as with water the normally small loss in the sweat is not under control and must be met by varying input.

(2)   sodium excretion tends to be larger when the output of urine is large, whether from increased water intake or from renal disease. Obligatory sodium losses may occur in chronic renal failure when the kidney is not able to reabsorb sodium as well as in health. The patient with chronic renal disease and excess sodium loss must maintain a high intake of sodium, and if this fails will rapidly become sodium depleted. The kidney is almost the only route of sodium excretion, and correspondingly in situations where renal function is absent sodium overload is very likely unless intake is strictly controlled.

(3)   there is a large amount of sodium in bone which exchanges only slowly within plasma and interstitial sodium.

The *regulation* of sodium excretion in the kidney occurs in response to both the perfusion of the kidney, and the secretion of aldosterone by the adrenal gland (see Chapter I). Both of these are dependent upon the circulating volume, and emphasize the role of sodium in determining what the extracellular water, and hence the plasma water and the circulating volume, will be. *Assessment* of the sodium status of the patient involves both an assessment of the plasma sodium and the volume of the extracellular water. The one multiplied by the other gives the sodium. The former is precise but the latter very imprecise. The important point to remember is that a low plasma sodium does *not* necessarily imply a sodium deficit, nor a high plasma sodium a sodium excess. For example, the nephrotic patient may have a grossly expanded interstitial (and therefore extracellular) water with a low plasma sodium; but when all the 20 litres or so of oedema fluid are considered may have a total body sodium twice normal or more. Conversely, a baby or a patient in chronic renal failure fed large quantities of sodium in a situation of limited water intake, may become dehydrated with a high plasma sodium, even though the volume of extracellular water, and with it the body sodium, are depleted. The factors involved in sodium depletion and overload are as those for water (Table II).

Dehydration and saline depletion

It is important to distinguish between true dehydration (that is, an isolated deficit of water) and saline depletion (a parallel deficiency of salt and water) since obviously the treatment of the two states will differ. Many patients who are in fact saline depleted are referred to in the ward as "dehydrated". The difference is reflected in the presence of a raised plasma sodium, and the early appearance of severe thirst, in true dehydration; and the normal or even low plasma sodium in saline depletion, and the absence of thirst if the patient is conscious.

Potassium is overwhelmingly intracellular (Figure 13.6). The striking thing about this ion is how all the external balance, both input and output, must pass through the tiny amount of potassium in the plasma and extracellular fluid: 95% of the potassium lies within the cells and it requires very little change in the entry or exit of K^+ from the cells to release or take up large quantities of potassium. At the same time, the low concentration of potassium in the extracellular fluid is vital to the maintenance of membrane excitability in cardiac and ordinary muscle, nerve cells, and indeed to all cells. Normally this plasma K^+ is kept within the limits of $3.5 - 5.5$ mmol/l and if it falls below 2.0 or rises above 8.0 mmol/l then death from cardiac arrest is likely. We live on the brink of disaster with regard to plasma potassium, and when disease states arise the situation is very precarious.

POTASSIUM BALANCE

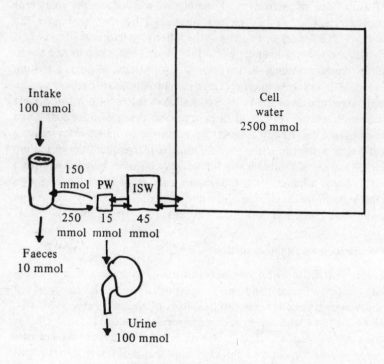

Fig. 13.6 Potassium balance for 24 h in a 60 kg individual. In contrast to sodium, almost all this cation is within cells. All exchange, however, as with sodium and water, must pass through the tiny amount of potassium in the plasma water, whose concentration must be kept within close limits because of the effect upon excitable membranes such as the heart, muscles and nerves. This very difficult task is normally achieved with great precision, despite the problems inherent in this arrangement. It can be seen that small changes in the amount of potassium leaving the cells could make a large difference to the concentration of potassium in the plasma (normally 3·5 – 5·5 mmol/l) and that this, rather than external balance will determine the plasma potassium concentration. There is no easy way of measuring the total amount of potassium in the cells.

Many factors besides external balance regulate the entry and exit of potassium from the cells, particularly the acid-base status of the cells, the sodium balance, and whether the cell is building up protein or breaking it down. It is unfortunate that in many patients with acute renal failure both acidosis and tissue protein breakdown conspire to release potassium from the cells, which may result in hyperkalaemia and death (see Chapter II) even if there is no intake of potassium. The situation is made even more difficult because, unlike sodium, the quantity or concentration of potassium within the cells cannot be assessed; the only samples we have are blood, which tells us only what the *plasma* potassium is doing. This is of course important, but tells us less than nothing about the intracellular potassium, since the plasma potassium may move in the opposite direction – e.g. upwards when the cells are losing potassium – and we have no way of telling what is going on. Measurement of external balance, and in patients with chronic disorders the exchangeable potassium (K_e) using radioactive potassium are all that is available.

In chronic renal failure, hyperkalaemia is rarely a problem except in situations of acidosis, because potassium (unlike sodium, which is only reabsorbed) undergoes section as well as reabsorption in the renal tubules. This secretion increases up to 20-fold in uraemia under the influence of aldosterone, and excess potassium may also be secreted into the gut.

III CLINICAL MANAGEMENT OF ELECTROLYTE DISORDERS

The clinical management leads naturally out of the physiological and clinical points just discussed. Although it is convenient to discuss water, sodium and potassium separately, in most patients multiple problems occur together. However, this does not alter the basic approach of trying to assess these three separately.

(1)   what is the present status with regard to water and potassium?

(a) the patient will be weighed; if previous weight is available this will give information as to what has just been happening; if not it will provide a valuable baseline for future management. Temperature, pulse and respiratory rate will all give useful information.

(b) the doctor will assess the circulation and hydration/volume as best he can, clinically. This will always require the recording of the arterial blood pressure lying and erect, the observation of the JVP and possibly the insertion of a central venous pressure line (see below).

(c) blood is sent to the laboratory for estimation of plasma electrolytes.

(d) if the urine volume is not known, or a specimen cannot be obtained for analysis the patient may be catheterized (Chapter VII).

(2) what has been happening? (Table II)
The doctor will obviously take a detailed history, particularly directed towards previous intake (if any) events such as operations, infections, gastrointestinal events, evidence of previous renal disease. Previous fluid balance charts etc., will be invaluable, if available.

(3) what is happening now?
the observations of weight, cardiovascular measurements, temperature and respiratory rate will be repeated, as ordered and an intake and output chart begun. All urine passed should be saved, and in many patients with gastrointestinal disease it will be necessary to save, measure (and often send for analysis) gastrointestinal aspirate, fistula fluid etc.

(4) what should be done to correct the present disorder and cope with continuing situation?

the crucial thing is repeated measurement and appropriate adjustment of intake. The initial management will usually be based upon guesswork, and only after several hours' observation and the result of tests will the true nature of the situation become evident.

The regime that the doctor orders will be based upon his initial estimates of what the principal problems are, whether he can deal with these or must continue in their presence (e.g. chronic renal failure); whether the patient has too much or too little total water and circulating volume, too much or too little Na^+, or too much or too little potassium; and what expected losses or gains may be. He will need to modify all this in the light of the output figures accumulated over the next 12 or 24 hours, and will have to decide which route or routes to use. This principally revolves around whether the patient and his gut can manage the anticipated quantities of water and electrolyte. In many renal patients he will need to consider the patient's nutritional needs, and perhaps intravenous feeding (see Chapter XII) for all or part of this. If the patient is on dialysis then *fluid losses or gains during dialysis must be cumulated with the ward fluid balance chart* where possible, otherwise these charts become meaningless. This holds for both peritoneal dialysis and haemodialysis. Electrolyte losses or gains during dialysis (except by the intravenous route) unfortunately cannot be estimated, since the change in concentration of the dialysate is, in either case, too small to record.

IV INTRAVENOUS LINES AND CENTRAL VENOUS PRESSURE RECORDING

The insertion of simple peripheral intravenous line will not be discussed in detail here, and the local procedure book should be consulted for their care. However, the management of central lines is a common problem in renal patients, especially during acute illnesses, and this will be discussed in detail.

Central venous pressure measurements

The arterial blood pressure has been measured in clinical practice for over 60 years, and gives information on the *resistance* (arterial) side of the circulation. The arterial blood pressure tells us mostly about the tone of the arterial wall muscle, and about cardiac output; the product of the one pushing against the other, being the blood pressure (Figure 13.2). However, this ignores one other variable: the *volume* of circulating blood. However hard the heart works, or however much the arterioles constrict, if a huge amount of volume has been lost (for example as external blood loss) then the blood pressure will fail. But this only happens, especially in young fit patients, when the blood loss is very great. A normal blood pressure may therefore conceal a grossly deficient circulating volume.

More recently, attention has turned towards the *capacitance* (venous) side of the circulation, to see if changes in circulating volume can be detected before they become critical. Also, when the heart fails to eject blood efficiently, the volume of the venous side of the circulation increases and the signs of congestive heart failure appear. Finally, if the circulating volume is over expanded because of fluid retention or too high a rate of intravenous infusion, the volume of the venous side of the circulation will increase. The degree of filling the venous side of the circulation is therefore of great use in detecting volume losses or circulation overload, and in assessing the performance of the heart.

Veins have less muscle in their walls, and the pressure within them is very low, only a few centimetres of water, compared with 10 or more centimetres of mercury (which is thirteen times as heavy as water) in the arterial side of the circulation. Measurement of *pressures* in the venous part of the system can give a good idea of the *volume*, or degree of filling of the venous reservoir; indeed, sometimes the pressure within the right atrium is called the *filling pressure* of the heart. More usually, it is called the *central venous pressure* or CVP. This has been exploited for many years by looking externally at the level of the jugular venous pulse with the patient at 45°, but this is not possible in all patients, nor is it possible to assess how much deficit there may be if the venous pressure is invisible in the neck.

To measure the CVP we must have a fairly wide-bore tube inserted into the right atrium – or at least the vena cava – so that the tube itself does not introduce too much artefact into the measurement. There are several routes to the right atrium which are used in clinical practice (Figure 13.7).

(1)   via the basilic vein from the arm. The basilic vein on the inner side of the arm is better than the cephalic on the outside, since the latter passes by a sharp bend into the thorax through a fascial sheet (the clavipectoral fascia) which is often difficult to pass.
(2)   via the internal jugular vein into the superior vena cava.
(3)   via the external jugular vein down into the superior vena cava.
(4)   directly into the subclavian vein. This can be done entering the vein either above the clavicle or below the clavicle, and each route has its advocates.

The details of inserting the catheter can be found in books on intensive care, and are best learned by watching and assisting an expert. For the insertion of the catheter, a sterile trolley will be required, together with the cannula to be used by the doctor inserting the line. Today, some form of wide-bore, thin-wall needle which is commercially available presterilized is usually employed to pierce the vein, and through this is passed the catheter supplied, after which the needle is withdrawn. The length of cannula will depend upon the site of insertion (e.g. 24″ (60 cm) from the arm, shorter if the jugular or subclavian are used). In patients in whom the peripheral veins have been used for previous cut downs or venepunctures, it may be necessary to expose the vein by a cut down and insert the cannula under direct vision. More often in such circumstances, the doctor may prefer to use a direct subclavian or jugular puncture, unless these veins have also been used previously.

Requirements for insertion of a CVP line

Dressing pack
Sterile graduated manometer
Three way tap
Needle/cannula as requested
1 × 2 ml syringe

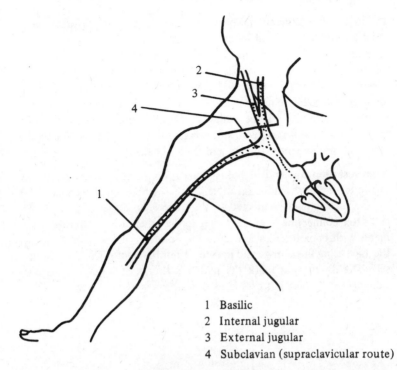

1 Basilic
2 Internal jugular
3 External jugular
4 Subclavian (supraclavicular route)

Fig. 13.7 Routes of access for right atrial (central venous) lines. The most commonly used is the basilic vein (the cephalic vein lateral to it can also be used, but there are problems in negotiating the cannula into the thorax from the arm by this route). All three routes using the veins above the clavicle are popular, but all three have disadvantages. Some doctors prefer to insert the cannula into the subclavian vein going *below* the clavicle (i.e. nearer the heart). See text.

1 × 5 ml syringe
1 × No. 1 needle
Sterile gloves
Mask
Lignocaine 1%
Hibitane 1:200 in spirit or iodine cleaning fluid
I.V. infusion set, plus litre bag or bottle of fluid (0·9% saline or isotonic glucose as requested)
Sodium citrate 3·8%
Levelling device (e.g. spirit level)
Marking pencil
Adhesive tape

The insertion and manipulation of the cannula must be performed with strict asepsis, since it will lie in the blood stream and infection on the cannula leads to septicaemia. Insertion is usually performed with the patient lying flat, or in the case of the subclavian line, even head down. This is because if the pressure in the right atrium and great vein is low, air may enter the veins once the needle is inserted, especially during inspiration. However, some patients with high central venous pressure may not tolerate lying down, and it is safe to insert a line via the basilic vein with the patient sitting up and the arm below the level of the heart.

After insertion, the end of the cannula is connected via the three way tap to (i) the intravenous infusion (ii) the manometer. It is best to set up the infusion set connected to the three way tap (see Figure 13.8), and after connecting the manometer to the other arm, to fill this manometer with heparinized saline or citrate solution via the rubber bung of the tap, using the syringe and needle. Often the doctor will do this himself. The doctor will mark the patient's thorax at a point to be considered 'zero'. This is to some extent arbitrary and the exact position

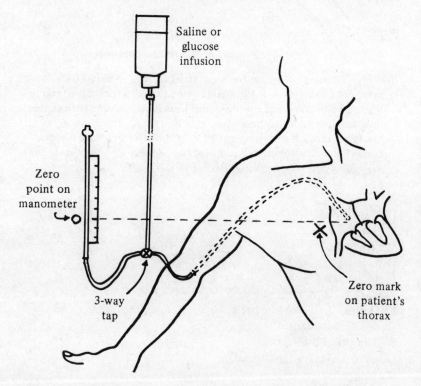

Saline or glucose infusion

Zero point on manometer

3-way tap

Zero mark on patient's thorax

Fig. 13.8 Reading the level of central venous pressure. See text.

does not matter, *so long as it is maintained the same* throughout the use of the cannula. The position of the catheter may be checked by obtaining a straight PA X-ray of the thorax.

Immediate problems

There are few immediate difficulties associated with basilic vein or jugular CVP lines, except local bleeding. However, the insertion of subclavian lines can cause considerable problems, principally:

(1) massive haematoma formation
(2) pneumothorax
(3) haemopneumothorax

and the patient needs careful observation after insertion to see that the site of insertion is causing no trouble (e.g. bleeding), and that the respiration is not becoming embarrassed or the patient cyanosed.

Subsequent care

The detailed care of CVP lines varies from hospital to hospital and unit to unit. The following is a general account and the local procedure book should be consulted to verify details.

(1) The venous pressure is read off the manometer, at intervals indicated by the doctor, and charted.
(2) Between readings, the line should be kept patent by a *slow* infusion of saline or isotonic glucose. Protein containing solutions, blood, and fat emulsions are *not* suitable.
(3) Whenever the patient's position is changed, the zero level of the manometer must be readjusted.

(1) *Reading* the manometer involves switching the three way tap to connect the manometer and the cannula. The level of saline in the manometer will fall (or rise) until the pressure within the right atrium is reached. If the cannula is in the right place, and is patent, the level will swing a little with each respiration (the respiratory excursion). The level is noted, the three way tap turned to infusion again. Each time it will be necessary to top up the saline level in the manometer using the rubber bung and sterile saline from the syringe. This ensures that the level in the manometer is higher than the right atrial pressure and that at the next reading the level will fall, flushing through the tap with saline. Normal values are usually 5 - 10 cm water. Less than zero and more than 15 cm definitely abnormal.

(2) The *infusion* running through the tap should be used only for maintaining the system open. Because it is running at a slow constant

rate, it is not very suitable for giving drugs by infusion. Blood and plasma intravenous amino-acid or fat solutions should not be used.

(3) *Rezeroing* simply involves raising or lowering the manometer so that the zero point on the scale is level again with the 'zero' mark on the patient's chest.

The CVP will fall, or be zero or less if the circulating volume falls. This may come about from external or internal losses of blood or protein rich fluid (e.g. proteinuria or gut fluid in ileus), or from pooling of blood in parts of the circulation, particularly in the gut. It is therefore more correct to say that the CVP reflects adequacy of *effective* circulating volume.

The CVP will *rise* in several circumstances, the commonest of which are circulatory overload from fluid retention and/or too much intravenous fluid; and failure of the heart to eject a volume equal to the venous return at a normal filling pressure (heart failure). Remember that we are measuring only *right* atrial pressure, and that while this usually reflects the *left* atrial pressure, strictly we can only assess right ventricular performance with a CVP. Left atrial pressures *can* be measured, but this is of more importance in patients with cardiac problems rather than difficulties with circulating volume. The easiest method is to pass an even longer catheter into the right atrium, through the right ventricle into the pulmonary artery (A 'PA' line). This catheter can then be wedged into the pulmonary circulation for measurement of the 'wedge' pressure, which reflects the left atrial pressure fairly accurately. This requires mechanical recording, and will usually be supervised by a doctor or technician.

Problems with CVP Lines

(1)   The commonest problem is *blockage* of the lines. This can sometimes be flushed through by syringe, or by changing the tap. A fixed reading which does not swing with respiration is usually the earliest sign. Sometimes the catheter needs to be withdrawn a little.

(2)   *Misplacement* of the line. Commonly the line may pass through the tricuspid valve and lie in the right ventricle or even the pulmonary artery, giving a false high reading. Occasionally it may pass from the arm up into the neck, and good readings cannot be obtained from this site. Usually the position of the catheter will be checked by X-raying the chest.

(3)   *Infection* of the line is particularly common in debilitated uraemic patients such as those in acute renal failure. It is not wise to

leave a CVP line in longer than one week, especially if the line is also being used for intravenous feeding.

(4) Sometimes the infection is associated with *thrombosis* of the superior vena cava, which is of course a major complication.

(5) *Artificial ventilation* of patients makes the readings obtained by CVP line in the right atrium no longer an accurate indicator of venous filling. This is especially so when positive end-expiratory pressure (PEEP) is used. In general, higher pressures will be recorded than with the patient off ventilation.

HYDROGEN IONS AND ACID-BASE BALANCE

This is a large and complex subject which it is impossible to review in full here. However, it is so important that the basic principles must be summarized, even though nurses are not usually involved directly in this treatment.

Hydrogen ions (protons, H^+) are very reactive ions (charged particles) which are generated in huge quantities as a result of normal metabolism. In disease states this production may increase still further. Almost all of the hydrogen ion in the body is produced – there is very little in food under normal diet. The production of hydrogen ions in a healthy adult is about 35,000 mmol/day, that is 35 moles: enough to fill 20 2-litre Winchester bottles with the most concentrated fuming hydrochloric acid!

This hydrogen ion results from several sources:

(1) breakdown of carbohydrate for energy. Glucose is metabolized by a complex series of steps using oxygen to produce, finally, CO_2 and water. The CO_2 dissolves in the cell water to form carbonic acid, H_2CO_3, which in turn dissociates into H^+ and bicarbonate, HCO_3'.

(2) similarly, oxidation of fat for energy leads to CO_2 and water.

(3) a much smaller breakdown of compounds containing sulphur (S) and phosphorus (P) such as some proteins and phospholipids, to form sulphuric acid and phosphoric acids.

(4) breakdown of purines from DNA to form uric acid.

(5) formation of organic acids such as lactic acid.

The body excretes most of this huge quantity of hydrogen ion as CO_2, through the lungs. Therefore the majority of H^+ is *produced* as the result of CO_2, and also *excreted* as CO_2. The lung is the major excretory organ for H^+ in the body.

What about the kidney? The lung can only excrete that amount of hydrogen ion which can be excreted as CO_2, and is usually referred to as "volatile" hydrogen ion; this is discussed further below. CO_2 is the compound (called the anhydride) which forms carbonic acid in solution and in turn may be reformed from it. A small amount of the hydrogen ion (about 70 out of the total 35000 mmol each day) is formed from the metabolism of sulphur and phosphorus compounds. The anhydrides of sulphuric and phosphoric acids are SO_2 and P_2O_5; the former is an intensely irritant gas, and the latter a solid at body temperature. The metabolism of S- and P- containing compounds, together with some organic acids and uric acid, leads to hydrogen ion that *cannot* be excreted as the appropriate anhydride through the lungs. Although only a tiny fraction of the total (70 out of 35000 mmol/day) it is of disproportionate importance. Between them, the lungs and the kidneys regulate the excretion of hydrogen ions.

As discussed in Chapter 1, the kidney can get rid of hydrogen ions in two forms.

(1) H^+ itself is secreted by the tubules. H^+ can be concentrated up to 600-fold compared with plasma, accounting for the greater acidity of urine (pH 5 – 6) than of plasma (pH 7·37).

(2) NH_4^+ is secreted by the tubules.

The secreted H^+ meets in the tubular fluid, HCO_3' filtered from the plasma through the glomerulus; it combines with this and normally there is no free bicarbonate in the urine, but an excess of free H^+ in solution. The renal tubules reabsorb filtered sodium in exchange for each H^+ secreted. In addition ammonium (NH_4^+) is formed from H^+ and ammonia (NH_3) secreted into the tubular fluid, itself derived from an amino ($-NH_2$) group from an amino-acid (glutamine). This allows excretion of a greater amount of hydrogen ions than could be achieved by secretion of the H^+ itself, and is of importance in states of chronic excess of hydrogen ion. Thus:

Every day	35000 mmol H^+ formed as CO_2	35000 mmol H^+ excreted as CO_2 } lung
	70 mmol of H^+ formed as H_2SO_4, H_3PO_4, H. lactate, H. urate etc.	30 mmol H^+ excreted as H^+; 40 mmol excreted as NH_4^+ } kidney

But how and in what form does the H^+ arrive at the lungs and the kidneys? If this enormous quantity of H^+ produced daily was simply added to the body fluids, the hydrogen ion concentration would rise to very high levels, and all metabolic and transport processes (which are very sensitive to small change in H^+ concentration) would cease immediately. For a multi-celled organism such as ourselves to survive, it must have a mechanism of "concealing" the H^+ on its way to the lungs and kidneys in the cell water, interstitial water and circulation, from the site of production in the cells to the organs of excretion. This concealment is achieved by *buffering* the H^+. A definition of a buffer and its action is discussed in the glossary (p. 311). In essence, a buffered solution is one which maintains its H^+ concentration constant, despite the addition (or subtraction) of hydrogen ions. Mammalian body fluids are buffered at a very low concentration of free hydrogen ions (about 40 nmol/l – less than one millionth of the concentration of sodium, for example).

Any mixture of a weak acid and a salt of the acid can act as a buffer. Remember that an acid is the compound which can give up hydrogen ions to form a base:

$$H^+ \quad + \quad A' \quad \rightleftharpoons \quad HA$$

proton   base   acid

The acid is *not* the hydrogen ion itself, although conversationally we often use it as though this were the case. Acid is *not* what may eat holes in clothing or burn the skin; this is the result of the free H^+ undergoing chemical combination. A "strong" acid exists almost totally in solution as H^+ and A'. A "weak" acid in contrast, exists as HA and can thus act as a buffer (see glossary).

Table III   HYDROGEN ION BALANCE

Hydrogen ion in diet	0
hydrogen ion production	35 000 mmol/day
hydrogen ion excretion	35 000 mmol/day
total body buffering capacity for hydrogen ion	2 000 mmol
amount of hydrogen ion in body (normal)	100 mmol
amount of free hydrogen ion in body	0·0015 mmol

Table III summarizes some facts about hydrogen ion production and buffering. Several facts emerge from a study of this Table:

(1)   the large amount of H^+ produced.

(2)   the speed with which it is excreted – at any one time only 1/350

of the daily production and excretion, on average, is in the body.
(3)   that only one twentieth of the body's buffering capacity is used up at any one time.
(4)   on the other hand, the system is vulnerable in that the daily production exceeds the buffering capacity 20-fold.
(5)   how successful the buffering is: 99·999% of the hydrogen ion in the body is buffered, only 0·001% is free H^+.

From the kidney point of view, the system is less critically balanced. It would take about three weeks (ignoring other problems) to accumulate a fatal dose of H^+ in complete renal failure, whereas if breathing stops CO_2 retention would lead to a similar state in minutes rather than hours.

The lungs and the kidneys do not, of course, function independently. It is possible, in the short term, to use the lungs for excretion of hydrogen ions which the kidney cannot excrete because of temporary excess, or disease. Finally however this "debt" must be paid off by excreting the "non-volatile" ion through the kidney. Also, the lungs and the kidneys cooperate in a very precise regulation of the small amount of free hydrogen ions in tissue fluids, on a minute to minute basis. The fashion in which this is achieved can be stated with varying degrees of complexity, the equations referring to blood plasma, since this is the fluid to which we have access for measurement. However it must be remembered that most of the hydrogen ion is buffered *within* the cells by weak acid systems other than the carbonic acid system usually discussed; principally weakly acidic amino-acids in protein which is present in large quantity within cells, including red blood cells.

The simplest way to put this relationship is:

$$\text{hydrogen ion concentration varies as } \frac{\text{lungs}}{\text{kidneys}}$$

using [ ] to represent concentrations, and inserting the aspects of the CO_2 system controlled by lung and kidney, we get:

$$[H^+] = \text{a constant} \times \frac{P_{CO_2}}{[HCO_3']}$$

$$[H^+] = k. \frac{P_{CO_2}}{HCO_3'}$$

because CO_2 dissolves in whole blood to form H^+ and HCO_3' we can write

$$[H^+] = k. \frac{[H_2 CO_3]}{[HCO_3']}$$

This is the equation described by Henderson which describes the behaviour of *all* acids and bases in solution: using the HA description of an acid we met above

$$[H^+] = k. \frac{[HA]}{[A']}$$

Later, Hasselbalch preferred to use the pH notation for expressing the hydrogen ion concentration (see glossary), so that the Henderson-Hasselbalch equation reads:

$$pH = pK. + \frac{[HCO_3']}{[H_2 CO_3]} \quad \text{or } pH = pK. + \frac{[A']}{[HA]}$$

The equation is the "other way up" because pH is the *negative* logarithm of H^+.

The implications of all this are very great but beyond the scope of this text. However, you can see that the $[H^+]$ (or pH) will regulate the ratio of HCO_3' to $H_2 CO_3$ in the blood, and vice versa. Thus, if the $H_2 CO_3$ changes because of changes in ventilation of CO_2, the kidney can keep the hydrogen ion constant in the blood by altering the excretion of bicarbonate; and if the excretion of acid or of bicarbonate by the kidney changes then this may be compensated for by altering the amount of CO_2 breathed off.

This accounts for the familiar deep breathing of the patient retaining H^+ in renal failure. CO_2 retention is usually referred to as *respiratory* acidosis, H^+ production or retention from organic acids, $H_2 SO_4$ etc. as *metabolic* acidosis. In disease situations, all three will be measured (pH, HCO_3' and P_{CO_2}) usually by an apparatus such as that described by Astrup and his colleagues.

It is easy to see, also, that each of the three components may alter either up or down, giving six basic pathological situations in acid-base pathology. *Hydrogen ion* may be produced in excess (as in diabetes or hypoxaemia from pneumonia) or fail to be excreted (as in renal failure); or on the other hand lost from the body in excess as in vomiting or aspiration of the very acid gastric juice. CO_2 may be retained in excess in chronic lung disease, or blown off in excess in over-ventilation from a variety of causes. *Bicarbonate* may be lost from the gut in states of malabsorption or diarrhoea, or administered in excess in the treatment of acidosis.

Doctors attempt to manipulate the situation e.g. by giving intravenous bicarbonate, or by altering the setting of artificial ventilation. States of excess H^+ (acidosis) are much commoner in clinical practice than states of alkalosis (hydrogen ion deficit) but the latter are no less important. In every situation, it is important to try to analyse the factors that led to the disorder of acid-base metabolism, and to treat these primary events if possible. In renal patients, this often involves both renal impairment and secondary problems such as acute or chronic lung disease.

Suggestions for further reading:
Cameron, J. S. (1970) Disorders of electrolyte and water metabolism. *Medical Treatment. A textbook of therapy in four volumes.* (Eds.) Maclean, K., Scott, G. W. London: Churchill.

Clarke, D. B., Barnes, A. D. (Eds.) *Intensive Care for Nurses.* 2nd Edition. Oxford: Blackwell.

Emery, E. R., Yates, A. K., Moorhead, P. J. (1973). *Principles of Intensive Care*, London: EUP.

Harvey, R. J. (1974). *The Kidneys and the Internal Environment.* London: Chapman and Hall.

Pitts, R. F. (1974). *Physiology of the Kidney and Body Fluids.* 3rd Edition. Chicago: Year Book.

Warren, C. P. (1971). *Fluid Balance. Water, Salt and Blood.* A Nursing Times publication. London: Macmillan.

Wilson, R. F. (1973). *Fluids, Electrolytes and Metabolism.* Springfield: C. Thomas.

CHAPTER XIV

Peritoneal dialysis

All forms of dialysis depend upon the same principles. The terms "haemodialysis" and "peritoneal" dialysis are misleading since in both cases the blood is the fluid from which the unwanted waste products of metabolism are removed. Before considering the practical details it is worth dealing with these principles which apply equally to acute and maintenance dialysis.

I THEORY OF DIALYSIS

Dialysis is usually defined as the *transfer of solutes across a semipermeable membrane*[1] down a concentration gradient. The first membrane used was parchment, but we now employ either one of the body's own membranes (the peritoneum) or artificial membranes, usually of cuprophan. Dialysis of substances from the blood is called *haemodialysis*. "Renal dialysis" does not exist and the term is an abuse of the language; it is the blood, not the kidneys, which are dialysed.

Any substance in solution tends to move from regions where it is in high concentration to regions where it is in low concentration. This is a consequence of random diffusion (the movement of the molecules) and is faster the higher the temperature. This is true of any naturally occurring compound or ion, and also of drugs and poisons. In both peritoneal dialysis and in haemodialysis the blood is brought into contact with a solution, dialysate, from which it is separated by a membrane.

This membrane may be artificial or natural but in either case is very permeable to small molecules and ions. The small molecules will travel across the membrane in the direction of their concentration gradient,

---

[1] one which permits the passage of small molecules, such as urea or sodium, but not large molecules such as proteins, or formed elements such as red cells, white cells or bacteria.

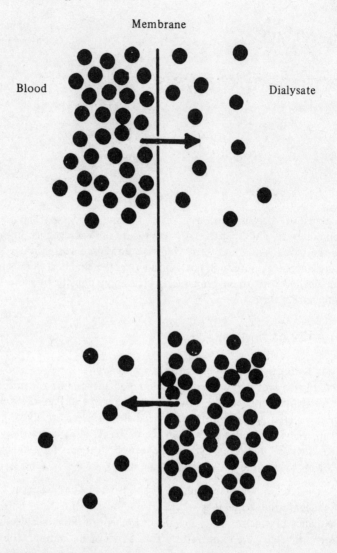

Fig. 14.1 The principles of dialysis. Above, a substance is shown in greater concentration in the blood than in the dialysate. The net transfer of this substance will be across the membrane into the dialysate. There will also be a small tendency for water to pass from dialysate into the blood.

Below, a substance is shown in greater concentration in the dialysate; in this case the reverse will be true and the substance will enter the blood with the removal of a small amount of water into the dialysate.

into or out of the blood, entirely depending on the size of the concentration difference between blood and dialysate, upon the temperature, and the area of contact between blood and dialysate. Peritoneal dialysis of course takes place at body temperature and any haemodialysis of blood outside the body is more efficient at blood heat than at room temperature. Obviously, if the blood were dialysed against a small reservoir of dialysate, then the concentration of all the substances in solution would approach and finally equal that of the blood. Therefore it is necessary to present fresh dialysate to the blood, either by changing the peritoneal dialysis fluid or by providing a continuous flow of fresh dialysate in the haemodialyser.

By adjusting the composition of the fluid used as dialysate, any substance can be made to enter, or leave the patient during dialysis, or remain in equilibrium. In this way the excretory and regulatory functions of the kidney may be replaced, although rather clumsily. There remains one problem: water. Water also tends to flow in the direction of its concentration gradient. This sounds ridiculous at first, but one can think of water as being dissolved in its solutes just as one can think of solutes dissolved in water. The concentration of water is greatest where the solution is dilute, that is where the total amount of dissolved substances (osmolarity) is low; and the concentration of water is low in strong solutions, where the osmolarity is high. Generally we wish to remove water from the patient so we ensure that the dialysate is at least as concentrated as the patient's blood; usually it is stronger than the blood. This is most exploited in peritoneal dialysis. Put another way, we use the osmotic pressure of substances dissolved in the dialysate (usually glucose) to "suck" water out from the patient.

We can also use another pressure to remove water: hydrostatic pressure. This is easier than osmotic pressure because it can be perceived. Water will move across a membrane according to the hydrostatic pressure differences across the membrane. Again, if we wish to remove water from the patient we can "push" it across by raising the pressure in the blood compartment, or "pull" it across by reducing pressure on the dialysate side. This cannot be exploited in peritoneal dialysis, but is the standard way of removing water in haemodialysis. Remember that the substances dissolved in whatever water is removed also come across the membrane.

So far we have considered the dialysis of the *blood*. When it returns to the heart, from either the peritoneum or from the haemodialyser, its composition approaches that which we would like, and is approximately that of the dialysate. But the blood is only a small part of the body water. Next, exchange takes place between the blood and the extracellular fluid (ECF), substances such as urea again moving down their concentration gradients. This exchange takes place rapidly since the blood vessels present no barrier. Finally, the urea or other substance will diffuse out of the cells into the ECF. This proceeds rather more slowly, and we cannot accelerate it. So that we dialyse the blood over and over again, whilst removing substances gradually from the whole body water. in summary:

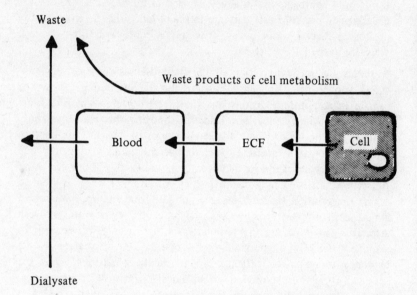

Fig. 14.2   Waste products of cell metabolism, such as urea, acid and creatinine, are dialysed from the blood into the dialysate during both haemodialysis and peritoneal dialysis. However, these substances come from cells, and the blood returning from the peritoneum, or from the haemodialyser, then exchanges with wastes in the extracellular fluid (ECF). This in turn exchanges with the waste products in the cells. The process of removing waste products from the body thus involves three changes. Obviously the concentrations of wastes in the cells may lag behind those in the blood and to a lesser extent, the extracellular fluid. If the difference between these concentrations becomes large, water may pass in the opposite direction to the passage of waste products, that is, into the cells.

It is possible to perform dialysis *too* fast, because if the extracellular urea concentration is dropped too rapidly, urea cannot pass out of the cells fast enough (urea is present in greater quantity than any other substance that we are removing and so is the most important). No susbstance can exchange across the cell membranes as fast as water, so that if there comes to be significantly more urea inside the cells than outside them, water will pass down its concentration gradient INTO the cells. The cells will then swell, which is of little importance except in the brain. This is for two reasons: urea exchange is particularly slow from the brain and the brain is inside the fixed box of the skull. If urea is removed too fast, then cerebral oedema will occur, with drowsiness, headache, EEG changes and possibly convulsions. This is called *"dialysis disequilibrium"* and may also occur if the patient's sodium concentration in blood, ECF and cerebrospinal fluid is higher than the dialysate sodium concentration. Obviously, the more powerful and rapid the dialysis, the more likely is this to occur; it is therefore seen with powerful haemodialysers, very uncommonly with peritoneal dialysis. One way of minimizing disequilibrium is by adding large quantities of glucose to the dialysate; this exchanges into the ECF, into the cells and tends to keep them at the same concentration while the urea and sodium pass out.

II PERITONEAL DIALYSIS

The first peritoneal dialysis dates back to 1877 when Wagner conducted experiments in rabbits. It was not until 1923 when Ganter performed the first peritoneal dialysis on uraemic rabbits and guinea pigs with anuria, produced by ligation of the ureters. Ganter also attempted peritoneal dialysis in humans in 1923, on a patient with ureteral obstruction due to carcinoma of the uterus. In 1938 Wear and colleagues dialysed five patients for periods of two to eight hours. The introduction of plastics and antibiotics made peritoneal dialysis a practical treatment, and today it is used regularly for both acute and chronic renal failure.

Technique

In this technique the membrane used is the peritoneal membrane, which has a rich blood supply. This blood can be used for the transfer of solutes into and out of the body. The dialysing fluid (dialysate) must therefore be placed in the peritoneum and withdrawn. This could be done continuously through an entry and an exit cannula into the peritoneum, but this technique has not proved popular; instead, volumes of dialysate are run into the peritoneum, allowed to equilibrate briefly with the blood perfusing the peritoneal membrane, and then run out again. The dialysate must be sterile, to preserve the relative sterility of the peritoneum. The technique, although possible in theory for many years, did not become practicable on a large scale until quantities of sterile, reliable, pyrogen-free fluids, non-irritant plastics and disposable PVC giving sets became available.

(i)   Setting up the dialysis

Suggested trolley
Swabs
Skin cleaning fluid, e.g. Hibitane in spirit or iodine
3 (paper) towels
Gauze squares
1% lignocaine
10 ml syringe Nos. 1 and 25 needles
Knife and No. 11 blade
Gloves
Scissors
Peritoneal dialysis catheter
(McGaw Adult "Trocath"[1], Braun 43.2002 or 43.2003)[2] or other
   suitable)
Peritoneal dialysis set (Travenol R61L, Allen and Hanbury's or other
   suitable set)
Peritoneal dialysis drainage bag (Aldon 3 litre, or Aldon 1·5 litre
   urine drainage bag)
Large skin stitch
Masks
Dripstand

(a) The giving set (Figure 14.3)   First the *giving set* must be prepared.
This consists of a large double drip set to which two 1-litre bags of
dialysing fluid are to be attached. From the common tube of the
double drip set is an additional tube running off sideways; this will be
used to siphon off the fluid from the peritoneum. The whole tubing
should be filled with whatever fluid is to be used for the first exchange.
An 'Aldon' urine drainage bag is cut just above the junction of tube and
bag, and the outflow tube plugged into it. Alternatively a Baxter or
Aldon peritoneal dialysis bag (3 litre) may be attached, or a 2 litre
container or measuring cylinder.

(b) The dialysing fluid   The dialysing fluid is prepared sterile and must
remain so. The usual solution used is provided in one litre bags (or
bottles) and contains normal plasma electrolytes (sodium 130 or 141
mmol/l), plus glucose 1·36% but no potassium, urea, phosphate or sulphate, since all these are usually present in excess in renal failure. All
bags must be warmed to body temperature before use (between heating

---

[1]   obtainable from Chas. Thackray, Ltd., Leeds.

[2]   obtainable from Armour Pharmaceutical Co., Eastbourne.

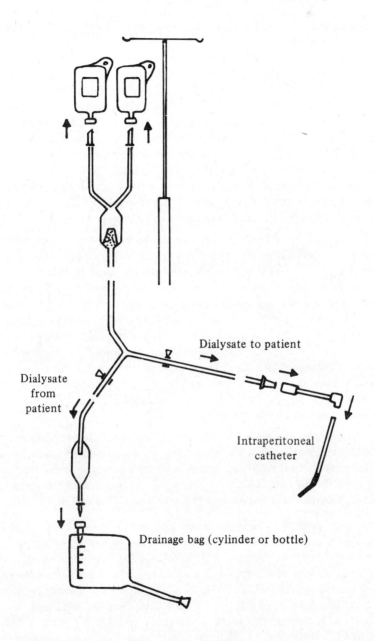

Dialysate to patient

Dialysate from patient

Intraperitoneal catheter

Drainage bag (cylinder or bottle)

Fig. 14.3 The components of a system for performing peritoneal dialysis. The diagram is not to scale, neither the relative sizes of the components nor the distance between them, which have been shortened.

258 Nephrology for nurses

pads or special warmer) or the patient may become very cold and drainage problems may ensue. Usually 500 u or 1000 u of heparin/l is added to them to prevent the protein washed off the peritoneum clotting in the catheter or tubing. If the patient's plasma potassium is not high, the doctor will order up to 5 mmol K^+ to be added to each litre bag (up to 2·5 ml of 20 mmol/10 ml solution). Before adding anything to the bag its top must be swabbed with either methylated spirit, ether or its equivalent. This is also necessary before stabbing the dialysis set into the bag. Each bag should be prepared individually when required, and not prepared in batches and then incubated for longer periods. This helps minimize bacterial multiplication in the bags should contamination occur. A mask and disposable gloves should be worn, and any additions should be checked carefully and written on the bag.

If the patient is oedematous from overhydration or heart failure *water* can be removed from the patient by using the dialysing fluid containing 6·36% glucose. This very strong solution attracts water from the patient into the peritoneal cavity and 5, 10, 15 or more litres of water can be removed. Its use may be dangerous and *a watch must be kept on the blood pressure and pulse hourly if the 6·36 g/100 ml solution is used* because hypotension and shock may result if fluid is withdrawn from the patient too quickly. Above all, the nurse must not confuse the 6·36 g% solution with the 1·36 g% solution, and use the former unwittingly when the usual solution has been the one ordered. This is made more likely by the fact that many commercially available fluids are poorly distinguished by their labelling.

Peritoneal dialysis solutions containing sorbitol (a slowly metabolized sugar-like compound) are now available, for use in patients with known diabetes, or those who develop carbohydrate intolerance during dialysis. At present they are available only in 10 litre containers (Peritofundin Is and IIs obtainable from Armour Pharmaceutical Co. Eastbourne).

(c) **The peritoneal catheter** There are several types of peritoneal catheter, but all are made of inert plastic, and consist of a long, fairly rigid tube with an open end and multiple perforations for several centimetres back from the end. The most widely used types have a central removable stillette, which is sharp and permits insertion of the catheter into the peritoneal cavity; the stillette may then be withdrawn. Supplied with the catheter in the same sterile packing is a piece of PVC tubing to connect the catheter with the "giving" limb of the peritoneal dialysis set.

(d) **The insertion of the catheter** The procedure is explained to the patient, if conscious, who is placed comfortably in bed, sitting up at about 45°. Premedication with pethidine may be ordered by the doctor. The bladder should be empty and, if palpable or percussable, must be emptied. Occasionally catheterization may be necessary for this. In any case the patient is offered a bed-pan or urinal. Some patients may need the area between the umbilicus and symphysis pubis shaved. The skin is cleaned and about 10-15 ml local anaesthetic (1% lignocaine) is injected in the midline into the linea alba, between the umbilicus and the symphysis pubis; usually about two-thirds of the way from the pubis. If the patient is very fat a long needle such as a cardiac or lumbar puncture needle, will be needed to anaesthetize the peritoneum. The doctor makes a stab incision in the skin at the anaesthetized site, and pushes the catheter through into the peritoneal cavity with a screwing motion. Once in, the stillette is withdrawn and the catheter advanced towards the pelvis. It is secured in place with Elastoplast or a stitch. Some catheters have a protective metal disc or stud around the catheter, which sits at the skin surface and effectively prevents accidental movement, either in or out of the peritoneum. Several inches of catheter will project from the abdomen; on no account should this be trimmed. The connecting tube is pushed on to the protruding catheter and connected to the giving set. With the out-flow clamped off, one litre of fluid is run in, and the patient's reaction noted; there should be only minor discomfort. As soon as the litre is in, the inflow is clamped off, the outflow is released and the fluid siphoned off to see that the system is draining adequately. The doctor will usually adjust the catheter position at this time to ensure good drainage. Drainage is improved by keeping the bag at the end of the outflow as low as possible, since this increases the siphonage.

Alternatively, an *indwelling silastic catheter* is available for long term peritoneal dialysis. There are a variety of silastic catheters, but the Tenkhoff indwelling peritoneal catheter is most widely used. The catheter consists of silastic tubing 55 cm long; the last 20 cm has numerous staggered perforations of 0·7 mm in diameter, or even smaller. The catheter is inserted under general anaesthetic by means of a specially designed trocar, or by laparotomy. This catheter is ideal for long term peritoneal dialysis which is only feasible if infection is consistently avoided.

The catheter has a dacron felt cuff which is bonded to the silastic tube in an effort to close the sinus tract at the skin level. Tissue grows into the felt, stabilizing the catheter and forming a biological barrier against infection. A second dacron felt cuff is located just outside the peritoneal cavity closing the sinus tract at that level. After implantation, the catheter is fitted with a syringe adaptor piece which is closed between dialyses by a disposable rubber cap. Strict aseptic technique must be used when connecting and recapping procedures are undertaken.

Drugs given into the peritoneum via the dialysis fluid are absorbed almost as quickly as by intravenous administration. The usual procedure must be followed in obtaining the doctor's signed prescription for them and in checking the drugs into the bags before setting them up.

(ii) Running the dialysis

From then on, one or two litres of fluid is run in at regular, frequent intervals as directed by the doctor; usually only 5 - 10 minutes will be taken to run it in. The fluid is then left in the peritoneal cavity for about five minutes to equilibrate with the capillary blood of the peritoneum and draw off the metabolic wastes and then ten or twenty minutes allowed for drainage. After this, another litre or two litres of fluid is run in, and the procedure repeated for as long as is necessary. The doctor will indicate the rate of exchange he would like achieved. A balance of fluid run in and out is very important, since the volumes involved are very large. Up to 50 litres or more may be exchanged into and out of the patient in 24 hours, and this is greater than the total body water. The balance may be recorded for each exchange (or if the large drainage bags are used, for every second exchange). The balance for that particular exchange (or exchanges) is recorded, and cumulated with the results of the exchanges to date on a suitable form.

It is important to note that the balance of both the individual exchanges and the cumulated balance may be positive or negative, and to see that arithmetic errors of sign (+ or −) do not occur. The balance of the 24 hours for the dialysis should be entered into the general fluid balance chart.

Apart from the volume of the dialysate returning from the peritoneum, the nurse should note whether it is bloodstained, and especially if it becomes turbid; this happens very rapidly in the presence of serious peritonitis. She should also observe whether the patient is comfortable during the running in of the fluid, and whether his abdomen remains undistended and free from more than minor tenderness.

Dialysis is usually performed throughout the 24 hours until the blood urea, electrolyte balance and fluid state are under control.

Thereafter dialysis may be performed intermittently, e.g. for 8 - 12 hours a day, leaving the catheter in place between times, and taking down the giving set; the set should, in any case, be changed daily. The following precautions are necessary if dialysis is interrupted:

(1)   The end of the connection tubing must be kept sterile, e.g. by covering it with sterile gauze, or by spigotting it firmly.

(2)   When finishing, the catheter and connection tube must not be left full of the peritoneal outflow (which contains protein and will clog the catheter); but about 10-20 ml of heparinized saline (1000 u in 250 ml) should be injected. Even so, the catheter may need rinsing with heparinized saline when dialysis is begun again, to avoid drainage difficulties.

(3)   When dialysis is restarted a new administration and drainage set should be used.

Time	In (ml)	Out (ml)	Balance*	Cumulative* balance	K+ (mmol)	Glucose (g%)	Orders/ Remarks
3.30	1000	900	+100	+ 100	4	1·36	
4.00	1000	700	+300	+ 400	4	1·36	
4.30	1000	600	+400	+ 800	4	1·36	
5.00	1000	600	+400	+1200	4	1·36	change to
5.30	1000	1050	− 50	+1150	4	6·36	6·36%
							glucose
6.00	1000	1400	−400	+ 750	4	6·36	(doctor's
6.30	1000	1300	−300	+ 450	4	6·36	initials or
7.00	1000	1600	−600	− 150	4	6·36	signature)
7.30	1000	1300	−300	− 450	4	6·36	

* + refers to fluid retained by the patient
  − to fluid lost by the patient.

(iii)   General nursing care

Patients on peritoneal dialysis are relatively immobilized during the procedure and are therefore subject to all the usual hazards of bed rest. If well enough they should be got out of bed twice daily for exercises. If dialysis can be carried out in a chair, so much the better. Attention to pressure areas is vital. Because of protein loss into the dialysis fluid a good protein intake must be maintained and the patient should be encouraged to eat an almost normal diet (see Chapter XII). Fluids allowed during dialysis will depend upon urinary output (if any), blood pressure and general state of hydration; they are normally restricted to 1500 ml per 24 hours. Sodium and potassium intakes may need to be restricted in some patients. Supplements of water soluble vitamins are also necessary. The patient should be weighed daily. The importance of accurate fluid balance records cannot be overstated. Observations of temperature, pulse, respiratory rate and blood pressure will be taken as directed by the doctor, usually four hourly, more frequently for a severely ill patient, or if the strong (6·36%) solution is being used (see above). Daily specimens of dialysate are sent for culture, and blood taken at least daily for electrolytes and urea.

Blood transfusions are sometimes given to the anaemic patient during peritoneal dialysis, especially those in acute on chronic renal failure. 6·36% solution is used at this time and where possible, packed cells are given, to minimize the amount of extra fluid given.

(iv)   Difficulties

(a)   Non-return of fluid

(1) At the beginning it is common for less than one litre of the first exchange to return, especially if the catheter is not placed low in the pelvis. Also, if the patient is dehydrated or saline depleted, two, three or four litres of fluid may be taken up and not returned. Accordingly, if the first litre is not returned a further litre is run in and then a third, watching for distension and discomfort. If three litres are not returned and are present in the abdomen, then the catheter or catheter position must be changed. If the catheter is initially misplaced between the layers of the abdominal wall, fluid will run in but there is usually no drainage. The misplacement may be recognized by (a) difficulty in advancing the catheter, (b) pain on advancing the catheter, (c) severe diffuse pain on running in fluid, (d) tense painful abdomen, (e) if the catheter is withdrawn, it is seen to be sharply kinked or bent to a near right angle. The catheter is best reinserted at a site away from the first because peritoneum is stripped away from the abdominal wall near the site of original insertion.

(2) Later in the dialysis, non-return may be due to a change of the patient's position or may indicate clotting or blockage of the catheter. This should be withdrawn gently or advanced a centimetre or two after cleaning with ether, and, if necessary, replaced by the doctor. This can often be done through the hole already made without further ado. Clotting should not happen if *heparin* is used, but is made more likely by infection. The introduction of air into the closed drainage system will cause drainage difficulties and must be guarded against.

(3) After discontinuing dialysis for a period. This calls for the cannula to be flushed through with heparinized saline, 1000 u per 200 ml saline, to remove the protein clots.

(b) Pain on running in the fluid Some patients have more than minor discomfort throughout each run-in, probably due to stretching of old intraperitoneal adhesions. Initial severe pain should lead one to consider a misplaced catheter. If the solutions are not warm, colicky pain may occur. If pain is present each time the fluid is run in, it can usually be quelled with pethidine or antispasmodic. Occasional patients experience pain only with the strong (6·36%) glucose solution, especially if this is slightly brown from caramelization of the glucose. The development of increasing pain should suggest excessive accumulation of fluid within the abdomen or the development of peritonitis.

(c) Leakage round the catheter entry is frequent in prolonged dialysis. Minor alterations in catheter position or angle of entry often stop leaks completely. A skin stitch at the hole of the entry may help. This should be reported and dealt with promptly since it predisposes to infection.

(d) Turbid fluid with or without pain or fever means peritonitis The doctor will add a broad spectrum antibiotic to the dialysate, and await the laboratory report from the daily specimen sent for microscopy and culture.

(e) Blood in dialysate Small quantities are frequent initially; bleeding later occasionally occurs. It is reasonable to stop adding heparin and continue dialysis. Major haemorrhage is extremely rare.

(v) Dangers

(a) Saline depletion ("dehydration") If the 6·36% solution is used knowingly or inadvertently the patient may be depleted up to 1·5 litres of fluid/hour. This can easily lead to circulatory collapse if continued at this rate. 6·36% solution should not be used without the doctor setting a limit either to the number of bags of 6·36% solution to be given, the time period during which they are to be employed, or the best negative balance to be achieved before stopping. Hourly observations of pulse and blood pressure must be made while this solution is used.

(b) Potassium If too much or too little potassium is added to the bags, the patient may have a cardiac arrest. All doses and quantities must be prescribed and checked for both quantity (mmol) and volume (ml) before adding.

(c) Catheter falling

(1)   into the peritoneum;
(2)   out

This usually occurs when MOVING THE PATIENT – e.g. on to a bed-pan. The security of the catheter should be checked first, and ideally a nurse should look after the catheter during the move.

(1)   is a serious matter which requires operation and is to be *avoided at all costs*. It is likely to occur in fat patients. Now that catheters have a blocking device on them this should not happen.
(2)   is inconvenient, delays the dialysis and increases the risk of infection.

(d) Perforation of the small intestine   can occur during the insertion of the catheter but this is very rare, even in patients with adhesions.

(e) Injury to blood vessels   in the abdominal wall or omentum occurs occasionally, and may lead to major haemorrhage.

(f) Acute hyperglycaemia   may be found in patients on peritoneal dialysis. Usually the blood sugar is about 10 mmol/l when the 1·36 g% (i.e. 1360 mg/100 ml) solution is being employed, and not above 20 mmol/l when the stronger solution is used. The doctor will check the blood sugar from time to time, and also if an unexplained deterioration occurs. This acute hyperglycaemia is of course common in known diabetics, but other patients may develop temporary acute diabetes under the stresses of their renal failure and the very large carbohydrate load arriving into the blood from the peritoneum.

(vi)   Automatic peritoneal dialysis machines

There are several automatic peritoneal dialysis machines on the market; an example is the P.D. 700, made by L.K.B. Medical. This automatic peritoneal dialyser can be programmed prior to the start of dialysis and it will then carry out the complete treatment with the minimum of supervision.

The dialysing fluid is drawn by suction through a heating tube and administered to the patient, allowed to stay in the patient for a set time, and then drained. The machine records and remembers the inflow and the outflow. There are a variety of alarms to eliminate risk of fluid retention, no inflow, high temperature, and air in the dialysate. This closed circuit minimizes the risk of infection. The dialysate tanks contain 10 litres of dialysate, and 500 units of heparin is added to each tank, and also potassium and antibiotics may be added under the doctor's instructions. Nurses must be very careful that they do not confuse the dosage of drugs added to the litre bag of dialysate, and a ten litre tank of dialysate.

With the introduction of the Tenkhoff silastic catheter and the automatic peritoneal dialysis machines, home peritoneal dialysis is now possible, and is in operation in several units in this country. Problems of sepsis and adhesions still present a problem. The loss of protein and amino-acids can be overcome by good nutrition. Children as well as adults have been placed on home peritoneal dialysis, and can achieve good growth.

(vii) Applications of peritoneal dialysis

(a) Acute renal failure Most patients in acute renal failure can be managed satisfactorily by peritoneal dialysis (Chapter III).

(b) Chronic renal failure Many patients in terminal renal failure can be placed on peritoneal dialysis as a preliminary to beginning regular haemodialysis. This is particularly valuable when it is not certain whether the patient has "acute on chronic" renal failure and renal function sufficient to support life may return.

(c) Poisoning Peritoneal dialysis may have a place in the management of the rare patient with an overdose of a dialysable drug who requires dialysis or haemoperfusion (Chapter XVI).

(d) Severe heart failure An occasional patient with intractable heart failure may benefit from peritoneal dialysis to remove oedema and correct electrolyte disturbances, especially as preparation for a valve replacement operation. Patients in acute or chronic renal failure may also be suffering from heart failure as their main problem.

(e) Miscellaneous Peritoneal dialysis has been used in a number of conditions such as porphyria and acute respiratory distress in the newborn; the value of these applications is still undecided.

Peritoneal dialysis in children

Peritoneal dialysis is usually preferred to haemodialysis for acute renal failure in small children because it is so much simpler to set up, and arteriovenous shunts and dialysis present special problems in infants (Chapter XV).

Peritoneal dialysis is performed in children exactly as in adults, scaling down the apparatus and volumes. There are available special peritoneal catheters for children with smaller diameters and a shorter area of drainage perforations. Even these will be too large in some infants or neonates, and doctors use a variety of apparatus at this age; intravenous cannulae of various sorts, and small needles being the most popular. Because of small volumes used in infants, the giving set is usually assembled from various components commercially available. A calibrated paediatric infusion set with a 100 ml chamber in the drip line is particularly useful as the giving set, and a three way tap can be inserted into the line to allow connection of a drainage arm. This drainage arm is most conveniently connected to a sterile graduated measuring cylinder, since exact balance is of great importance in tiny children. In older children, the commercially available giving sets may be used. Volumes to be given may be scaled down on a weight for weight basis, e.g. if two litres per hour are cycled in a 70 kg man, then 500 ml per hour are cycled in a 20 kg child; but most children will tolerate amounts in excess of this without discomfort. Heat balance is very important, and a heating coil is often inserted into the system; the infant will usually be nursed in a weighing incubator and a continuous rectal temperature is recorded.

Peritoneal dialysis is a simple but extremely powerful and useful procedure. Its simplicity should not lead to a lessening of the care given to its execution. Correctly applied, a great deal can be achieved; misused or misapplied, a great deal of harm done.

Suggestions for further reading:
Boen, S. T. (1964). *Peritoneal Dialysis in Clinical Practice.* Springfield: C. Thomas.
Harrington, J. de L., Brener, E. R. (1973). *Patient Care in Renal Failure.* Philadelphia: Saunders.
Moxon, V. (1974). Peritoneal dialysis in a neonate. *Nursing Times*, 20.6.74.
Scurrell, A. N. (1973). Peritoneal Dialysis: a five year evaluation. *Nursing Times*, 19.7.73.

CHAPTER XV

Haemodialysis

The theory behind haemodialysis is the same as that underlying peritoneal dialysis and is discussed at the beginning of Chapter XIV.

HISTORY

Haemodialysis was first applied by Abel, Rowntree, and Turner in 1913,
in Baltimore. They made a semi-permeable membrane by pouring celloidin over tubes, which were removed once the membrane material had
set. The blood (from rabbits) flowed through these tubes whilst outside
the celloidin tubing the dialysate circulated. Heparin was first used by
Lim and Necheles in 1926 as an anticoagulant for haemodialysis and
this was an important step since all dialysis membranes to date are
strongly thrombogenic (i.e. clot promoting). It was not until 1943
when Dr. Willem Kolff introduced the first practical artificial kidney to
clinical medicine in the form of a rotating drum dialyser. The first pre-
sterilized dialyser was the twin coil, introduced again by Kolff in 1956.
This development meant that more hospitals could equip themselves
for haemodialysis. The main disadvantages of the twin coil dialyser
were that it required two units of blood to prime it, and the use of a
blood pump. Kiil and Leonard developed parallel flow, or "flat bed"
dialysers, which required no blood prime. A variety of flat bed dialysers
were developed and long term dialysis programmes were expanded. The
development in 1960 of the external arteriovenous silastic – PTFE
shunt by Quinton and Scribner, and later the Cimino-Brescia subcutaneous arteriovenous fistula, solved the problems of long term blood
access. By 1966, home dialysis programmes were being set up all over
the United Kingdom. Today, haemodialysis is considered a standard
form of therapy for patients in acute and chronic renal failure (see
p.106).

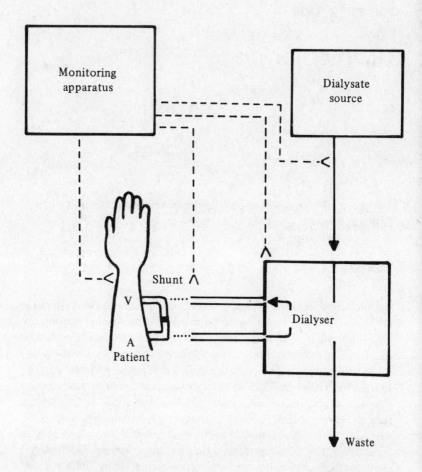

Fig. 15.1 The components of a haemodialysis system. Blood is taken from the patient by opening the *shunt* and connecting it to the blood lines of the *dialyser*. Blood travels through the dialyser and back into the patient; A = arterial end of shunt, V = venous end of shunt. In the dialyser itself, exchange takes place between the blood and the *dialysate*, across a cellulose membrane. The dialysate is produced in bulk, passes through the dialyser, and usually passes away to waste (although it can be circulated or re-used after regeneration). During the dialysis, the *monitoring* system measures a number of important aspects of the system, such as composition of the dialysate, whether there is a leak of blood in the dialyser, and various pressures within the system.

HAEMODIALYSIS

Any system of haemodialysis has a number of component parts – see Figure 15.1.

(i) The patient.

(ii) The shunt or fistula, providing access to the patient's blood stream.

(iii) The dialyser (artificial kidney).

(iv) A source of dialysate (dialysing fluid).

(v) Monitoring equipment.

This section concentrates more on the shunt than the detailed operation of various dialysis equipments, because the shunt may be encountered in a variety of clinical settings apart from specialized units, such as on general wards.

Blood access

Before haemodialysis can take place, blood must be removed from the body, passed through the dialyser and returned to the body. This means that access to the circulation, either from vein to vein or the artery to the vein (the shunt), must be established. The principle methods of blood access used are the arteriovenous shunt and the arteriovenous fistula. The arteriovenous shunt is used mainly for small children, and patients in acute renal failure who require haemodialysis. Adults and older children in chronic renal failure requiring long term haemodialysis usually have a fistula surgically constructed. *The Quinton-Scribner PTFE-silicone rubber shunt* (Figure 15.2) is the commonest type of shunt in use at the moment. It was introduced by Quinton and Scribner and is usually called by their names. The shunt is made of silicone rubber ("Silastic") tubing, with PTFE ("Teflon") vessel tips and connector, and may also be referred to by materials of which it is constructed. Basically it consists of a connection between an artery and a vein, through which the blood flows when the shunt is not being used for dialysis. Part of the shunt lies subcutaneously, part outside the skin for access (Figure 15.2). The surgeon places the vessel tip of the appropriate size in the artery, attached to a length of silicone rubber tubing. This may be shaped to have a curve, and a "step" to bring it up through the skin, or may be a simple length of straight tubing (straight shunts are sometimes described as Ramirez shunts). A similar piece of PTFE with tubing attached is tied into the appropriate vein. The tubing is brought out through stab incisions in the skin, usually on either side of a single longitudinal incision. The other ends of the tubes are pushed over a simple PTFE connector and blood can flow from artery to vein. Some doctors use metal or plastic stabilizers to attach the shunt when a patient is manipulating his or her own shunt. The Buselmeier shunt is a further variation, eliminating the PTFE connector.

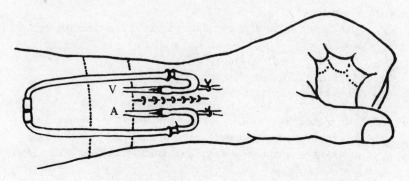

Fig. 15.2 The PTFE-silicone rubber external shunt of Quinton and Scribner. A PTFE tip is placed in an artery, and another in a convenient vein. Silicone rubber tubing is slipped over the tips and brought out through the skin. During dialysis, blood is taken from the artery and returned to the body via the vein. Between uses, as here, the two tubes (arterial and venous) are slipped over another piece of PTFE tubing so that blood circulates directly from artery to vein. The commonest site is the arm, as shown in the diagram, but the leg may also be used. It is usual to employ peripheral sites such as the radial or posterior tibial arteries, but in children, or in patients who have needed several shunts because of the clotting problems, the brachial or even the femoral artery may be employed.

(a) Shunt insertion Sometimes the doctor will elect to place a shunt under local anaesthetic and sedation, sometimes under general anaesthetic. If the latter, the usual precautions about intake of food and liquid before the procedure must be observed. The patient's consent is obtained, he is gowned, identified and placed on a stretcher for transfer to the operating theatre or ward treatment room where the shunt is to be inserted.

The shunt may be placed in the arm or the leg. The commonest sites are from the radial artery to a forearm vein at the wrist, and the posterior tibial artery and the saphenous vein at the ankle, but almost any peripheral artery and vein may be used. The surgeon can adapt the tubing ingeniously to lie straight from a variety of awkward sites. Clearly, however, there is a limit to the number of potential shunt sites although in practice it is rare to use them all up. For the patient on maintenance dialysis the care of the shunt is of the greatest importance since it is literally a life line.

The shunt arm or leg to be used will be selected, and it is important that venepunctures and intravenous infusions are avoided in this area. The limb is shaved from wrist to elbow or ankle to knee, prepared with antiseptic and towelled as directed by the doctor.

Care after shunt insertion

(1) Observe the general condition of the patient if a general anaesthetic has been given.

(2) Analgesics and antibiotics are given as directed by the doctor.

(3) The shunt is observed regularly for clotting (see below) and bleeding. Usually a pressure dressing will be applied to the limb and unless there is good reason this should not be disturbed for 48 hours at least. A dressing is then applied over the shunt wound and held in place with a bandage. This dressing should not constrict the flow of blood in the shunt or the vessels in the limb. Tight elastic stockings should not be worn and men should not wear suspenders. If the dressing becomes wet, or dirty, or the shunt is infected, then the dressing may need changing daily: otherwise twice or three times weekly at dialysis is sufficient. Micropore adhesive tape is placed over the PTFE bridge to reduce the risk of two parts of the shunt being pulled apart accidentally.

(4) Two shunt clips must be attached to the dressing AT ALL TIMES to clamp the tubing should haemorrhage occur, or the shunt require declotting.

(5) The shunt limb may be splinted or placed in plaster backslab according to the wishes of a surgeon, to prevent the tissues moving round the subcutaneous part of the shunt. Leg shunts: crutches are used after the first 48 hours to avoid weight bearing for the first 10 days since healing may be slow, especially in new patients who have been in renal failure for some time and who may be wasted and ill.

(b) Shunt observations As soon as possible these will be carried out by the patient on regular dialysis himself, but in the case of a patient with acute renal failure and in the early stages of a patient's period of regular dialysis the nurse will make these observations.

Most of the observations described can be made without removing the dressing applied to the skin surrounding the points of emergence of the tubes. These areas should not be exposed (except at the time of dressing) unless it is necessary to do so to make an adequate examination.

A shunt which is working satisfactorily should have:

(1)   no pain, tenderness, swelling, redness or discharge at the site.
(2)   a continuous column of homogeneous pink blood in the silicone rubber tubing.
(3)   detectable warmth in this tube.
(4)   a detectable pulse in the tube and often in the vein receiving blood from the shunt.
(5)   a murmur audible through the stethoscope over the vein or in the area adjacent to the shunt.

(c) Complications   Two of the main complications which shorten the life of a shunt are *clotting* of blood within the shunt and *infection* of the tissues around the shunt. *Haemorrhage* is rare. Treatment is satisfactory only if it is started at once.

(1) Clotting   Shunts have a greater tendency to clot in some patients than in others. Such patients will need to examine their shunts more frequently. Clotting in all shunts occurs with greater frequency:
(1)   for 3 days after insertion or after another operation.
(2)   for 12 hours after dialysis is completed.
(3)   if local or general infection is present.
(4)   if mechanical problems (i.e. increased resistance in the vein) are present.
(5)   if the limb or the patient is cold.
(6)   after a clotting episode has been treated.

In "high risk" patients and at the "high risk" times, the shunt should be examined every hour during the day, as late as possible at night and as early as possible in the morning. Many patients wake themselves during the night to examine their shunts. Any suspicion that all is not well should prompt more frequent observation.

Clotting will be indicated by any or all of the following features:

(1)   Dark, separated or fragmented blood.
(2)   Pain and tenderness in the area.
(3)   Coldness of the shunt.
(4)   Loss of the pulse and/or murmur.

If there is any doubt about the diagnosis both sides of the shunt should be clipped and opened. A small amount of blood is squeezed out from the end of the silicone rubber tubing, and when the shunt is reconnected a small air bubble will be seen trapped within the shunt. When the clips are removed (first venous, then arterial) the bubble should move rapidly through the venous side. If the bubble does not move, or is sluggish, then the declotting procedure is carried out after informing the doctor.

Action: declotting a shunt

This is a sterile procedure and is often trying for both nurse and patient. Full aseptic precautions must be taken, using masks and sterile gloves whenever a shunt is opened. Declotting may be carried out by the doctor, the suitably trained nurse, or the trained patient. Declotting a shunt requires finesse, knowledge and experience, and should not be undertaken by those ill-equipped to perform it.

Procedure: wearing sterile gloves and a mask.

(1)   Remove the dressing; clean the shunt tubing and surrounding skin. Apply the shunt clips and open the shunt. *'

(2)   Remove Teflon connector.

(3)   With forceps ease the clot from both ends if possible. Often the whole clot may be withdrawn.

(4)   If one side bleeds (rare) fill this side slowly with *warm* heparinized saline (mix 2000 units of heparin in 200 ml of saline); 5 ml should be used and repeated every 30 minutes.

(5)   The other side should then be declotted. If both sides are clotted, then deal with the arterial side first.

(6)   Using a 20 ml syringe, suck on the shunt. This is usually effective on the arterial side but not on the venous side.

(7)   If this fails, insert a declotting guest catheter so that its tip reaches the upper end of the shunt but does not go into the artery or vein. Rinse the shunt with the heparinized saline (as above) so that any clot lying in the tubing is washed out.

(8)   Apply suction again.

(9)   As each side is declotted it should be filled with heparinized saline as in 4 above.

(10) If these measures fail to dislodge the clot it may be necessary to push fluid into the blood vessel. First wash out air bubbles in the shunt tubing by passing the declotting catheter up and injecting saline through it. Then inject *warm* heparinized saline into the shunt. On the *arterial* side, a 5 ml syringe should be used and on the venous side a 20 ml syringe. The injection should be carried out rapidly. As soon as the clot is felt to "give" suction should be applied again. *Never* inject more than 3 – 5 ml because larger volumes may reflux into cerebral circulation. The patient may experience pain during this manoeuvre.

(11)   When the venous side will admit fluid, draw up 5000 units of heparin into a 20 ml syringe. Fill the rest of the syringe with *warm* heparinized saline. Inject this mixture into the vein.

(12)   If both sides have been declotted, the shunt should be reconnected. Assess the flow rate by observing the progress of a small bubble of air left in the shunt.

Next

(1)   Inject subcutaneous heparin 12 500 u every 12 hours until the patient's next dialysis.
(2)   Observe the shunt regularly.
(3)   Dialyse patient as soon as possible.

If these procedures fail, the doctor may decide to inject substances which dissolve fibrin into the venous or arterial side of the shunt. These include streptokinase, urokinase, bacterial fibrinolysins and heparin-like compounds. Sometimes this allows an otherwise irreversibly clotted shunt to function subsequently. It is usual to be able to declot the arterial side of the shunt, but if the venous side cannot by any means be declotted then the doctor will have to revise the venous cannula.

(2) Infection   Infection ordinarily develops more slowly than clotting and unless you are suspicious of infection when the dressing is changed, inspection will be sufficient to ensure that early treatment can be begun.

Infection reveals itself by any or all of the following changes in the limb at the shunt sites:

(1)   Pain or tenderness.
(2)   Redness or increased warmth.
(3)   Swelling.
(4)   Discharge appearing on the dressing.

Action   Inform the doctor. A swab will be taken for culture and, if the patient has a raised temperature, blood cultures should also be taken. Antibiotics will then be started as the doctor directs. Usually a bactericidal, broad spectrum antibiotic or antibiotic combination will be used until the antibiotic sensitivity of the organism is known.

(3) Bleeding   This is rare. It will be indicated by any or all of the following features:

(1)   Damp, soaked, warm dressing.
(2)   Sudden fatigue, breathlessness, pallor, sweating and palpitations.
(3)   Local pain and swelling if internal bleeding appears suddenly.

Action

(i) External (i.e. if the shunt is pulled open by accident)

(1) Apply shunt clip to each side of the shunt.

(2) Adopt procedure for routine dressing, taking particular care to clean the ends of the silastic tubing.

(3) Close shunt by re-inserting connector tube into silicone rubber tubing. If connector tube is bent or damaged, use a new one.

(ii) Internal

(1) If the swelling is around the venous tip, apply shunt clip.

(2) If the haemorrhage is on the arterial side do NOT apply shunt clips.

(3) Apply firm bandage and hold the limb above the level of the heart.

(4) Inform the doctor.

(d) The life of the shunt This is very variable, from a few days only to several years in patients on regular dialysis. The arterial tip lasts much better than the venous tip, so that it is usual for the venous tip to undergo several revisions before the whole shunt need be shifted. The tip is replaced, either further up the same vein or in another vein. The commonest cause of losing a shunt is clotting, and this most invariably starts at the venous end. This is partly because the vein frequently develops a narrowing just .beyond the PTFE tip, which may eventually obstruct the flow through the shunt. An avoidable tragedy occurs when, due to late recognition that the shunt has clotted, or late treatment, the arterial end also clots irreversibly and a new shunt has to be inserted elsewhere instead of a venous tip revision. The doctor may elect to revise a venous tip early when, before irrevocable clotting has occurred, it is clear that the shunt is giving persistent trouble and is likely to clot in the near future.

Infection round the venous end of the shunt is a serious matter which may itself lead to clotting, but infection round the arterial end is an emergency. The infection may lead to erosion of the vessel wall with external bleeding. Sometimes this is preceded by a "blow out" or aneurysm formation at the venous tip, and again this is a serious matter requiring immediate attention by the doctor.

If the doctor elects to treat the arterial infection without surgical intervention, the nurse must be aware of the possibility of haemorrhage from the artery and have a tourniquet or sphygmomanometer cuff immediately available. Usually a new shunt in another limb is necessary.

The PFTE-silicone rubber shunt made regular dialysis possible, but has many disadvantages for really long-term use. A number of patients do not seem to be able to maintain patent shunts for any length of time, even with anticoagulants. The number of shunt sites is limited, even with careful revision. The external portion of the shunt is a constant reminder to the patient of the fragile nature of his existence and its exposure may lead to his general anxieties concentrating on the shunt itself. Especially at times of infection and clotting, it is a source of pulmonary emboli. Because of these difficulties, another type of shunt is now extensively employed in regular dialysis:

The Cimino-Brescia subcutaneous arteriovenous fistula (Figure 15.3) The pre-operative preparation is as for the insertion of a PTFE-silicone rubber shunt. Frequently a fistula is placed in both arms. If the patient needs haemodialysis before the fistulae have been in place for a minimum of four weeks, then a leg shunt may be inserted and removed when the fistulae are established. Post-operatively, the fistula should be observed hourly for 12 hours, to check that there is a "thrill" present and to see that there is no bleeding. Sutures are removed after two weeks. A small proportion of fistulae fail to work, but once established their life is almost indefinite, since as one arterialized venous channel closes another tends to open. The patient is free of the external silicone rubber which may clot at any time, as well as all the other complications previously mentioned. For home dialysis, this type of fistula is used by the patient himself. Children with fistulae either needle themselves, or one of their parents actually insert the needles. There are a variety of suitable fistula needles on the market.

The careful insertion of thin-walled, wide bore needles into the fistula for dialysis is obviously very important but, equally, so is the removal of the needles. At the end of dialysis Protamine 50 mg is given very slowly into the venous line (the line carrying the blood back to the patient from the dialyser) during the "wash back". This reverses the anticoagulant action of heparin. After the patient is disconnected from the dialyser, the needles should be removed one at a time. Each needle should be pulled out quickly and smoothly and immediately digital pressure applied over a dressing at the needle site. The ideal position is with the thumb over the needle site and the fingers under the arm; pressure should be applied for a few minutes until the bleeding has stopped. This procedure prevents bruising and the patient losing blood. If however the bleeding does not stop, a sample of blood should be sent to the laboratory for Protamine titration and more Protamine given intravenously if necessary. A doctor must be informed. It is not necessary to dress the limb between dialyses as the needle sites heal very rapidly.

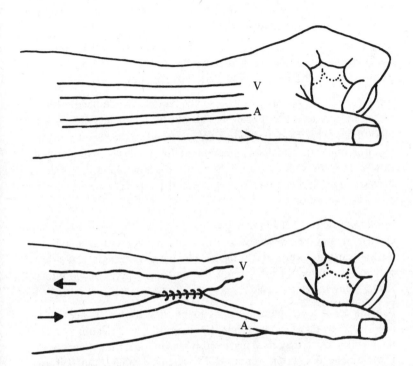

Fig. 15.3 The subcutaneous arteriovenous fistula of Brescia and Cimino. An artery and a vein (here the radial artery and the cephalic vein) are mobilized, incised and sewn together. Usually this is done side to side as shown here, but the artery may be cut and used end to side, especially if it has previously been used for a Quinton-Scribner shunt. The vein is thus arterialized, dilates and develops a rather thick wall over a period of one to six weeks, when it is ready for use. The arm, and to a lesser extent the hand, become covered with a dilated complex of veins from which a thrill can frequently be felt. These veins can be needled for use during dialysis. It is usual to place the "arterial" needle, from which blood is to be taken, near the anastomosis, and the "venous" needle further up the arm. Because the flow through the arterialized vein is great, there is little pressure difference between the "arterial" and "venous" needles and a blood pump is necessary to make blood flow through the dialyser, even when it has itself a low resistance. It is rarely necessary to revise Cimino fistulae, which are nearly always placed in the arm; they can, however, be placed in the leg if necessary.

In case of haemorrhage from a needle site (on the ward) apply digital pressure as described above and call for medical assistance.

If the fistula becomes infected the patient will be advised to insert the needles at another site well away from the infected area. Treatment with antibiotics will begin and the fistula may require dressing.

Single needle cannulation (Figure 15.4) is a new technique (described by Twiss, Kopp and others) which may be used to simplify the problem of blood access in cases of complication to the fistula site.

The principle of operation The single cannula is equipped with a Y piece, and blood is transported in and out by alternately clamping the blood lines. The magnetic clamps are controlled either by the pressure monitor, the time circuits or a combination of the two. During the inflow phase, the venous clamp closes the outflow blood line after the dialyser, and during the outflow phase the arterial clamp closes the blood line ahead of the pump.

In patients with poor blood vessels, or in whom fistulae inserted have clotted, it may be necessary to insert subcutaneous Dacron tubes or bovine carotid artery grafts on to the patients venous and arterial system. These may then be needled in a manner similar to an ordinary fistula using a special needle.

Patients are often apprehensive about inserting the fistula needles and need a great deal of encouragement and support, while learning to insert the needles. Once they have mastered the technique, they generally find it preferable to an arteriovenous PTFE-silicone rubber shunt. The great advantage of the fistula is the freedom from the constant worry that their shunt may clot at any moment, and this helps to make the patient's life off dialysis more normal.

Temporary shunts for acute dialysis

Simple cannulation of a peripheral artery or vein may be all that is necessary for one or two haemodialyses. Some doctors insert the catheters by direct surgical exposure. Others use the Seldinger technique that radiologists employ for arteriograms. A wire is inserted through the skin into the vessel and then a catheter is passed over it and the wire removed. Between use the catheters are kept open by slow infusions containing heparin. Alternatively, a double lumen catheter may be inserted through a cutdown onto the femoral vein. This has one hole at the tip and another further down. This is passed up into the inferior vena cava, and blood drawn from the end hole and returned through the side. Between times, the catheter can be used for drawing blood,

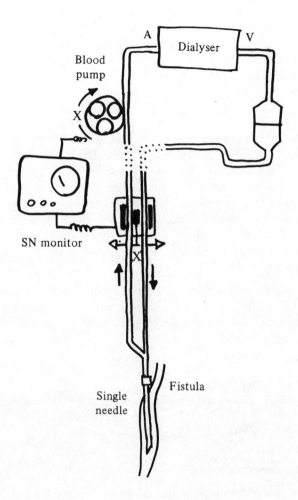

Fig. 15.4 The "single needle" system. A single needle is inserted into the patient's arteriovenous fistulae. This is connected to the dialyser blood lines through a Y-piece. The blood pump and two clamps are connected, so that the blood pump reverses direction at a predetermined interval at the same time as one line is clamped and the other is released. This permits blood to be pumped out of the patient and then back into the fistulae through the same needle.

maintaining a central venous pressure recording and for intravenous infusions. This type of catheter has the advantage that it can be put in very rapidly and does not result in loss of an artery, but it is difficult to mobilize a patient with this type of catheter *in situ*, and infected clot tends to form on the end. Many doctors prefer to use the PTFE-silicone rubber shunt for acute renal failure as well as for regular dialysis since the nurses and doctors are familiar with its use.

The dialyser

The dialyser, often inaccurately called an "artificial kidney" is the apparatus by which the composition of the blood is adjusted towards normal. A great variety of dialysers are in use at the moment, and it is probable that better and more efficient models will be in use shortly. All have the object of presenting a small volume of blood over the maximum surface area, to membranes on the other side of which flows the dialysing fluid. The principles of dialysis apply equally to haemodialysis and peritoneal dialysis, which is really haemodialysis using the peritoneal blood vessels.

At the time of writing there are a variety of disposable coil and "flat bed" dialysers which are fairly expensive, and a range of dialysers which may be re-used. The initial cost of the re-usable type is high, but the running costs are low. There are basically three types of dialyser:

(1) The "flat bed" dialyser e.g. the Meltec Multipoint, the Kiil, the Gambro Lundia etc.
(2) The coil dialyser e.g. the Travenol Ultraflow II, Extracoporeal, etc.
(3) Hollow fibre dialysers e.g. Cordis-Dow.

The ideal dialyser

(1) The cost of the purchase and operation should be low.
(2) The system must be safe, reliable and simple to operate.
(3) The circulating blood volume must be low: a maximum of 300 ml in the dialyser and lines. In paediatric dialysis, not more than 10% of the blood volume of the child, should be in the dialyser and lines.
(4) The blood circuit should be disposable.
(5) The minimum clearance of small molecules (e.g. urea) should be 150 ml/min at average blood flow; clearance of larger ("middle") molecules should also be good.
(6) The membrane burst rate should be low.

(1) Flat bed dialysers (Figure 15.5)   At the time of writing, the majority of units in the United Kingdom are now using the Meltec Multipoint dialyser which is designed on the same basic pattern as the Kiil. It comes in three sizes: the Mini 0·61 m², the Midi 0·77 m², and the Maxi 1·07 m² surface area. The Meltec Multipoint is a two layer, flat bed dialyser. Three boards made of polypropylene are sandwiched with four disposable Cuprophane membranes. The membranes are supported by a series of tiny pyramids, unlike the original Kiil design which had parallel straight grooves. The whole dialyser is clamped together and rendered water and air tight. The dialyser is built and checked for patency, then sterilized, usually with 2% formalin (0·8% formaldehyde and water).

A FLAT BED 'KIDNEY'

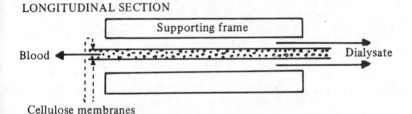

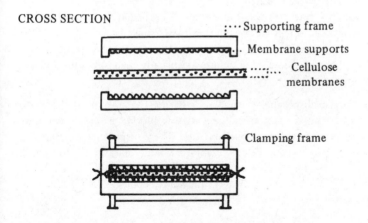

Fig. 15.5   A "flat bed" dialyser. Blood passes in a thin film between two cellulose membranes. On either side, dialysate passes in the opposite direction. Exchange (dialysis) occurs across the cellulose membrane. For use, the frame of the dialyser and the two membranes are clamped together. In the type of flatbed dialyser designed by Kiil, there are two sets of membranes, one above the other, in a single clamping frame, it is thus a "two layer" dialyser.

Before use, the formalin is dialysed out by running water through the dialysate compartment for one hour prior to dialysis. Then the venous and arterial blood lines are attached to the dialyser, and the blood circuit is primed with a sterile solution of heparinized normal saline.

After dialysis, the dialyser is formalinized again. The dialyser can be used like this for three to six dialyses, and then it must be stripped down and rebuilt. The low resistance of the dialyser gives an unrestricted blood flow, and therefore eliminates the need for a blood pump, except for patients with an arteriovenous fistula.

Different dialyser sizes are used for patients of different body weights:

Dialyser Size

Body weight	*Meltec Multipoint*	*Priming volume + blood lines*
17 – 20 kg	0·61 m^2	220 ml
20 – 30 kg	0·77 m^2	240 ml
Over 30 kg	1·07 m^2	270 ml

During dialysis, the dialysate flows through the dialyser to waste after simple contact with the blood. Water may be removed from the patients blood by negative pressure applied to the dialysate compartment of the dialyser. This is most usually done by a drain (effluent) pump, which pulls the dialysate through the kidney. The negative pressure in the dialysate compartment (often referred to as "suck") can be adjusted by partially occluding the dialysate flow from the dialysate reservoir to the flat bed dialyser. These adjustments are usually made by a control on the dialysis monitor.

There are also disposable multilayer dialysers. The advantage of these is that there is no contact with the patient's blood on the membranes, which reduces the risk of serum hepatitis. These disposable dialysers are very compact: for example, the Gambro Lundia dialyser (Figure 15.6) is 8 × 9 × 67 cm, compared with the adult Kiil or Meltec 1·07 m^2, which is 98 × 39·5 cm. However, they are expensive, approximately £10.00 each (1975 prices).

The number of hours dialysis needed on flat bed dialysers varies from 30 hours a week down to 18 hours a week depending on the unit policy. Patients at home usually dialyse overnight.

(b) Coil dialysers   In coil dialysis, the blood is passed through a bag of Cuprophane membrane wound in a spiral with a flexible meshwork

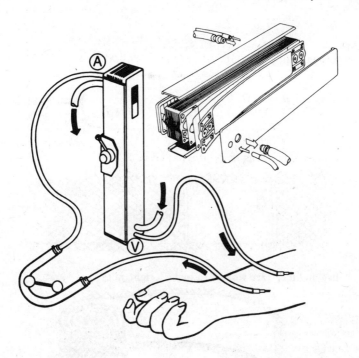

Fig. 15.6   A flat bed dialyser (the Gambro "Lundia ®"). The dialyser is
mounted vertically for use (left). On the right are shown the numerous layers of membrane across which blood and dialysate flow.

support to form a coil (Figure 15.7). The coil is encased in a rigid plastic shell. The flexible mesh membrane support keeps the membrane bag
flat so that a thin layer of blood is presented to the dialysate, which is
pumped through the mesh, usually at right angles to the flow of blood.
There are a variety of coils made by firms such as Travenol, Extracoporeal, Avon, Dasco etc. ranging in size from a membrane surface area
of 0.3 m^2 to 1.5 m^2. All coils require a blood pump because the resistance of the coil is too high for the patient's blood pressure to be able to
push the blood through unaided. To remove water from the patient,
the principle of hydrostatic pressure is again employed. The pressure in
the coil is increased either by increasing the blood pump speed, or
partially obstructing the outflow on the venous side of the coil (for
example, with a gate clip), so increasing pressure within the coil. If the
total pressure of the blood on one side of the membrane is greater than
the pressure of the dialysate on the other side of the membrane, then
filtration of water occurs from the blood into the dialysate.

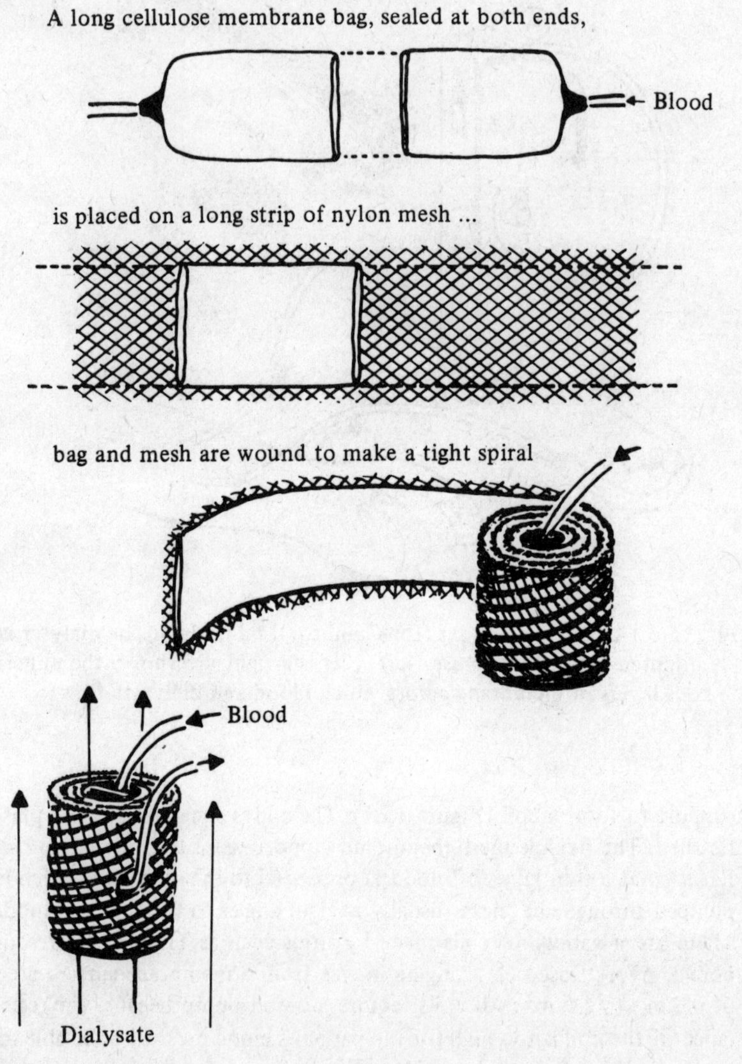

A long cellulose membrane bag, sealed at both ends,

← Blood

is placed on a long strip of nylon mesh ...

bag and mesh are wound to make a tight spiral

← Blood

Dialysate

Fig. 15.7   The blood lines are brought out for convenience, and the finished coil is then placed in the machine so that the dialysing fluid passes through the interstices in the mesh, past the blood which flows inside the now flattened bag. The flattening greatly increases the area of blood in contact with the dialysing fluid. In the most popular type of coil kidney, two such bags are wound into a broader strip of nylon mesh; hence the name "twin-coil".

(c) Hollow fibre dialysers In this design the membrane surface is presented to the blood in the form of a large number of very fine capillary tubes, through which the blood flows. The dialysate flows in a single chamber around the capillary tubes, and dialysis takes place between the blood and dialysate as in other forms of dialyser. The main advantage of hollow fibre dialysers is their small size, which is less than 30 cm long and a diameter of 8 cm for a dialyser of a surface area of $1 \cdot 5$ m^2 available for dialysis. Their disadvantage is the tendency of blood to clot in the very fine capillaries of membrane which it traverses, with consequent increased dialyser blood loss, and more important, loss of dialyser performance throughout dialysis or on re-use.

Ultrafiltration refers to the filtration of fluids and dissolved solutes across a semi-permeable membrane, due to high pressure within the system.

The larger the surface area, and the more permeable the membrane, the more rapid the ultrafiltration of water.

The advantage of the coil dialyser is that it is quick and simple to set up, and the number of hours on dialysis may be shorter e.g. 3 – 8 hours. The coil dialyser is also disposable, so helping to reduce the danger of serum hepatitis. Again, the main disadvantage is the price: most coils are approximately £11.00 each (1976 prices).

The use of dialysers for acute and regular dialysis:

(1) For acute renal failure Most units use a coil dialyser, because the patient will not require more than a few hours dialysis on each occasion, and for a period of only a few weeks. The convenience and potency of a coil dialyser outweigh any cost considerations under these circumstances.

(2) For regular dialysis The question of cost and convenience are both important, and no dialyser at present available satisfies both requirements. Most units employ the multipoint flat bed dialyser for home dialysis, and the Gambro and coil for unit regular haemodialysis, because of the dangers of cross infection and serum hepatitis. However, disposable dialysers can be employed in the home, re-using to minimize costs.

The dialysate

Dialysate is a mixture of a concentrated solution of chemicals and de-ionized or soft water i.e. does not contain more than a trace of calcium.

Dialysate mmol/l			*Normal serum mmol/l*		
Sodium	=	135	Sodium	=	136 - 145
Chloride	=	100	Chloride	=	96 - 106
Acetate	=	35 - 40	Bicarbonate	=	24 - 30
Potassium	=	0·1	Potassium	=	3·5 - 5·0
Calcium	=	3·0	Calcium	=	2·25 - 2·65
Magnesium	=	0·5	Magnesium	=	0·7 - 0·9
Glucose	=	10	Glucose	=	2·5 - 5

The dialysate composition is given as an example, and may vary from unit to unit. Dialysate is either mixed by hand or by specially designed proportionating systems, such as the Dylade, Lucas, Cambridge, Drake Willock etc. A proportionating system such as the Dylade blends dialysate continuously by taking small quantities of a concentrated solution and large quantities of de-ionized or soft water, and mixing them in exactly the right proportions. The dialysate is then pumped through the dialyser.

Monitoring

Any dialysis system must be able to run relatively unsupervized, especially if the system is to run overnight without attendance while the patient is asleep in his own home. The dialysis technique is powerful and errors in its performance may harm, and even kill, the patient. The monitoring system measures a number of events that are important to the patient's safety: for example, whether the patient's blood is leaking through a burst membrane into the dialysate. The system also measures the pressure in the dialyser and blood lines and will alarm when predetermined limits have been reached or exceeded. There is an audible alarm and the blood pump is stopped, during both these alarms, as it would be dangerous to continue pumping blood into the dialyser. The dialysate in the proportionating systems is also switched off or diverted, and an audible alarm sounds, when the alarm system indicates that the dialysate has been mixed incorrectly, or if the temperature is incorrect. Should any of these alarms by faulty or fail, apparatus switches automatically to an "alarm" state. This is referred to as a "fail safe" system. Some important alarms and monitoring systems are duplicated.

Haemodialysis systems

Each of the components – dialyser, dialysate and monitoring, can be combined in a number of different ways, so that the number of different possible layouts is large. In practice, they are usually variations on a few basic layouts. For regular dialysis, the machines most widely used carry out the manufacture of the dialysate and the monitoring. The commonest systems in the United Kingdom are the Dylade, the Cambridge and the Lucas. With these machines one can use the Kiil or the Meltec, or disposable flat bed dialysers like the Gambro or, with certain attachments, a coil. However, the coil is also used with a portable system taking only coils, e.g. the Travenol RSP dialyser. The RSP monitors only the dialysis, and the dialysate must be made up by hand in a large tank containing 120 litres of dialysate. So there is no need for elaborate plumbing to obtain de-ionized or soft water at a rate of 500 ml per minute throughout the dialysis.

One of the newer haemodialysis systems to be used is the REDY. The main features of this machine are:

(1) Plumbing modifications are unnecessary.
(2) Requires no water de-ionizer or softener.
(3) May be used anywhere there is a power supply.
(4) Provides mobility.

The principal of the REDY is that of *adsorption* of dialysate. About a gallon of dialysate is prepared from any drinkable water, and concentrate. The used dialysate passes through a cartridge where the waste products of metabolism are adsorbed and the dialysate returned to normal levels to be re-used. The main aim with this system is to reduce the amount of dialysing fluid required.

With this system, patient dialysis can be performed at any location with access to an electrical outlet and some drinkable water. Disposable dialysers, such as hollow fibre, coil or the flat bed can be used with this particular machine.

Applications of haemodialysis

These are similar to those of peritoneal dialysis.

(a) Acute renal failure Although many patients can be managed adequately with peritoneal dialysis, some patients, as noted in Chapter III, must have haemodialysis. These are patients in whom peritoneal dialysis is unsuccessful or undesirable, for reasons such as old intraperitoneal adhesions, or recent operations with potential or actual fistulae, burst abdomen, biliary surgery or foreign materials (such as an aortic graft) within the peritoneum; and those "hypercatabolic" patients whose tissue breakdown is so large that peritoneal dialysis does not provide optimum control of the blood urea and potassium. Which patients are haemodialysed, and which have peritoneal dialysis, will be decided by the doctor in the light of his previous experiences and preferences.

(b) Chronic renal failure Maintenance dialysis is almost exclusively done by haemodialysis at this moment. The care of the patient receiving maintenance dialysis is dealt with in Chapter VIII.

(c) Poisoning A very few patients severely poisoned with drugs which can be removed by dialysis, may require this treatment. Haemodialysis is especially valuable in the patient with shock and circulatory collapse (see Chapter XVI).

(d) Severe heart failure As with peritoneal dialysis, salt and water can be removed and patients can be prepared for cardiac surgery by this means.

Haemoperfusion

Haemoperfusion is the passage of blood through various absorbent materials, including charcoal. The clinical use of hydrogel-coated charcoal columns for the removal of barbiturates and glutethimides from severely poisoned patients has been found to be preferable to haemodialysis.

Before haemoperfusion can be performed, access to the patients circulation is required in the form of an arteriovenous shunt or temporary cannulation, as used for patients in acute renal failure, as discussed in this chapter.

Haemodialysis in children

A small, but increasing number of children are now on regular haemodialysis at home and in hospital. Until recently, arteriovenous shunts were used for blood access in children requiring regular haemodialysis, but unfortunately these shunts are prone to clotting, and over a period of time may require revising, until the child no longer has any shunt sites left. Now, the majority of children over the age of 10 years use arteriovenous fistulae for access. The children are encouraged to run their own dialysis, including the insertion of the fistula needles. In some cases, one parent may need to insert the needles. Children under 10 years usually have fistulae inserted in their forearms and a leg arteriovenous shunt placed until they are old enough to use their fistulae. Children adapt surprisingly well to fistula and dialysis training.

Dialyser size in relation to the child's weight, is no longer a problem in the children weighing more than 15 kg. As described earlier, there are a range of multipoints and flat bed dialysers for paediatric use. A number of disposable flat bed dialysers and coil dialysers are now made in special paediatric sizes. The problem, however, is how to dialyse infants and small children; special paediatric arteriovenous shunts must be used, as well as very small dialysers. It is important that not more than 10% of the infants blood volume should be in the blood lines and dialyser at any one time. The company Extracorporeal manufactures a special paediatric coil with a priming volume of only 65 ml and with the blood lines the total priming volume of 120 ml. The Rhône-Poulenc dialyser can be adjusted to have one, two, three, or any number of layers, each 0·075 m². These children and infants are usually in acute renal failure, and few units perform regular dialysis in this age group.

COMPARISON OF PERITONEAL DIALYSIS AND HAEMODIALYSIS

These two techniques are complimentary rather than alternative. One technique is better for some problems, the other for different situations. Some of the factors which influence the use of the two techniques at present may be summarized (Table I).

Table 1   FACTORS INFLUENCING DIALYSIS TECHNIQUES

	Haemodialysis	*Peritoneal dialysis*
Equipment:	Expensive	Cheap*
Running Cost:	Expensive	Equally expensive
Speed of first setting up:	2 hours	20 minutes
− subsequently	1½ hours	5 minutes
Staff training needed:	Extensive	Brief
Convenience:	depends upon local facilities	
Efficiency:	Very high	Much less
Risk of infection:	Low	High
Time for which patient immobilized:	Short	Long

*unless automated machines are used.

Suggestions for further reading:

Bailey, G. L. (1972). *Haemodialysis: Principles and Practice.* New York: Academic Press.

Bell, P., Calnan, J. S. (1974). *Surgical Aspects of Haemodialysis.* London: Churchill-Livingstone.

Cameron, J. S. (1973). The treatment of chronic renal failure in childhood by regular dialysis and by transplantation. *Nephron,* 11, 230.

Harrington J. de L., Brener, E. R. (1973). *Patient Care in Renal Failure*. Philadelphia: Saunders.

Nosé, Y. (1969) *The Artificial Kidney*. Philadelphia: C. V. Mosby.

Robinson, J. D. (1972). *Modern Urology for Nurses*. London: Heinemann.

Treatment of Renal Diseases. Nursing Times Publication. December 1972. London: Macmillan,

Whelpton, D. (1974). Renal Dialysis. London: Sector Publishing Ltd.

(see also the reading list for Chapter VIII).

CHAPTER XVI

Drugs and the kidney

Drugs are nearly always given by nurses, and nurses are usually the first to observe their expected or unwanted effects with regard to the kidney and renal disease. Drugs may be said to fall into two categories:

(i)   those which act on the kidney itself
(ii)   those which act elsewhere in the body and which are excreted wholly or partly through the kidney.

I DRUGS ACTING ON THE KIDNEY

(i) Diuretics and their action

Usually diuretics are given to promote urine flow when disease has reduced it. This may happen in a variety of states, for example in heart failure, in liver disease, as well as in the nephrotic syndrome. The kidney is in fact usually working efficiently when it retains sodium, and with it water, to form oedema. The problem is that the hormonal instructions to the kidney leading it to retain sodium are partly inappropriate. This happens principally when there is poor renal perfusion with blood (as in heart failure) or in hypovolaemia (for example in the nephrotic syndrome and in liver disease). The kidney responds to the hormonal and vascular "instructions" but the result, because of the abnormal conditions, is an uncomfortable oedema which we wish to remove. Conventional diuretics interfere with the reabsorption of salt in the renal tubule (Chapter I) so that more salt and water are carried out into the urine. All the *thiazide diuretics* act in this fashion, as well as *frusemide, ethacrynic acid, amiloride* and *bumetanide*. All except amiloride have the disadvantage that along with the salt and water diuresis, which is looked for, comes an unwanted loss of potassium, which in many cases must be supplemented in the diet. *Frusemide* leads to an acid urine and may produce a rise in the plasma bicarbonate. The thiazides also alter hydrogen ion secretion but in the opposite direction; hydrogen ions are retained and a mild acidosis produced.

Other diuretics with a different mode of action include *spironolactone*, which inhibits the action of aldosterone on the renal tubule, and the agents which inhibit ADH inhibitors are rather poor diuretics clinically but the actions of *alcohol* and the *theophylline* in coffee on urine flow are well known, socially. Theophylline increases blood flow to the kidney and also makes smooth muscle relax.

Osmotic diuretics There is another important situation in which diuresis of a rather different sort may be obtained. When kidney function is imperilled by severe heart failure, or when acute renal failure is feared, an *osmotic diuresis* may be induced deliberately. Osmotic diuresis is of course one of the features of chronic renal failure (Chapter VI). If any substance which cannot be reabsorbed, or which overwhelms the capacity of the tubule to handle it, is filtered at the glomerulus in large quantity, then not only water but also electrolyte will be carried down the nephron. This occurs because any concentrated solution will attract water, by virtue of the osmotic pressure it exerts. This increases the quantity and rate of flow down the nephron, so that electrolyte reabsorption is limited. Glucose (and urea) can act as osmotic diuretics if the blood level becomes high enough but the usual osmotic diuretic given is mannitol, a compound related to glucose. This, unlike glucose, is neither broken down in the body nor reabsorbed at all, so that it can exert the maximum effect.

Concentrated mannitol solutions (25%) may crystallize out at room temperature, and before they are injected into the intravenous infusion the solution should be inspected for crystals, and if they are present, the bottle of mannitol placed in warm water until they dissolve. Under conditions of impending renal failure or poor renal perfusion with blood, the osmotic diuretic will keep a good flow of urine through the tubules and this protects the tubules from blockage and cessation of urine flow. The dangers are electrolyte and water depletion.

(ii) General

We should not forget that drugs which improve cardiac performance (such as digoxin) are diuretic since they improve renal blood flow.

This will not only increase the filtration rate, but inhibit aldosterone and angiotensin release, and so permit a free excretion of salt and water. Synthetic hormones will also act on the kidney as do their natural analogues. Aldosterone is too expensive for general use, but 9 alpha fluoro hydrocortisone may be used to promote sodium retention in patients with Addison's disease and poor adrenal function. Similarly, antidiuretic hormone (pitressin) may be used to cut down the water diuresis of the patient with pituitary failure and diabetes insipidus. This is available as an injection, aqueous for intravenous use and as the tannate in oil for intramuscular injection. Care must be exercised in using the latter preparation since the ADH collects as a brown scum on the bottom of the ampoule and unless mixed or dissolved before injection, is likely to be left behind when drawing up the oil. For long term use in patients with pituitary failure it is also available as snuff and as metered aerosol.

Antibiotics are of course used to treat urinary infection and are discussed in Chapter V and the use of prednisolone and other immunosuppressive drugs are discussed in Chapters IV and IX.

II TOXIC EFFECTS OF DRUGS ON THE KIDNEY

Many drugs have a toxic effect on the kidney. For example, virtually all antibiotics – even some familiar friends such as penicillin may on occasion bring about renal failure. In general, renal damage by drugs comes about in three ways:

(1) By a direct toxic action on the renal tubules. These are vulnerable to a number of toxic substances, for example to metals in free and conjugated form and to many antibiotics.

(2) By a sensitivity reaction, acting on the small blood vessels, including those of the glomeruli. The anticoagulant phenylindanedione (Dindevan) and the gold compound use in the treatment of rheumatoid arthritis (sodium aurothiomalate) are examples of drugs which may do this.

(3) By producing an interstitial nephritis, i.e. inflammation and fibrosis of the connective tissue supporting the nephrons. Many antibiotics produce this type of injury, as does the abuse of analgesics (Chapter X).

III THE EXCRETION OF DRUGS BY THE KIDNEY

Any drug which remains in simple solution in the plasma will be filtered at the glomerulus and excreted by the kidney if not reabsorbed by the tubules. Only if it is broken down elsewhere in the body or is fixed in tissues very rapidly will there be *no* excretion through the kidney. Some drugs are excreted entirely by this route and some other drugs (such as the penicillins) are actually *secreted* by the tubules as well as being filtered, and are therefore cleared from the body very rapidly. This tubular secretion of drugs may be blocked by the drug probenecid.

All this means that in patients with impaired renal function drug dosages must frequently be modified, and drugs never given without considering what effect the renal impairment might have on the amount remaining in the body. Some drugs have harmful effects which depend on the concentration they reach in the plasma – for example, the destructive effect of streptomycin and related drugs on the auditory nerve. With these drugs, extreme caution is necessary in renal failure. In passing we may note that precisely the same situation exists for drugs broken down in the liver, and liver failure.

IV   THE TREATMENT OF POISONING BY FORCED DIURESIS

The other situation in which the clearance of drugs by the kidney is of importance is, of course, the sad one of deliberate or accidental self-poisoning. Very frequently this occurs in patients who are already under treatment with a variety of sedative, antidepressive or tranquilizing drugs. The other main group of drugs used in self-poisoning are drugs readily obtainable without prescription, such as aspirin. The full management of these patients is beyond the scope of this text but includes:

(i)   diagnosis
(ii)   general management of the unconscious patient
(iii)   support of the respiratory and cardiovascular systems
(iv)   removal of the drug from the body
(v)   psychiatric support and treatment after recovery.

We are here considering only the fourth of these: *removal of the drug from the body*. In the treatment of self-poisonings, both nurses in general wards and intensive care wards may be involved, since apart from general supportive measures, several techniques are available which may help removal of the drug:

(i)   forced diuresis
(ii)   peritoneal dialysis (Chapter XIV)
(iii)   haemodialysis (Chapter XV)
(iv)   charcoal haemoperfusion (Chapter XV)

In general only drugs which are removed from the body principally by the kidney and which remain in simple solution in the plasma (not bound to plasma proteins or fixed to tissues) are suitable for these techniques. Only an extremely small proportion of poisoned patients need be *dialysed*, or have charcoal haemoperfusion. These patients have usually taken massive doses of drugs, and their renal circulation is so impaired that excretion will not occur by this route. Alternatively they may be patients with renal disease. One immediate problem facing the doctor is that it may not be at all clear what drug or drugs the patient has taken, and forced diuresis or dialysis may be performed in the hope that a drug has been taken which can be removed by these techniques.

Only a few patients in deep coma need *forced diuresis*, which is not without danger. The decision as to which patients should be submitted to forced diuresis is a difficult one for the doctor. The nurses' task is to see that this arduous technique is carried out as efficiently and as safely as possible. The account below is a simple scheme which has been used with success, but there are many individual variations which doctors in different hospitals employ. In particular, there is considerable disagreement at the moment as to the best regime for forced diuresis in aspirin poisoning, because of the acid-base problems in this state. The drugs for which forced diuresis has been shown to have a definite place are:

(1)   long acting barbiturates (such as phenobarbitone)
(2)   salicylates, including aspirin.

The situation with regard to other drugs is very confused. The shorter acting barbiturates (amylobarbitone, quinalbarbitone, butobarbitone, pentobarbitone) and phenytoin (Epanutin) are removed to some extent and the doctor may wish to try the treatment in patients poisoned with these drugs. However, a number of drugs may be taken in self-poisoning for which forced diuresis is of little use; these include phenothiazines, amitryptyline, diazepam (Valium) and chlordiazepoxide (Librium).

An outline of forced diuresis

(i)   An intravenous infusion is set up, usually connected to a CVP manometer. Blood is taken for baseline electrolytes, pH and blood gases. A catheter is passed into the bladder (Chapter V) to record the rate of urine flow. The doctor will assess the renal function by one or more of the tests detailed in Chapter XI. Sometimes the patient will be oliguric because cardiac function needs support, and diuresis cannot be begun until this is provided. Occasionally renal function is poor, and remains poor (for example in patients with pre-existing renal impairment) and diuresis will not be possible.

(ii)   Urine flow is stimulated, either by a diuretic (such as hydrochlorothiazide or frusemide) given into the intravenous infusion, or an osmotic diuretic such as mannitol is given (see above). A brisk diuresis is then seen.

(iii)   Infusion of intravenous fluid is continued. Up to 500 ml or even 1 l/h may be given, the urine flow being stimulated by repeated injections of diuretic or mannitol as directed by the doctor. Often this will be every two litres of fluid or so. A typical régime might include variations upon:

>   540 ml 0·9% saline or M/6 lactate, followed by
>   540 ml 5% dextrose, then
>   540 ml 5% dextrose, with 20 mmol (1·5 g) of KCl added – in rotation.

The object is to *match the excretion of water, sodium and electrolyte induced by the diuretic and leave the patient in balance.* The blood and urine electrolytes will be estimated as requested by the doctor, and he will alter the infusion accordingly. Both phenobarbitone and salicylates are excreted more readily in an alkaline urine, and the nurse should check the urine pH with BDH universal indicator paper to see that its pH is about 7·5 – 8·5. The doctor will vary the amount of M/6 lactate in the regimé according to this simple measurement, reinforced by measurements of the actual blood pH. Bicarbonate as the molar solution (8·4% (1 mmol/l)) may be added to the infusion instead of molar lactate.

Observations

It is seldom necessary to continue the forced diuresis for more than 24 hours. Apart from the usual observations of pulse, respirations, temperature and level of consciousness the nurse will frequently have a central venous pressure line to keep open and to observe. To begin with most observations will be on an hourly basis. The pressure areas of unconscious patients are peculiarly vulnerable. The patient may need assisted ventilation, in which case the care of a cuffed tube, or less commonly a tracheostomy, may be added to that of the catheter. Accurate recording of fluid input and output is of course essential. In some units the patient will be nursed on a weighing bed and this will be recorded. The likelihood of recovery in the patient with severe poisoning largely rests with the quality of the general nursing and medical care that he or she receives.

Suggestions for further reading:
Curtis, J. R., Williams, G. B. (1975). Drug administration in renal failure. *Clinical Management of Chronic Renal Failure.* Oxford: Blackwell.
Linton, A. L., Lawson, D. H. (1970). Antibiotic therapy in renal failure. *Proceedings of the European Dialysis and Transplantation Association*, 7, 371.
Reidenberg, M. M. (1975). Drug metabolism in uremia. *Clinical Nephrology*, 4, 83.

CHAPTER XVII

General social and ethical problems

Many of the topics discussed in the chapter – for example, the care of the dying – are by no means peculiar to patients with renal disease. However, the success of renal transplantation, the limited availability of both transplant donors or regular dialysis have raised problems which are already a daily feature in the practice of renal medicine. There is no doubt that these difficulties will become more widespread as other expensive, time-consuming techniques are developed which cannot be made available to all. We can only pose the questions and indicate some of the answers or part-answers that have been suggested; or which we ourselves have found useful in coping with these dilemmas.

SELECTION OF PATIENTS FOR REGULAR DIALYSIS TREATMENT

At the moment only a small proportion of patients reaching terminal renal failure are offered this type of treatment. Although facilities for both regular dialysis and renal transplantation have expanded and are expanding rapidly, it is likely that demand will always exceed the supply of available dialysis places and donor kidneys. Ideally, something like 7,000 patients should be treated every year in the United Kingdom (54,000,000 population) for terminal renal failure. Frequently the doctor and nurse are faced with the melancholy situation of the patient for whom no treatment is available, although he could well benefit from it.

The selection of patients for dialysis or transplant programmes is a controversial subject since it places upon the doctor the insoluble problem of who should be treated and who allowed to die. At first, it was suggested that impartial bodies of lay and medical people could select the patients for dialysis and transplant programmes, after considering all the problems of personality and social worth offered by the candidates. This has, perhaps fortunately, proved impossible in practice. Patients rarely present themselves in a state where assessment is possible, and along with several others so that a choice may be made. A place may be filled on a dialysis or transplant programme this week with one patient, and as a result, a patient whose very existence is unknown to the doctors making the choice dies the following week. No direct comparison is possible. Many units have now adopted the attitude of accepting patients on a "first come, first served" basis, providing that certain medical criteria are satisfied.

Some of the factors the doctor may take into consideration in selecting patients are:

(i) Is there a medical reason why the patient should not be accepted, or should be given lower priority? Such as the presence of a systemic disease affecting not only the kidneys but other organs, or coincident disease, particularly of the cardiovascular system.

(ii) Is the patient too old or too young? This is arbitrary, but few patients over 60 or 65 years are accepted, and not all units will accept children.

(iii) Has the patient, and his or her spouse, the temperament to stand the stresses of regular dialysis, particularly if home dialysis is contemplated?

(iv) Who will suffer if the patient dies? Many doctors attempt to give priority to patients with family responsibilities.

The "ideal" patient for maintenance dialysis would be a young man or woman (aged less than 40 and more than 20) with family responsibilities and a roomy house, a stable job and marriage, a tough temperament, without systemic or coincident disease and who, although in terminal renal failure, has been well looked after and is capable of rapid rehabilitation from the many metabolic and nutritional problems of this state.

Such patients are all too rare in practice! Most patients are too sick with their terminal illness for a detailed assessment to be possible, especially of their mental state and capacity. In addition, taking these factors into consideration means we are making value judgements on individuals which we are ill-equipped to make, and which are as distasteful after the hundredth decision has been made as after the first. There is no easy solution to this problem.

THE PROLONGATION OF LIFE BY ARTIFICIAL MEANS

A number of objections can be raised, from a variety of viewpoints, that substitution therapy is in itself not something which should be attempted. How justified are we in prolonging the lives of a privileged few? The first objection, that the quality of life obtainable after transplantation or on maintenance dialysis is not worth having in terms of quality, is clearly untenable; contact with patients undergoing these procedures is all that is required to convince one that the patients would rather continue with their present existence than die. More, they have a positive zest for life, knowing perhaps more sharply than any other group of people how fragile and precious it is.

The second objection, that this is too expensive a procedure for the country to afford, has some truth in it. However, to maintain the dependents of those kept productive on dialysis, and especially those successfully transplanted, would in the long run be more expensive than treating the patients. In terms of cost and effectiveness few medical treatments (none of them for fatal chronic disease) are more effective or have been carefully costed. We may say we can no longer afford comprehensive medical care, which may become true as more and more useful treatments for more and more diseases, expensive in time, money and personnel, become available. It may be argued, justifiably, that the money would be better spent on preventing or ameliorating renal disease than in dealing with its terminal phases. There is certainly logic behind this suggestion and ideally, one would like to do both. The emotional pressures, however, from those *now* dying of renal disease are such that although reasonable, this attitude is not tenable in practice. If we were more certain of preventing renal disease this argument would have more force. The only variety of renal disease we appear to be within sight of preventing is chronic pyelonephritis beginning in childhood. The cost of this prevention is still speculative, and even by the most generous estimates only one quarter of the patients being taken on to dialysis and transplant programmes have pyelonephritis; the majority of patients with pyelonephritis are over 65 years of age.

Finally, looking at the problem on a larger scale, how justified are we in maintaining these patients at a cost of which we are well aware[1], when the world is overpopulated and two-thirds of it underfed? There is no answer to this argument, which is part of the much larger question of the developed world's responsibilities to its less prosperous neighbours.

[1] See opposite page

TRANSPLANT DONORS

Recently there has been much publicity about the donation of organs from the newly dead for transplant purposes. This has raised a number of questions:

(i) What is death?

Until recently it was sufficient to say that death occurred when "vital functions" ceased. The vital functions referred to were heart beat and respiration. Now it is possible to maintain respiration almost indefinitely, and to maintain heartbeat, or at least circulation, for a limited period. Also, patients whose independent existence without these supportive measures is impossible may or may not have brains which are capable of working again. These two considerations lead to the idea of "brain death" which is a conceptual advance but leaves one no nearer the solution of the practical problem since it cannot precisely be defined. A flat EEG tracing has been widely advocated as a suitable criterion and has been adopted as law in France, but although generally useful does not remove the possibility of a patient being abandoned whose brain can recover. Better are tests designed to examine the function of systems located in the brain stem. These include vestibular reflexes, and also the ability of measured concentrations of CO_2 in the blood to stimulate the respiratory centre. That is, the patient's ability to begin or attempt ventilation, when support of the ventilator is withdrawn, is examined.

These problems are difficult enough when it is simply a question of how long one carries on with respiratory support in a patient with brain

---

[1] It is difficult to cost any form of treatment accurately because this depends so much upon how much of the overheads and support activities are included in the costing. At the moment, a patient on Kiil dialysis in the home uses about £1100 of disposable materials each year. To this must be added a proportion of the costs of maintaining the Unit where he or she was trained, and who provide medical support and supervision. This amount will vary with the number of patients maintained by the Unit, but will not be less than £500 and is more likely to be over £1000 at the present time. When each patient goes home the equipment necessary and its installation will cost over £3000, depending on the type of machine.

For comparison it would be useful to give the cost of a renal transplant and the subsequent supervision of the patient. This is even more difficult to estimate since so much of the activities concerned with transplantation take place within the hospital and are absorbed in the routine costs. Again, the more transplants done the less each will cost. Including the cost of a pretransplant period of six months dialysis, a renal transplant costs, very approximately, between £3000 and £6000 (1976 prices).

damage, they are even sharper when the possibility of transplanting organs from the patient arises. And it is from just such patients that the most viable and most useful grafts can be obtained, because the moment of probable death can be known in advance, since it will usually be shortly after respiratory support is removed. The transplant operation can be planned in advance and kidneys or other organs with the minimum ischaemic time obtained. In renal transplantation it is fortunate that we can use organs taken from a patient who has by any criterion died, but a further difficulty has arisen over the timing of organ removal in patients maintained on ventilators. The difficulty of deciding who is and who may not be recoverable in this group of patients with brain injuries has already been discussed. Even when a decision has been reached that the patient has irrecoverable brain damage, there still remains the problem of whether the kidneys should be removed whilst the patient is maintained on the ventilator, and has a beating heart. At the moment it is normal practice in the United Kingdom to switch off the ventilator, wait until the pulse ceases or the ECG is flat, and then proceed to remove the kidneys. In France and Scandinavia it is normal practice when irreversible brain death has been diagnosed and the patient is to be used as a donor, to remove the kidneys first. The real problem here is that no one is completely convinced that we can diagnose irreversibility with *no* chance that an occasional mistake will be made. Even if a small doubt remains, public confidence is bound to be shaken somewhat, and despite the need for such organs removed from what have been termed "heart-beating cadavers" it is possible that a change to the French and Scandinavian model may lose more than it may gain.

At present a patient is "officially" dead when two doctors, – one qualified at least five years and neither associated with the transplant team – are willing to declare so. It is usual in cases involving irreversible brain damage for one to be a neurologist. This is the best we can do at the moment, if an irreplaceable source of good kidneys for transplantation is not to be lost.

Cadaver donor transplantation

It might be thought that it is the right of any individual to specify what should happen to his or her body after death. In fact, present laws limit this rather severely and the body after death may come into the disposal of the nearest relative, or under the care of the coroner. Very few people leave instructions as to what should happen to their body after death, which often occurs unexpectedly and possibly far from home.

The suggestion that it should be possible to use organs from the body of someone newly dead without specific permission is thus not such a large step as might seem at first sight. However, if either by precedent established in court, or by Act of Parliament it becomes possible to take organs unless specifically instructed not to, then it will become necessary to have some machinery for those who object to "opt out" and register their objection.

The alternative suggestion is that those who wish to donate their kidneys (or other organs) after death should "opt in" by carrying a card stating this. To a limited extent this is already in operation in a number of countries including the United Kingdom, where transplant donor cards signed by the individual concerned and their nearest relative are available. The problem here is twofold. Until a high proportion of the population carry such cards, the chances of finding one on someone involved in a car accident are small. A more important difficulty is that in Britain, unlike some states in the USA, the card is not a legal document but merely a statement of intent. The Human Tissues Act (1961) still governs the use of bodies after death in the UK, and in theory at least this implies seeking the formal permission of the person in charge of the body to take organs. This has, however, not been tested in court. The person in charge will normally be the nearest relative but may be the coroner.

Surveys indicate that at least 75% of the population are willing for their own or their relatives' kidneys to be taken, and it must be admitted that one of the major blocks to the free availability of kidneys is the apathy and perhaps distaste of the medical professions in general, and doctors in particular, with regard to organ donation. In this respect the profession lags behind public opinion.

The ethical problems of *living donor transplantation* are in some ways even more complex, although they have received less attention than cadaver donation. The main problem centres round the risk to a healthy individual of having an anaesthetic, undergoing a (for him) unnecessary operation, and living thereafter with only one kidney. No case of the death of the donor as a result of the removal of the kidney or the operation have yet been published, despite over 10 000 live donor transplants. However, the risk of even an anaesthetic only is finite although very small, and sooner or later a death must occur. Will this one death outweigh the good done to the other recipients? So far as subsequent risks are concerned, insurance companies do not normally load individuals with only one kidney although the risk of injury or disease in the remaining organ is still present. A particular problem is that many kidney diseases are familial, and it is sometimes difficult or impossible to know whether a particular form of nephritis may occur in other members of the family. Certainly this is a problem which has been underestimated in the past.

Against this must be judged the benefit to the donor of an act whose emotional importance can hardly be exaggerated. Whilst there are many donors who would suffer if denied the opportunity, equally there are many who offer because of family pressures or who later regret what was an impulse, reconsidered later. It is important that the medical staff try to provide a situation in which only those donors whose motives are beyond question have the opportunity to donate. This can usually be achieved by talking to the prospective donor alone and if he or she expresses doubts, the family and others may be told that the graft is not possible because of technical considerations: for example, tissue type. However, one must not forget that some guilt in the possible donor is inevitable once the suggestion has been raised, especially if the potential recipient should die.

In a fair number of families the possibilities of using a child or adolescent under the age of 18 years may arise. Most doctors feel that this is not a decision that parents can make on behalf of their children (as they legally must in this situation) nor one that a child or adolescent should be asked to make. It is policy in most units not to use minors as donors, even in the situation of identical twins, nevertheless, a few transplants from children as young as six years old have been performed in the United States.

THE DYING PATIENT

A more perennial problem than these recent important questions is the care of the dying patient. This is particularly difficult when a patient is dying of chronic renal failure, and a place is not available (or has not been offered) on a regular dialysis programme; or where a successful peritoneal dialysis is stopped because no future can be seen for the patient after a period of maintenance. One must remember that death in uraemia is peculiarly unpleasant until the patient actually becomes comatose. With modern management this may be very little before death itself.

Today, with improved medical care death is less a part of most families' experience. It is also less acceptable. This arises partly because massive publicity for medical advances has led people to believe that something can be done in every instance, and partly because of the declining number of those for whom death is the prelude to a firmly anticipated, happy after-life. Many patients with renal disease die at an age when most people can expect a number of years of active life; either in childhood, adolescence or early adult life. Most of them die in hospital.

Care of the dying patient may be considered for convenience under a number of headings, most of which overlap to some extent:

(i) Emotional problems of staff looking after the dying patient
(ii) The patient: relief of symptoms:
relief of anxiety;
answering specific questions
(iii) The relatives. information;
support
(iv) The role of the medical social worker and chaplain.

Consider these in order:

The emotional problems of staff looking after the patient

This has been put first, not because the staff are more important than the patient but because as Cecily Saunders says:

"We will never help the anxieties of others if we do not try to understand and handle our own."

It is very difficult to be objective when a patient is dying, especially one on whom care has been lavished and for whom affection is strong. This is doubly true when the patient dies early in life. Indeed, complete objectivity is impossible since caring is part of the nurse's or doctor's job. The important point is to use these emotions to generate the care the patient needs and should receive. Beyond a certain intensity, further emotional involvement may become an obstacle rather than an aid to the care of the patient. Even if the patient cannot be saved, the nurse must make it her duty to ensure his comfort, freedom from pain and anxiety, and that the death, when it comes, is comfortable and has dignity. She can feel sure that in doing this her contribution is by no means negligible. Achieving the emotional stability which can allow a nurse and doctor to face the hurt of their patient's death is part of the process of becoming a useful member of a medical team. It is useful to think of oneself as a member of a group concerned with the dying patient, all of whom are striving their best. Each individual must find his own path to this according to their personal beliefs and temperament.

The patient: relief of symptoms and anxiety

It is important to ensure that unnecessary suffering is avoided. Often the nausea, vomiting and confusion that may precede death is treatable. One must avoid pain, although a painful death is less common than one in fear and confusion. Anticipation of pain can remove its threat. Fear should always be foreseen and forestalled or allayed, and the biggest fear is of the unknown. Lack of information about what is going on is far more common than fear of the death itself. Explanation and simple reassurance can achieve a great deal. Above all, *some* information must always be supplied to direct questions even if this is a part truth or on occasion an untruth. It is very important that the nurse ensure that what she and other members of the team tell the patient should correspond. Even if nothing sinister is apprehended by the patient, the confusion brought about by differing statements may cause anxiety in itself. It is therefore important to meet frequently to decide an agreed policy for each patient.

It is also very important that the patient should not feel himself abandoned. Many people, even those trained to work with the sick and dying, withdraw unconsciously from the patient who is going to die. Medical staff, and especially nursing staff must ensure that no impression of this is evident to the patient. For example, if a patient on peritoneal dialysis is to have this dialysis stopped it is better to do this by changing the bags much less frequently, to continue the charting and observations. To remove the peritoneal catheter and shift the patient to an area where he receives less nursing attention can be a barbarity. This may be true even where the patient is aware of dying and is reconciled to it. Care must continue to the very end and this is valuable not only in its human comfort to the patient but also in the feeling that it gives to the nurse. She can feel that she is contributing to the care of the patient in a very positive fashion. No patient should ever die frightened or alone. Powerful drugs are now available which can make the patient's state more tolerable to him, even if it cannot be improved. These include the narcotic drugs and chlorpromazine. Judiciously used, they are an enormous help but should never be used as a substitute for the human contacts just discussed. It cannot be too strongly emphasized that narcotic drugs of addiction are not only of use in the patient with severe pain; their ability to allay anxiety is unique. Unfortunately, morphine itself tends to produce excessive drowsiness and frequent vomiting. It is for these reasons that many doctors prefer heroin. Some combine it with cocaine to combat the sedation produced by the narcotic.

Doctors will usually use these drugs in doses which are necessary to render the patient free of anxiety or pain. On occasion these doses may be large enough to shorten the patient's probable period of survival. Most doctors are willing to employ them in this fashion, but deliberate *euthanasia* is something which, although much debated, has little relevance to the actual situations encountered in clinical practice. The hypothetical patient who is so much discussed – conscious, in intolerable circumstances from pain or other suffering, whom doctors fight to keep alive – is virtually a myth. Many times one sees that when a patient in a terminal illness ceases to struggle for his life, he dies rapidly, even if the doctor, perhaps misguidedly but directed by his instincts, attempts to save him.

Direct questions   The direct question "am I going to die?" is often asked. Some patients ask this question and anticipate a reassuring answer, even though fundamentally they are aware that they are dying, because they are unable to handle the enormity of the thought. Others, especially those anticipating an after-life, genuinely wish to be told the truth. Others will be satisfied if the seriousness of their situation is stated unemotionally, and the undoubted fact is restated that one can never say when or how a patient may die. Occasionally it is simply a cry for information – any information – and indicates a failure of communication or comprehension. One must always remember that the sick patient may well take in little of what is said at the first hearing, and repetition is usually necessary. The problem is to try to anticipate what the real meaning of the question may be. Again, it is vital that all members of the medical and nursing staff are aware of what is felt to be best for the patient. Often discussion with the closest relative or relatives will help in deciding what is the best course to take as to what to tell the patient.

It is as necessary to listen to the patient as to talk to him. Often anxieties can be released simply by the presence of a sympathetic ear. Many patients wish to talk and find that they cannot say the things they wish when their relatives visit, especially in a public ward. Under these circumstances the nurse may be a vital communicant.

The relatives

The first reaction of relatives to a sudden unexpected death may be disbelief. This may be followed for a brief period by the need to blame the death onto someone – sometimes the medical staff, sometimes the family doctor, sometimes unrelated events in the recent past. The nurse needs to recognize both these reactions and cope with them. The relatives must be kept informed of what is happening when a death can be anticipated. As with the sick patient, so with the worried relative; it will often be necessary to cover the same ground again and again, adjusting language to the level of comprehension before understanding can be achieved. The relatives should be made to feel a part of the group looking after the dying patient and can provide much of the security and contact needed. Sometimes a problem arises if a relative is so distressed by the situation that he cannot handle his own emotions. Again, the nurse can do a great deal when this does arise by stressing the positive role the relative can play in comforting the patient. She can also reassure the relative that everything that can be done is being done. Many relatives' worry arises not so much from fear for the patient himself but from guilt that they could themselves have in some way prevented the illness, for example, by heeding earlier what then appeared to be innocuous symptoms, or by preventing some incident to which they attribute the illness. Specific reassurance on these points may bring great relief. However, the bitterness of the situation when all that could be done is *not* being done cannot be blunted (as when no dialysis place is available for a suitable patient in chronic renal failure).

Once death has taken place it is important that someone who has been concerned with the care of the patient should see the relatives rather than a stranger, however sympathetic.

The role of the chaplain and medical social worker

Many patients will wish to talk with someone about their problems. Specifically, if they are practising members of an organized religion then the priest of that faith or sect may be of great comfort. Even those of intermittent faith find that approaching death – even if not consciously admitted – brings about the desire to discuss their spiritual problems. Again, contact with another human being helps spread the load providing comfort to the dying patient. The rôle of the medical social worker in states of bereavement is discussed in Chapter VIII.

Suggestions for further reading:
> British Transplantation Society (1975). (Ed.) Brent, L. The Shortage of organs for clinical transplantation; document for discussion. *British Medical Journal*, 1, 251. See also *British Medical Journal* editorial on the report (1975), 1, 230.
> Calland, C. H. (1972). Iatrogenic problems in end-stage renal failure. *New Eng. J. Med.*, 287, 334.
> Creighton, H. (1974). Legal problems related to transplant management. *Dialysis and Transplantation*, June 1974, p. 34.

Illich, I. (1974). *Medical Nemesis*. London: Calder and Boyars.

Illich, I. (1976). *No Placebo. The Nightmare of Medical Progress*. London: Calder and Boyars.

Lancet Editorial (1975). Kidneys for transplantation. *Lancet*, ii, 164.

Parsons, V., Snowden, S., Bewick, M. (1973). Ethical problems surrounding dialysis and transplantation. *Proceedings of the Royal Society of Medicine*, 66, 913.

Reinhardt, J. B. (1971). The doctor's dilemma: whether or not to recommend continuous renal dialysis or renal homo-transplantation for the child with end-stage renal disease. *Journal of Pediatrics*, 77, 505.

Schowalter, J. E., Ferhoff, J. B., Mann, N. M. (1973). The adolescent patient's right to die. *Pediatrics*, 51, 97.

Tietz, W., Powars, D. (1975). The paediatrician and the dying child. *Clinical Pediatrics*, 14, 585.

Glossary

In the text, terms with which the nurse may not be entirely familiar have been avoided as far as possible. However, some technical, physiological and biochemical terms are unavoidable, and those most likely to be unfamiliar to the nurse, or which may cause difficulty, are defined briefly here. Many of these terms are not, in fact, used in the text but this glossary may prove useful if they are encountered on ward rounds, books or case notes.

Acid A substance which releases hydrogen ions (protons, H^+) in solutions.

$$HA \rightleftharpoons H^+ + A'$$
$$\text{acid} \qquad \text{base}$$

strong acids exist almost entirely in the form $H^+ + A'$ (dissociated); *weak* acids mostly in the form HA (undissociated). Acid is excreted through the kidney as H^+, and as ammonium ($NH_3 + H^+ = NH_4^+$ ammonium), and through the lungs as CO_2 and water ($H^+ + HCO'_3 \rightarrow H_2CO_3 \rightarrow CO_2 + H_2O$).

Acute cortical necrosis Infarction (death by blocking of the blood supply) of the cortex of the kidney.

Acute tubular necrosis The appearance of damage to the renal tubular cells frequently seen in patients with acute renal failure.

Aldosterone Hormone secreted by the adrenal cortex which acts on the renal tubule, stimulating sodium reabsorption and potassium loss.

Angiotensin Hormone which acts on the renal tubule to influence the reabsorption of sodium. It also stimulates the adrenal cortex to release aldosterone (q.v.) and makes the smooth muscle of arterioles contract.

Antidiuretic hormone (ADH, pitressin, vasopressin) Hormone secreted by the hypothalamus and stored in the posterior part of the pituitary (the neurohypophysis) which influences the amount of water passing through the distal tubules and collecting ducts of the kidney. It permits water to pass out of the ducts, so that under its influence concentrated urine is formed.

Anuria No urine flow in the absence of retention of urine.

Antistreptolysin O titre (or ASOT) Amount of antibody in the blood against a particular streptococcal antigen (O).

β-blocker Class of drugs which block the β-receptors of the autonomic nervous system. Often used for high blood pressure. May be divided into β_1 and β_2 blockers according to action.

Buffer A buffered solution is one which accepts addition or subtraction of H^+ ions with little or no change in its H^+ ion concentration (pH). One can therefore add H^+, or OH' ions, to such a solution without altering its H^+ concentration. Most buffer solutions consist of a weak acid (that is, one which in solution exists mostly as the form HA, rather than $H^+ + A'$) and a salt of the acid. In the extracellular fluids the principal kation is sodium, so more buffering systems in this compartment may be considered as weak acid + sodium salt. Consider the weak acid carbonic acid and sodium bicarbonate in solution together, with hydrochloric acid then added:

$$H_2CO_3 \quad H_2CO_3 \quad H_2CO_3 \quad H_2CO_3 \cdots\cdots\cdots\cdots\cdots\cdots$$

$$\Updownarrow$$

$$HCO_3' \searrow \quad HCO_3' \quad Na^+$$

$$H^+ \quad \boxed{H^+Cl'}$$

most of the carbonic acid is undissociated (H_2CO_3) and the free hydrogen ion concentration is low (H^+). The added hydrogen ion combines with bicarbonate to form additional H_2CO_3

$$H_2CO_3 \quad H_2CO_3 \quad H_2CO_3 \quad H_2CO_3 \cdots\cdots\cdots\cdots\cdots\cdots$$

$$H_2CO_3 \rightleftharpoons HCO_3' \quad Na^+$$

$$H^+ \quad Cl'$$

in effect, one gets NaCl and H_2CO_3 from HCl + $NaHCO_3$ and the bicarbonate concentration of the solution falls but *the H^+ concentration remains constant.*

The importance of there being a *weak* acid present is clear: if H_2CO_3 remained largely dissociated in solution as $H^+ + HCO_3{'}$ then there would be little or no buffering effect.

The importance of buffers in body fluids is that their actual hydrogen ion concentration changes little even though large amounts of H^+ are being added to them as a result of cell metabolism.

"Cellophane" and "Cuprophane"   proprietary names of cellulose membranes used in haemodialysers. Cuprophane is only half as thick as Cellophane.

Complement   A complex system of proteins forming 10% of plasma protein. When anti-body adheres to antigen (for example, bacterial cell wall antigen or lymphocyte HL-A antigen) complement proteins are activated sequentially and result in actual disruption of the cell wall (cytolysis). In addition the complement system forms substances which attract white blood cells to the site of inflammation, and increase capillary permeability. It is therefore of first importance in resistance to infection, but also in tissue typing, in the injury of glomerulonephritis and in rejection of transplanted kidneys. Complement components are numbered C1 to C9.

Concentration gradient   The rate at which the concentration of a solute differs with distance. The larger the concentration gradient, the more rapidly will the solute move from the region of high concentration until equilibrium is reached.

Dialysate   Dialysing fluid. Usually contains electrolytes in the concentrations expected in the plasma, but little or no potassium, no urea, phosphate or sulphate; and an excess of bicarbonate, lactate or acetate.

Dialyser ("artificial kidney")   An apparatus in which dialysis takes place. Usually blood is dialysed, hence *haemodialyser* and *haemodialysis*.

Dialysis   Transfer of electrolytes and other dissolved substance across a semi-permeable membrane, i.e. one which allows small molecules to pass, but not large molecules (such as proteins) or cells.

Diuresis; diuretic   High flow of urine; substance which stimulates a high urine flow.

Electrolyte   A substance which, when it dissolves in water, forms charged particles (ions).

Enhancement   Technique of treating the recipient in order to block antibody against transplants; used in experimental transplantation, potentially useful in human grafts.

Erythropoietin Hormone secreted by the kidney which stimulates red blood cell production by the bone marrow.

Glomerular filtrate The solution formed from the blood by pressure filtration through the glomerular capillaries. It contains almost no protein and no cells but otherwise its composition is nearly that of plasma.

Glomerular filtration rate (GFR) The rate of formation of glomerular filtrate; usually about 120 ml/min, or 180 l/day.

Glomerulonephritis A group of diseases affecting the glomerulus of the nephron. Usually all glomeruli are affected. Sometimes the changes are too subtle to be detected even by electron microscopy; in other patients, the glomerular capillary walls are thickened (*membranous glomerulopathy*) and in others, an excess of glomerular cells pre-dominates (*proliferative glomerulonephritis*). If the process leads to gross scarring of the kidney, the condition is called *chronic glomerulonephritis.*

Glomerulus The filter of the nephron, made up of a number of capillary loops covered by a layer of thin tubular cells.

Heterograft (or xenograft) Transplant between different species, e.g. baboon or pig to man.

Histocompatibility Identical tissue antigens, sometimes therefore called histocompatibility antigens (see HL-A).

Homograft (or allograft) Transplant between two individuals, not identical twins.

"Hyperacute" rejection (immediate, accelerated, early failure) Rejection of a grafted kidney within minutes or hours of grafting.

Immune enhancement see enhancement.

Immune tolerance see tolerance.

Immunosuppression (or immunodepression) Inhibition of the immune defence mechanisms. These mechanisms are principally dependent on cells and upon circulating antibody, and both are inhibited by immunosuppressive drugs. Immunosuppression permits foreign tissue to remain within the body (e.g. a grafted kidney) but may also permit foreign organisms such as viruses, bacteria, yeasts or fungi, to multiply within the body and colonize it.

Ion A charged atom or molecule; in physiology these are usually in solution or water (positive ions$^+$ = cations, negative ions$'$ = anions).

Ischaemic time Time spent by a grafted kidney without a circulation during transfer from donor to recipient. The *warm ischaemic time* is that spent at or near body temperature in the donor before excision, and in the recipient before the vascular anastomoses are complete. The *cold ischaemic time* is the time spent at a low temperature, usually that of iced water (4° C).

Lymphocytotoxic antibody Antibodies used for tissue typing which, if complement is present, kill lymphocytes bearing certain HL-A antigens. Such antibody may circulate in potential transplant recipients following immunization by blood, pregnancy or a failed tissue graft.

Lymphocytotoxic cross-match Test used in tissue transplantation, when the donor's lymphocytes are exposed to the recipient's serum; if lymphocytotoxic antibodies are present, the donor's lymphocytes are destroyed. This indicates that a graft between these two individuals is unlikely to succeed.

Membranous glomerulonephritis (membranous nephropathy, extramembranous nephropathy, membranous change) A type of primary renal disease characterized by diffuse thickening of the glomerular capillary walls. The thickening affects the basement membrane, hence "membranous".

Metabolites Products of metabolism.

Milliequivalent (mEq) One thousandth of an Equivalent (Eq). Both are units for expressing the chemical combining power of a substance. The equivalent weight = atomic or molecular weight/valency. The reference substance in hydrogen, where

$$\frac{1.}{1} = 1 \quad 1 \text{ g of hydrogen} = 1 \text{ Eq, one } 1 \text{ mg of hydrogen} = 1 \text{ mEq}$$

23 mg of Na^+, 39 mg of K^+ are equivalent to 1 mg of hydrogen since their atomic weights are 23 and 39, and their valency one. With calcium (which is divalent) one must divide the atomic weight (40) by $2 - 40/2 = 20 -$ to obtain the equivalent weight. The chemical combining power of most substances in solution is expressed as mEq/l of water.

Millimole (mmol) One thousandth of a mole (M). This is the unit for expressing the quantity, or concentration (mmol/l of water) of substances which are not ionized when they dissolve in water (e.g. glucose, urea). It is analogous to the milli-equivalent (mEq), which see for explanation. One millimole = molecular weight in milligrams.

Nephron The functional unit of the kidney, consisting of a glomerulus and a tubule. There are 1000000 nephrons in each kidney.

Oliguria Low urine flow.

Osmotic pressure, osmosis, osmolarity, osmolar, milliOsmoles When substances dissolve in solution the concentration of particles, whether charged or not, is expressed as the *osmolarity* (or osmolality – for practical purposes these are the same). The units used are milliOsmoles (1/1000 of an Osmole) per litre (mOs/l). The importance of the number of particles in solution is the tendency of water to pass to regions of high osmolarity (*osmosis*). This tendency can be balanced by hydrostatic pressure and is therefore called *osmotic pressure*. All body fluids (except urine) are in osmotic equilibrium, that is, their water contains an equal number of particles in solution.

pH Concentrations of acid (H+) in solution are often expressed on the pH scale. pH = $- \log_{10}$ × hydrogen ion concentration. This means that an H^+ concentration of 10^{-7} Eq/l = pH 7. 10^{-5} Eq/l = pH 5 and so on. The higher the number on the pH scale, the less the hydrogen ion concentration (which is confusing). The normal pH of the blood is about 7·3 - 7·4, of the urine 4·8 - 8·0.

Prime, priming dose Dose of substance or drug required to saturate the body water. Used of heparin, and of substances (such as inulin) used to measure renal function. It is also used (*priming volume*) for the amount of fluid (saline or blood) required to fill a haemodialyser at the beginning of dialysis.

Recirculating single pass Dialysis system in which part of the dialysate is recirculated through the dialyser, then passes away to waste. Usually the net flow is small, and the recirculating rate large.

Rejection The process by which grafted tissues are attacked and destroyed. The final event in rejection is the blockage of the small blood vessels supplying the graft. Various events lead up to this blockage, including vascular damage by antibodies and lymphocytes directed against the graft and complement thrombosis involving platelets and fibrin, then organization of the thrombus by collagen (scar).

Renin Hormone secreted by the kidney, which acts on a blood protein to release *angiotensin* (q.v.).

Shunt A communication between artery and vein through which blood flows. In patients with chronic renal failure, it usually means the silicone rubber – PTFE (polytetrafluorethylene – "Teflon") external shunt for access to the circulation if repeated haemodialysis is required.

Single Pass Dialysis system in which dialysate passes through the dialyser to waste.

Solute Substances in solution (dissolved).

"Suck" Colloquial term used for the negative pressure used in haemodialysers to remove water from the patient's blood during its passage through the dialyser.

Tissue type Description of those tissue antigens thought to be present in a transplant donor or recipient. These antigens are identified by *in vitro* tests involving the patient's lymphocytes and antisera. The antisera contain antibodies which react with the various tissue antigens, and kill cells which possess the particular antigen they recognize (cytotoxic antisera). The best recognized antigens have been allocated numbers in the series HL-A, e.g. HL-A1, HL-A2, etc. Others still have provisional designations, e.g. W36, TY.

Tolerance, Immune tolerance A state where the recipient is able to sustain without immunosuppressive drugs a graft containing foreign antigens. These could be human HL-A antigens or foreign species antigens, such as pig or baboon. Tolerance of organ transplants unfortunately has yet to be produced reliably in man, but may become one of the important developments in the near future.

Ultrafiltration The process of separating water and solutes from a solution through a membrane. Occurs in both the renal glomerulus, and in the artificial kidney (see "suck").

Urea A product of the metabolism of protein. Urea is formed from the nitrogen of the protein, and is in terms of quantity, the most important end product of protein metabolism in man.

LIST OF ABBREVIATIONS WHICH MAY BE ENCOUNTERED IN PATIENT'S NOTES, TEXTS, OR OTHER MATERIAL DEALING WITH RENAL DISEASES AND THEIR MANAGEMENT

A	arterial (used of arteriovenous shunts for dialysis)
ADH	antidiuretic hormone
AGN	acute glomerulonephritis

ALG	antilymphocyte globulin, prepared from ALS
ALS	antilymphocyte serum
ARF	acute renal failure
ASOT	anti-streptolysin O titre
Au antigen	Australia antigen (correctly HB_s)
BUN	Blood urea nitrogen, usually in mg/100 ml. This is about half the blood urea, and is similarly employed.
C	complement. C1, C3 etc: components of the complement system
CH_{50}	complement activity, expressed in units of 50% haemolysis of red blood cells in test system (hence H_{50})
CGN	chronic glomerulonephritis
CRF	chronic renal failure
CMV	cytomegalovirus
$C_{subscript}$	Urinary clearance of the substance specified in the subscript, e.g. $C_{creatinine}$ etc.
CVP	central venous pressure
UV/P	$= clearance. \dfrac{\text{Urine concentration} \times \text{urine volume}}{\text{plasma concentration}}$
dl	decilitre (100 ml)
EB	Epstein-Barr virus (glandular fever virus)
ECF	extracellular fluid
ECW	extracellular water
ESR	erythrocyte sedimentation rate
FDP	fibrin degradation products
GFR	glomerular filtration rate
GN	glomerulonephritis
HAA	hepatitis-associated antigen (correctly HB_s)
HB_s	hepatitis B surface antigen
HL-A	system of tissue antigens thought to be important in transplantation
HSP	Henoch-Schönlein purpura
HSV	herpes simplex hominis virus
HUS	haemolytic-uraemic syndrome
ICF	intracellular fluid
ICW	intracellular water
Ig	immunoglobulin
IgA	immunoglobulin A
IgG	immunoglobulin G
IgM	immunoglobulin M
IVP	intravenous pyelogram
IVU	intravenous urogram (or IVP)

kcal	kilocalorie (obsolete)
kJ	kilojoule (replaces kcal in dietary energy)
K_e	exchangeable potassium
LD	lymphocyte-determined antigen
MJ	megajoule; unit of energy for diets.
MSU	midstream specimen of urine
MLC	mixed lymphocyte reaction
mosm	milliosmole
mmol	millimole
μmol	micromole (1/1000 millimole)
mCi	millicurie (measurement of radioactivity)
μCi	microcurie (measurement of radioactivity)
Na_e	exchangeable sodium
NOMS	national organ matching service
PAH	para-aminohippurate
PAN	polyarteritis nodosa
PCV	packed cell volume = haematocrit
PD	peritoneal dialysis
pH	unit of concentration (or activity) of hydrogen ions
PN	pyelonephritis
ppm	parts per million. Usually used in connection with dialysis of calcium concentration in water. 1 ppm (as calcium carbonate) = mg/100 ml
psi	pounds per square inch (1 psi = 53 mmHg). Used of water pressure in dialysis machines
PT	measure of film weight (and therefore thickness) in dialysis membranes e.g. **PT** 150 and **PT** 300 which is twice as thick
PTFE	polytetrafluorethylene, "Teflon", a non-wettable plastic used in arteriovenous shunts
PVC	polyvinyl chloride, a flexible plastic
RSP	recirculating single pass (of dialysate flow in haemodialysers)
SLE	systemic lupus erythematosus
SPA	suprapubic aspiration
TBW	total body water
Tm	the maximum amount of a substance that can be transported by the kidney tubules in a given time (usually expressed as mg/min) e.g. Tm_{PAH}, $Tm_{glucose}$.
TTP	thrombotic thrombocytopaenic purpura
V	venous (used of arteriovenous shunts for dialysis)

GENERAL READING LIST

There are several large medical texts dealing with the kidneys. These are, in general, too detailed for use by nurses looking after renal patients, but may need to be consulted for special topics:
  Renal Disease (1976) 4th Edition. Black, D. A. K. (Ed). Oxford: Blackwell.
  Diseases of the kidney (1973) 2nd Edition. Strauss, M. B., and Welt, L. (Eds). Philadelphia: Saunders.
  The Kidney (1974) 4th Edition. de Wardener, H. E. London: Churchill.

There are also several smaller texts which amplify the general topics mentioned in this book.
  A Short Textbook of Renal Disease (1970). Kerr, D. N. S., and Douglas, A. London: Pitman Medical.
  The Kidney (1971). Golden, A. and Maher, J. F. Baltimore: Williams and Wilkins.
  Postgraduate Nephrology (1974). Gabriel, R. London: Butterworths.

For problems dealing with dialysis and transplantation, the books and articles listed after Chapters VIII, IX, XIV, and XV should be consulted. The *Proceedings of the European Dialysis and Transplant Association*, the *Transactions of the American Society for Artificial Internal Organs*, and the journal *Dialysis and Transplantation* are particularly useful; especially the latter, which deals extensively with practical problems connected with dialysis and transplant nursing. Harrington and Brener (see Chapter XIV) is also a valuable source of further material.

For topics concerned with chronic renal failure, J. R. Curtis and G. B. Williams is a short text which can be recommended.

There are several texts dealing with renal disease in children.
  Pediatric Nephrology (1975). Rubin, M. I. and Barratt, T. M. (Eds). Baltimore: Williams and Wilkins.

Index